Also by David Falkner:

Great Time Coming: The Life of Jackie Robinson, from Baseball to Birmingham

The Last Yankee: The Turbulent Life of Billy Martin

Nine Sides of the Diamond

The Short Season

Sadaharu Oh: A Zen Way of Baseball

Joe Morgan: A Life in Baseball (with Joe Morgan)

L.T.: Living on the Edge (with Lawrence Taylor)

THE
LAST
HERO

Simon & Schuster
New York London Toronto Sydney Tokyo Singapore

The Life of Mickey Mantle

David Falkner

SIMON & SCHUSTER
Rockefeller Center
1230 Avenue of the Americas
New York, NY 10020

Designed by Levavi & Levavi

Manufactured in the United States of America

10 9 8 7 6 5 4 3 2 1

Library of Congress Cataloging-in-Publication Data is available.

ISBN 0-684-81424-2

Photo Credits:

Collection of Nick Ferguson: 1, 2, 3, 4; UPI/Bettmann: 5, 14, 26; AP/Wide World Photos: 6, 8, 9, 10, 13, 19, 20, 22, 24, 27, 28, 29, 31, 34, 35, 37, 38, 39, 40, 41; National Baseball Library & Archive, Cooperstown, N.Y.: 7, 17, 21, 23, 30; New York Yankees: 11, 12, 16, 18, 25; The Topps Company, Inc.: 15; Collection of Greer Johnson: 32, 33, 36. Title page photo courtesy of the National Baseball Library & Archive, Cooperstown, N.Y.

To Martin Isaacs

Prologue

It took 185 working days to build old Yankee Stadium. On the gala opening of the ballpark in 1923, Babe Ruth hit a home run ten rows deep into the right-field bleachers. For thirty-three years, beginning with that inaugural blast, no batter ever hit a fair ball out of the cavernous, three-decker park with its elegant cornice gingerbreading the roof that loomed up over the playing field. The men who tried included the Babe, Lou Gehrig, Jimmie Foxx, Joe DiMaggio, Hank Greenberg, Ted Williams, and countless others wearing uniforms of every stripe and every league. By the time Mickey Mantle stepped to the plate in the fifth inning of the first game of a Memorial Day doubleheader against the Washington Senators in 1956, hitting a ball out of the Stadium had become one of those invisible, insuperable challenges, an eleventh labor of Hercules, a task and a dream thought to be beyond the reach of human strength.

Mantle had had the best spring of his career. He was hitting near .420. He had already hit eighteen home runs, fourteen of them in the month of May alone, although he was playing in only his fortieth game of the season. The Senators' pitcher in that first game was Pedro Ramos, a right-hander the Yankees would acquire a decade later in the midst of a pennant drive. In an earlier game during that '56 season, there had been a touch of bad blood between Mantle and Ramos. Mantle had been singled out for retaliation after a Senators' batter had been hit by a pitch. Ramos made no attempt to disguise what he was doing when he threw a fastball that drilled Mantle in the middle of the back between the shoulder blades.

Mantle said nothing when he was hit. He glanced quickly at Ramos and then, in that peculiar way he had of seeming to contain all emotion—and pain—within himself, trotted on to first base with his head down and at an angle, as though signaling that what had happened was just part of the game.

But, weeks later, in the fifth inning at Yankee Stadium, Mantle had not forgotten. As he often did when he batted left-handed, he borrowed one of Hank Bauer's thirty-two-ounce bats, which he carried out with him to the on-deck circle (when he hit right-handed, he regularly borrowed a thirty-six-ouncer from Bill Skowron). Mantle watched Ramos carefully from a kneeling position, swishing a couple of extra bats around, studying the way Ramos released his pitches.

When he stepped into the batter's box, Mantle's mind was on making contact, hard contact. Later that afternoon, he would get his twelfth bunt single of the season, a daring two-strike drag bunt in the middle of a winning Yankee rally, but there was no thought of bunting now. He was locked on to Ramos like a hunter who had been stalking his prey for a month, waiting for the right moment.

Ramos was just as alert and focused on Mantle. He drove him back from the plate with one pitch, hit the outside corner with another, got him to reach for yet another outside pitch, then came inside again. He had him at 2-2, and then tried to get him on still one more low outside fastball. The pitch was low enough, but it caught too much of the outside part of the plate. The pitch was exactly where Mantle most liked it when he hit from the left side.

As he did always, he seemed to swing from the heels. No one among the more than 29,000 people who saw the game that day has ever commented on the sound the ball made coming into full contact with the whipping bludgeon of the bat. Players and reporters over the years always maintained that when Mantle hit a ball it somehow *sounded* different. This time there seemed to be no sound at all. The ball rose into the afternoon air like no other that had ever been struck in Yankee Stadium in three decades. Depending on the witness, the ball was a gunshot or a moonshot. Whatever it was, its velocity and altitude were too swift for the human eye. The ball struck the cornice above the third deck—the first time that had ever been done—only eighteen inches from the open spaces beyond the roof. "A skyscraper wallop," said *The New York Times,* adding some arithmetic to help bring to blow to earth: "The ball struck at a point 370 feet from the plate some 117 feet above the ground."

Mel Allen, the Yankee broadcaster then (and also in 1963, when Mantle hit another ball that almost cleared the roof), described the shot as a line drive that "just went up like an airplane taking off and it was out before you knew it. It wasn't a fly ball dropping down. It struck the overhang inches from the top of the Stadium and then rebounded all the way back to the infield." Allen said he got so excited he literally became speechless. His signature home-run call, "going, going, gone," was not even an impulse. "I didn't lose my voice," he said, "but the crowd was yelling and I just starting yelling with them."

How far would the ball have gone if it had cleared the roof? There are estimates—one made by an engineer—of up to 620 feet. No one knows. The ball is still traveling. It has, like a rocket that has moved beyond the earth's orbit, taken on wings of its own as it hurtles, weightless, through space to the borders of imagination and beyond. Mickey Mantle's life carried his fans with him in much the same way.

Chapter 1

Mickey Mantle Boulevard in Commerce, Oklahoma, is a nondescript road leading into and out of town, an arrow through the heart of the legend that floats above the town and above the memory of Mickey Mantle's life. As your eyes follow it to the distant horizon, the road seems to disappear into the heat of a summer's day, past weed-choked fields packed with black holes. The sky is empty, and the holes, along with piles of spent ore, called chat, are the physical remains of the Eagle-Picher Mine Company that once dominated the area.

The holes were once tunnels that crisscrossed parts of three states, running for miles all the way up to Joplin, Missouri, past Dust Bowl towns like Picher, Cardin, Miami, and Spavinaw, where Mickey Mantle was born to a mining family on October 20, 1931.

The lead and zinc mines were hellholes full of danger, illness, and death. The miners were not unionized in the late '20s and early '30s. The wages were low, but in the years of the Great Depression they were gratefully accepted. Thirty dollars a week was good pay. The horrors of the jobs that the men performed below ground were echoed in the cares and anxieties of those who waited above for the day's—or night's—shift to end. Sirens announcing an accident of some kind were a regular feature of life in the area; miners were often injured or lost their lives in explosions, cave-ins, and tunnel accidents.

Bill Mosely was Mantle's closest childhood friend. When Mosely was five, he lost his father in a mining accident. "My dad was a powderer, a dynamite man," said Mosely, "and after everyone left he set off the charge, but he didn't get out in time." Mosely, like Mantle, lived for a good portion of his early life in Commerce, and he remembered the sound of those sirens. "Whenever they went off, people heard them in all the little towns, and they would come together, and go over to the hospital to wait for the ambulances to come in."

Mickey's father, Mutt Mantle, was a shoveler in a mine called Blue Goose Number One. Mickey's cousin, Ron Mantle, who still lives in the area, recalled that "Mutt worked in the Blue Goose mine, and my dad worked at the West Side mine. It's hard to imagine what they had to do every day. When I was younger, I went down in the mines once. It was horrible. It was like crawling down a hole. It was damp and dark and dirty, and that's the way you came out of the ground every day. We used to go out and get my father whenever mom had the car. The miners would come out of there so filthy you'd barely recognize them. It was just dark, dark, dark. You talk to the people who are still left, the very few of them that are alive, they'll tell you the same thing. Most of 'em have some ailments now, since they were either hit by falling rock or they've got lung damage or whatever. My dad, like my Uncle Mutt, got to be a ground boss, and I remember on at least three occasions he had to go out during the night because they had an accident in the mines and they would call all the miners in and they would go down and rescue people. Once they had a fire they had to go fight down there. They lived with death every day."

The history of the Mantle clan, like that of so many who were born and labored hard on this land, is found more in the memory of its members than in public records. "Our family bloodlines run mainly to English beginnings," said Mickey, "with a sprinkling of Dutch and German. We go back five generations in America."

Mantle's mother and father were both raised in the Oklahoma-Missouri-Arkansas corner, in and around the town of Spavinaw. Mantle's grandfather Charlie lost his wife when the couple was still young, but not before they had had four children, three boys and a girl. The grandfather, a left-handed pitcher, supported his family by working at a variety of jobs, but he was principally a butcher. Other family members helped out caring for the children; the youngest, Emmett, was raised by an aunt and uncle.

According to those who knew him, Charlie Mantle was a sweet man. "I never ever heard him raise his voice," said Floy Norton, one of his daughters-in-law. "Mr. Mantle was just a very kind person, very there at all times for Mickey and just plain nice to everyone." Charlie Mantle fed others as well as his own kin out of his butcher shop, but he wasn't a miner—the one sure source of steady employment—so making ends meet was always tough. The Mantle family moved from Spavinaw to Commerce when Mickey was a child, and the grandfather went along, too. "He lived with Mickey's family in Commerce," said Max Mantle, a younger cousin of Mickey's who was around the family all the time. "He wasn't working when they moved to Commerce; he worked in a grocery store, he worked as a butcher, but not after the family moved." Like so many in the Mantle family, Grandpa Charlie died young—though not before he played a part in Mickey's early baseball education.

Mantle's father, Elvin (no one knows the origin of the nickname Mutt, except that he seemed stuck with it almost from infancy), was, in the words of cousin Ron Mantle, "an old hardrock miner who loved his kids. That's basically what he lived for, to raise his kids." But raising his kids meant, for him, a life in the mines rather than following in his father's footsteps.

Mutt tried his hand at other work before he went underground, but in the end it was mining that allowed him to take care of his family.

Mantle's mother's maiden name was Richardson. She may have been part Cherokee; Mickey was less sure of her family's origins other than that she, like his father, grew up in Spavinaw. As a teenager, Lovell Richardson ran away, married, and had two children before divorcing and returning to her parents' home until Mutt Mantle, whom she had surely known over the years, began courting her.

In a tiny hamlet like Spavinaw, Oklahoma, where everyone knew everyone, a runaway teen bride who had divorced and returned with two children in tow must have been quite a topic of conversation. Yet the taint of scandal made no difference to Mutt Mantle, and that was no small thing. Back in the twenties and early thirties, during the Depression years when Mickey was born and raised, the teaching of the Lord in rural Oklahoma was tailored to the hard lives of the parishioners. The values and codes of behavior were narrow and well defined. Every Sunday the churches in the tiny hamlets resounded with hymns and sermons that taught that this life is full of sorrow and deceit, but that Judgment Day is real and not far off.

Mutt's family was remarkable in that they were neither churchgoers nor, in any discernible way, religious. They raised their children on their own terms. But raising a family at all in that place and time meant inevitably turning to the mines. Mutt worked all the different, wretched jobs there were. He was a mule skinner, which meant he handled the mules used to pull the huge cans of ore that had been gouged from the veins of subterranean rock; he was a "screen-ape," a rock-busting, sledgehammer-swinging man; he was a shoveler, a hooker, and a ground boss. While serving as a ground boss, he often had to go below when someone got sick or there was an accident, or when a shift of busters and shovelers needed more men. He rode the great hooks down into the holes, and he came up riding the cans of ore to the surface. Pat Summerall, a longtime friend of Mantle's, said that on one occasion Mantle surprised him by telling him that Mutt "never died of cancer; it was emphysema." The miners, of course, breathed death every day of their working lives.

Even when the miners tried to forget what was underground, they could not, so they lived hard and they played hard, too. Their recreations were few but intense. They drank, they fought, and they brushed themselves off and went to Saturday night barn dances, where one of them would show off his special skills with fiddle or accordion. And they played baseball.

The miners—Blue Goose, West Side, and the other Eagle-Picher shafts—all had teams. They played on Sunday afternoons and sometimes on Wednesday evenings, before crowds of two and three hundred with a keg of beer waiting for the winning team. Mutt Mantle and his brother Eugene (Ron's father) played for Blue Goose Number One. Mutt was a pitcher, Eugene (or Tunney, as he was nicknamed) was a catcher, forming an all-Mantle battery—and a good one by all accounts. Mickey believed that if his father had ever gotten the breaks he had, he would surely have made the majors. Many contemporaries said Mutt could run; years later, when Mickey was on his way to a professional career, Mutt raced against his son and could stay with him stride for stride over a good stretch of ground. Other observers, less partial than Mickey, remembered Mutt as a good but not great player.

"We used to go out and watch the mining teams," said Nick Ferguson, a close childhood friend of Mickey's. "They had good teams and some real good ballplayers. Sherm Lollar played for one of them teams. Barney Barnett, who later started the league in which Mickey played, had one of those teams, it was Blue Goose I think. . . . Mutt played for the Blue Goose team, so Barney coached the father and then the son. Mutt was a switch hitter, too. Good player, but I don't think he was special. I remember one day watching Mutt play, there was a guy pitching who was ambidextrous, a guy named Montgomery, and they kept switching back and forth. Mutt would get up to bat one way, Montgomery would take off his glove and try to throw the other way. They came up with a rule that you could only jump around one time, so that took care of that. But I sure remember Mutt as a player; he was pretty good and he played real hard."

Mutt Mantle played baseball hard enough to bring it home with him; it was his passion, his answer to the mines, something to dream about. And he had a partner, a mate who genuinely shared his passion for baseball and then some. Mickey's mother was a homemaker, but one who did her housework while listening to broadcasts of St. Louis Cardinal games. The Cards were *the* team in those parts, the closest major-league team in the area (excluding the hapless St. Louis Browns, whom no one followed).

For those who did not live through the Depression, it is difficult to imagine the grip those hard times had on the people who did. The fears it provoked in that corner of Oklahoma and elsewhere in the Dust Bowl were especially intense. Young people openly wondered what there was to look forward to. "In Oklahoma back then when kids were growing up," Tunney Mantle's widow, Floy Norton, said, "we always had people come to the door in those days to try to get a little donation or somethin' to eat. The kids would see that and would laugh and say, 'When I grow up I'm gonna be a bum.' They thought that was funny. But it wasn't funny, because times was so bad in those days. And if you haven't lived when you don't make enough money to eat and feed your family, you don't know what I'm really talking about."

"See, where we come from," said Mrs. Norton's son, Max Mantle, "we were just poor, that's all, the whole area. You went down into the ground three hundred foot a day, and there just wasn't much else. You just try to get by the best you can, that's all. You knew you wasn't ever going to make much money, you just did what you had to do the best you could."

The discomfort Mickey Mantle showed in the face of fame

reflects this deeper sense that pervaded the area like alkali dust: that survival itself was the real goal, and a worthy one. Where he came from, your future was the mines—if you were lucky—or sticking your hand out, if you weren't. If you wanted or needed more, you were a hopeless dreamer.

Mutt Mantle was such a dreamer. By all accounts he was a quiet man, without airs or pretensions—a good neighbor, a good provider, and a survivor. But in ways that might be more recognizable today in the basketball dreams of urban youths, Mutt Mantle dreamed about the open spaces of country baseball, about the roads that led out of Spavinaw and Picher and Commerce, north and east to St. Louis and other big-league venues. However accomplished he was, he imagined himself at one point in his life with a major-league uniform on his body. In those miners' games, whether anyone knew it or not, he was playing for half a dream, the other half always missing, always out of reach. It is not known whether Mutt Mantle, in his baseball-crazy childhood, ever picked himself up and consciously sought the attention of major-league scouts for himself, as he would later, on his son's behalf. Regardless, the birth of his eldest son provided the missing half of his fading dream. He named him Mickey—not Michael or Elvin Junior, but Mickey, after the great Detroit Tigers catcher Mickey Cochrane, though no one has ever explained why Mutt, a stone St. Louis Cardinal fan, a pitcher, a hard rock miner, picked out a Detroit Tiger from Bridgewater, Massachusetts, as his favorite player. The mystery has long been part of the myth.

Neither mysterious nor mythical was the baseball education that followed. Mutt Mantle, not unlike other fathers, was determined to teach his son how to play. Unlike other fathers who played catch with their sons, though, he was working with a son so gifted and so different that their games of catch literally became a passport to another world.

Chapter 2

I remember the first time I saw Mickey Mantle play. He just looked different from other players. He was massive through the shoulders and chest. His neck, forearms, and thighs were thick as sides of beef. When he swung a bat, this sense of thickness was transformed into baseball's nearest equivalent to mass times the speed of light squared: pure, breathtaking power. What was special in that swing is hard to name, easy to visualize, and impossible for anyone who ever saw it to forget.

His swing was all-out, totally committed, a wondrous unleashing of every last muscle fiber in his body. Mantle, said one of his fans, "swung from his soul." Even when he missed a pitch, you could feel the totality of the effort in the last row of the bleachers. There was something scary to me about the fury of that swing; when I was a child, I thought it was his size I feared, but when I met him years later, I was shocked to discover he was not particularly tall. The programs of his day listed him at six feet. He was barely more than five feet ten inches. I realized then that he could have been five feet five inches or five feet two inches, and it would have made no difference; the purest expression of who he was was in that swing.

In fact, when Mickey Mantle was growing up, he was small and spindly, unusually so. His friends called him "Little Mick." Neva Mosely knew Mantle in the first grade, after the family had moved from Spavinaw to Commerce. "He was a cute, little, pigeon-toed, bashful kid," she said. "A shy little boy. He wore cowboy boots all the time—when some kids didn't have any shoes at all."

The Commerce grade school where Mosely and Mantle were classmates was tiny, the classes were small, and everyone knew everyone, parents and children alike. "We'd been there all our lives, growin' up together, all of our parents knew each other, it was just a nice situation." Their first grade schoolteacher was a woman named Mrs. Potorroff. "She loved every one of us like we were hers," Mosely said. "She was huge, about two hundred pounds, but nobody ever made fun of her because we all loved her."

Mantle, whom she would know all his life, was much the same then as he would be later on: "I remember him with a big grin, great big teeth, teeth too big for his mouth. Nothing seemed to bother him. He had a good start from home. His folks were very humble people; they seemed to accept things as they came along."

This description applied to everything except baseball, which was never always passively accepted but rather avidly pursued. His playmates and fellow school-age ballplayers remember the free hours they had together, at the schoolyard, in the alkali fields, and then at Mantle's home at 319 N. Quincy in Commerce. By any standard, the Mantle house was modest, little more than a one-story clapboard shack with two bedrooms, a postage-stamp-sized front porch and an adjoining garage barely large enough to cover a single car. The garage, made of rickety boards held together by sheet metal, was the backstop where Mantle learned that baseball was something more than child's play.

By the time Mickey was a second grader, Mutt Mantle was

exhorting him to "practice, practice, practice." Mutt brought home broken bats from his miners' games, shaved off the tops, nailed the broken parts together, and provided his son with bats a child could swing. Mantle remembered that his parents bought gloves for him, that his mother made him uniforms out of throw-away clothes, and that when it was time for him to get his first spikes, which the family could not afford, his mother took pairs of old shoes and screwed makeshift cleats into their soles. But nothing took the place of the hours devoted to training, father to son.

From the beginning, "Little Mickey" could hit with authority from the right side. Though none of his friends remember feats of power that early, Mantle himself said, "by the time I reached second grade I was hitting them pretty good from the right side." He was, in other words, a natural right-handed batter. But, Bill Mosely, who turned into something of an athlete himself, recalled that Mantle, like a lot of other right-handed hitting kids, seemed to have trouble when pitches came close to him. In their practice sessions, Mosely said, "Mutt used to break off a lot of curveballs." Mutt was throwing tennis balls, but even with those he could see that his skinny son had trouble standing in against a pitch that came at him and then broke toward the plate. Mickey has said endlessly that Mutt was a "prophet" in turning his son into a switch-hitter. Prophet or not, as an old semipro ballplayer and a switch-hitter himself, he understood perfectly that a breaking ball that forced a right-handed hitter to bail out was far easier for a left-handed hitter to follow.

At first, hitting left-handed had little appeal for Mickey. But his comfort and confidence grew, fueled by the daily practice sessions his father and grandfather set up for him when Mutt came home from the mines. At four or five in the afternoon, the father and grandfather would gather up Mickey and whatever friends were around and go out back to the tin-plated garage next to the house. Mickey would hit first from the right side, with his left-handed grandfather Charlie pitching, then from the left side, with Mutt throwing. The friends fielded and did some hitting, too. Mutt was still a young man, not yet thirty; Charlie Mantle was fiftyish, an old semipro player himself. When Mickey hit, the pitchers held nothing back, did nothing to let him simply tee off. He was a hitter, and his grandfather and father were pitchers who went after him, forcing him to concentrate, to face his own fears and inabilities. The sessions went on until dinner, two hours or more.

In 1967, a little more than a year before he retired, Mantle said about his father: "No boy, I think, ever loved his father more than I did. I was a good boy, really, who needed little disciplining, and I would do nearly anything to keep my father happy. He was a big, strong, stern-looking man, just a fraction short of six feet tall, lean and well-muscled, with the strong, gnarled hands of a miner, and dark, thick hair. . . . He never had to raise his hand to me to make me obey, for I needed only a sharp look and a word from him and the knowledge that I had displeased him to make me go and do better."

As time went on, Mantle was willing to acknowledge a little more. He recalled that when he was four, his father gave him one of the only beatings he ever had to administer. It was memorable, Mantle said.

"As clear as yesterday, though, I remember one incident from that period. We were sitting on the front porch. . . . In those days they used to haul water and ice to us on a truck. It would come by with a bucket for our use. A tank sat on two beams on the bed of the truck and these two beams stuck out. I jumped up and grabbed one of the beams, rode the underside of the truck for about half a block, thinking I was doing something great.

"When I got back to our yard, Dad was so mad he was shaking. He looked around for something to hit me with and all he could find was a piece of bailing wire and gave me five or six good licks across the ass.

"It was just about the only time he ever whipped me. Was about the last time he ever *had* to whip me, too."

Mutt Mantle pushed his son toward the dream of playing major-league baseball, but Mickey was hardly unwilling; the skinny, small, shy boy simply loved sports and games. He played whenever he could, at school recesses, after school, on weekends, on holidays, through the long, punishing Oklahoma summers; he played kickball, basketball, football, baseball, anything. One "sport" Mantle did not take to was swimming—and once it nearly cost him his life.

He and his friends regularly used to trudge out to the Neosho River, near town. There was a swimming hole there, removed enough from the road and from scrutiny to swim naked. Mantle did not swim but paddled around, using his friends to pull him along through the water as though he were a log. His friends kept an eye on him—until one afternoon when a young woman appeared on the riverbank, and Mantle and his friends, exposed and ashamed, all dove off in different directions. Mantle nearly drowned, plucked from the river as he flailed, gasping and choking.

His favorite games, though, were all related to baseball. One childhood friend remembers a game they played called "Broomball," though other friends insist that instead of a broom handle, they always used a bat and a tennis ball. Whatever it was called, it was a two- or sometimes three-man game; the games went on till dark, and for Yankee diehards, they contained a true irony: In these games, where the boys would pretend to follow the batting order of their favorite teams, Mantle in his early years invariably chose the Boston Red Sox. The reason, Nick Ferguson said, was simple: Ted Williams. "Mickey was a Red Sox fan and a Ted Williams fan because Williams was a pure hitter."

In the winter months or when the weather was bad, the children often went to the Mantle home because it was always lively, full of games and noise and camaraderie. Aside from Mickey, the eldest, there were his twin brothers, Ray and Roy, a younger sister, Barbara, and a brother Larry (Butch). In addition, Mantle's half-brother, Theodore, was sometimes around (an older half-sister, Anna, who died in her youth, was not raised by the family). "When Mickey was young, he was just the most happy-go-lucky and fun-loving kid you'd ever want to meet; in school, though, he was quiet, and because of it the teachers loved him," Nick Ferguson said. "We all had a happy childhood, I think. Nobody had any great expectations. We didn't have much, but we'd play all day long, either baseball, football, or basketball, and then if we couldn't play those, if we had to go inside, we'd put up a little hoop over a door or all five of us would play cards or dominoes. Mutt was a big card player. And we'd play Monopoly all day long. I don't know how Mrs. Mantle did it; she had five kids and then she put up with all of us underfoot at the same time."

The other branches of the Mantle clan had the same lively spirit. Uncle Tunney's house was a block from the school in Commerce; it inevitably became a beehive, especially during Mickey's high school years after Mutt moved his family out of town to a farm. The farmhouse was little more than a shack on rented land; there was no plumbing, and family members had to bathe in small zinc tubs. When the river flooded and the roads between Whitebird and Commerce were washed out, Mickey stayed with his aunt and Uncle Tunney, next to school. "My house was like a circus in them years," Floy Norton said. "I had a job in a garment factory then, we didn't have much and they didn't have much but I don't think that mattered at all. People were very close to each other at that time. And they spent a great deal of time with each other."

Nick Ferguson remembered breakfast time at Mantle's house. "I was down there all the time, I'd be there before breakfast," he said. "In those days they put out a great big economy-sized box of Post Toasties, they'd get boxes of wheat flakes, stuff like that to take care of Mickey, the twins, and Larry and Barbara and then anybody else like me who was over at the house. It took just one breakfast to finish off this great big ol' box, and all of us were gettin' bigger and bigger and needing more and more food.

Didn't matter. That's why they moved outside of town, I think, so Mutt could also run a small farm to feed everybody."

One of the twins, Ray Mantle, remembered the load of farm chores they all did. "We were real close, so maybe it was a little easier to do all them chores. We milked cows, we had pigs, we had chickens, we did it all while my dad was still working the mines," he said.

"When they all moved out to the farm," Nick Ferguson said, "we used to go out and help shuck corn and help out on the farm some. Mick did his stuff, but one thing he didn't like, no matter what he's said, he wasn't much of a rider. That could get to be a little funny. They had one horse out there that would try to take you right into the barn but nobody could get Mickey on that horse, he didn't want no part of that. Smart enough to stay off that horse."

Bill Mosely came out to the farm to spend time with Mickey during the summers, and he vividly recalled the energy and life that abounded in the household. It revolved around Mantle's mother, he said: "I remember running through that house and everything and there she would be ironing. It was real hot, and she'd have a towel wrapped around the top of her head. But she's also listening to the ballgame, listening to the St. Louis Cardinals game. Because, see, Mutt's out working, so she's writing down all of the scores, all of the plays, everything that's happened in the ballgame. You know, otherwise you couldn't get the news till the next day's papers, and they didn't give it all to you. So she's doing all that while she's looking after the cooking and the evening meal and trying to take care of all the kids, and then we'd sit down at the table, the big round table they had in the kitchen, and she'd run back every play, every inning of that ballgame, she'd tell you how this happened and that happened, she had it all right in front of her and she made it sound so exciting, too. And everybody had to know what went on; they'd keep asking for more and more and she'd just keep telling them like she had actually been at the game herself."

Nick Ferguson also remembers Mantle's mother as the center of life in the family, "and in ways no one ever talks about," he said. Her baseball knowledge was such, he said, that she, not Mutt, was the one who had "inside" things to say to her son. "She'd never raise her voice, you'd barely hear her, but she'd sort of whisper to Mickey about what he had done in games she saw. She'd say, 'You know, in that situation, if you bunted, you woulda done this or that, if you backed a little bit at second you'd have more room to take a ball, or on this hitter or that hitter you should maybe move over a little more.' She knew the game and she could always get him to think about what he was doing."

One time the family all piled into a used car they had just gotten, an old LaSalle, and took a trip down to Spavinaw to visit Mrs. Mantle's family. "While we were there, Mutt went off to play cards downtown. Well, after awhile, Lovell told me and Mick to go down and get him," Ferguson said. "We did. But he didn't want to go, he was still playing, and it was obvious he had had a few, so we went back. A couple of hours later she sent us off again to tell him it was now time to go home. Well, we got there and Mutt was kind of in a stupor. He had just had too much, but he started in saying they had drugged him and took all his money, and he was so out of it there was no way he could drive—and Mrs. Mantle had never driven a car in her life, and none of us could drive, either. But she says, 'Get in, I'm takin' us home.' So everybody got in the car, Mutt was out of it in the back, there were so many of us in the car that we were sitting all over each other, and Lovell puts the thing into first gear and sets out. We're laughing our heads off, Mickey's teasing her, 'Hey, ma, put 'er into second, put her into second,' but she just kept the thing in first and damn if she didn't get us all the way home safe and sound."

The simple and dependable rhythm of family life was shattered in 1944, when Charlie Mantle contracted Hodgkin's disease and died. His death was the first in a series of deaths young Mickey, then twelve, would see in the next few years. "Grandpa suddenly became old and feeble, almost overnight," Mantle said a few years ago. "My father would help him out of bed, support his wobbly legs that used to stride along South Quincy Street with so much vigor. What I'm absolutely sure of is that dad was worried sick over Grandpa's condition. . . .

"He died shortly after we moved. I never forgot that moment, standing beside the casket with my little twin brothers Ray and Roy, the three of us looking down on him, and my father whispering, 'Say good-bye to Grandpa.' "

Three years later, Tunney Mantle died. He was thirty-four. His death was even more shocking because he was so much younger. "In my dad's case, they thought he had appendicitis," Max Mantle said. "He went into the hospital and they had him on the table on July 4. When they cut him open they saw it was cancer and they sewed him back up, it was stomach cancer. Sewed him back up, and a month and a half later he was dead. He went from about 215 pounds down to about ninety."

Max Mantle said that his father's early death and those of his uncles changed his life. "It probably made me a different person. For a few years, I hid from everything. Yeah, I hid. I pulled my little mask down and I was a different person than I would have been. It's hard to explain. When something would happen, I would laugh it off when I shouldn't have, when I should have faced something."

Mickey was very much affected by these blows and by the death a few years later of his Uncle Emmett; he lacked the emotional armor that Max Mantle hid behind. "Mickey was always a sensitive person," cousin Ron Mantle said. "He was that way his whole life. He was always the first one of us who would cry. He laughed a lot. Everything good or bad that ever happened in his life, if you knew Mick, he cried over. Me, I'm the cold one, but Mick was something else."

Ron Mantle recalled the death of his Uncle Emmett in 1952 at age thirty-two. Emmett was the last and youngest of the brothers.

By then Mickey was a Yankee star. "We were all together and this doctor came along and said to us, right in the room we were in, it would be interesting to see if the cancer carried on to the next generation. Well, I know it scared the hell out of all of us at the time because all those men in our family had died in their thirties and that didn't leave much sense of security. And I know that hit Mick the hardest because he was so much more sensitive than the rest of us, so yeah, it left a mark on him all right. We're all the silent types, you know, so we never talked about it much, but it was a part of all our lives."

Chapter 3

Grade school and then junior high and high school in Commerce, Oklahoma, in the forties were no different than in thousands of other small towns in America. Mickey Mantle and his friends remembered school mainly for what took place outside, beyond the classrooms. Mantle did his schoolwork, but he lived for recess and afterward. By the time he was eleven, he was playing sandlot ball in and around Commerce. On Sunday mornings, he would hook his mitt through the handlebars of his bike, then peddle miles with his friends to catch a game for the afternoon. Or he'd walk, sometimes half a day, to ball fields in other towns. Because baseball was so popular, even ball games between children's teams were festive occasions. Mantle recalled the sight of people driving to dusty fields to see the games. Was it fiction, or was the fiction made from it? Mantle said, in 1985, "You'd see the dust coming up the road and dozens of old cars honking by. What a sight! They formed a circle around the field. Picnic baskets, egg crates, and whatnot would be dragged out of the backseats, pints of whiskey in back pockets, too; everybody laughing and hollering, then settling down to watch us play, so attentive, so respectful you'd think they were actually paying their way into the World Series."

Not quite. Mantle played in a sandlot league, the Pee Wee League, and then in one for twelve to fifteen year olds named after Gabby Street; the games were in little towns like Picher and Douthat, mining towns, where the crowds that gathered were mostly miners, ballplayers themselves, and their families. The games were hard played, like the miners' games, and as with those games, there was always a keg of beer waiting for the winner afterward.

"One of the guys we picked up for our team was named Delbert Lovelace, a kid from right outside Commerce," said Nick Ferguson. "You've heard of rabid fans and how they could get on ballplayers, well, they got on this kid Lovelace something awful. There was this one gal who was louder than anyone, she'd just stand up there screaming in this high piercing voice, 'Lovelady, Lovelady, Lovelady,' and all that stuff. It was somethin', I tell ya."

The uproar was no more disconcerting than the weird, stripped fields on which the games were played. The fields were actually waste sites, washed flat by continual flooding, made smooth by the baking sun, raised into swirling alkali dust by any kind of wind. "It's surprising we all don't have tuberculosis from that stuff, but all we'd do is beat the dust off our clothes," Ferguson said.

In 1944, as a thirteen year old, Mantle played second base for the championship Gabby Street League team from Douthat. By then, small as he was, he could do some things others could not. For one, he could throw as well as hit left-handed. Mantle and his friends were all amazed by the war time, one-armed outfielder for the St. Louis Browns, Pete Gray. The "tricks" Gray did to transfer a ball from his glove to his hand after making a catch—tossing glove and ball into the air, swiping the ball as it separated from the glove; tucking the glove under an armpit while rolling the ball down an arm—were tricks Mantle and his friends tried to imitate. "We used to watch those old Movietone newsreels that showed how he did it," Nick Ferguson explained, "and then Mickey could actually do it, just like he had one arm. He'd put his right hand behind his back, only use his left, and he was real good. He coulda thrown left-handed for real if he ever had to."

Another skill he had was throwing a knuckleball. There was an old catcher in the area who had played professionally and who knew how to throw the pitch, Ferguson recalled. "None of the rest of us could really do it, but Mick could, he could make the ball flutter and dip and dive. He won some big games pitching for us that year, too." It was a skill that Mantle never lost. Years later, with the Yankees, he used to torment teammates by throwing his knuckler during sideline warm-ups. One year he broke a teammate's nose throwing the pitch. Ferguson and other childhood friends believe that Mantle might well have made it as a pitcher if he had not been the hitter he was.

After Mantle's Gabby Street team won the league championship, there was a banquet held for the players. Gabby Street himself was the principal guest. It was the first contact any of the youngsters had had with someone who had actually played major-league baseball. Street told them stories, Ferguson remembered. "He told us about how he took part in this publicity stunt in the '20s where he tried to catch a ball with his bare hands that was dropped from the top of the Empire State Building. He said he caught one out of ten. And then he held up his hands. Our eyes got big as saucers. All his fingers on both hands went off at right angles from all those years of getting hit with foul tips, maybe even from trying to do stunts like the one he described."

All the while, Mutt Mantle kept tutoring his son. The late afternoon rounds of switch-hitting were as regular as paid work. The daily labor, the endless rounds from both sides of the plate, like the playing of scales, slowly separated Mantle's abilities from those of his friends. But now, as the prized pupil got older, the workouts included other phases of the game. Nick Ferguson remembers going to the Mantles' in the afternoons to work on double plays with Mutt. Mutt fungoed grounders and fly balls. But the big thing always was hitting, making sure that Mickey did not cheat by hitting from one side at the expense of the other.

"Mickey always had this thing when we went to games, see, he hated hitting left-handed, he always wanted to hit righty when he could, and if Mutt wasn't at the game, that's what he'd do," Ferguson said. "So we'd look out for him, and if we saw Mutt coming, we'd holler, 'Here he comes,' and Mickey would jump around to the left side. One time, Mutt came to a game and saw Mickey hitting the wrong way and he made a real fuss. Went to the coach and had Mickey taken right out of the game. He was dead serious about it."

But Mutt Mantle was never heavy-handed in the way he pushed his son. He was not the prototypical aggressive, domineering parent now so familiar as shapers of Olympic gymnasts, tennis prodigies, or teenaged skating stars. Save for the time he thrashed his son for riding that ice truck, Mutt did not raise his hand to him. He did not raise his voice or bend him into submission with lectures and admonitions. At games, if teammates or coaches got on his son, he would let them know, quietly but firmly, to back off. He intimidated by intimacy, by the way he would fix a look, drape an arm around a shoulder, or by removing his heavy steel boots when he came trudging up the road at the end of the day and then, in his bare feet, challenging his son to a race. Mantle says that his father won until a certain point, "when I knew I was faster but even then I still let him win." But Mutt's most persuasive hold on his son—and on his son's friends—came from a peculiar ability he had to get others to do what he wanted without seeming to ask for anything.

"He did it in such a nice way," said Bill Mosely. "You'd do things for him and never realize you were doing them. He kind of motivated you, that was all. He'd kind of look at you funny and that would go right through you, but I never noticed him ever gettin' on anybody. He just had that look about him. And everybody seemed to like him real well." Even with his children and their friends, he was a friend as much as an authority figure.

"Mutt was a great guy, hard living, hard playing," Nick Ferguson said. "He did his carousing around—I mean just drinking, you know, I'm sure he didn't chase around with women, but Mutt drank and he used to take Mick and us kids into the bars with him when we weren't even old enough to drink."

Oklahoma at the time was a dry state, and trips to those old miners' bars were a form of adventure and bonding. They were places where the miners could let go, share stories and laughs, and talk about anything from river floods to pennant races. The bars were nondescript rooms in old buildings in or just out of town, places like Finch's Bar, Killa Bar, the J-J Cafe, Lee's, the A-D Bar. The alcoholic content of beer was limited, by law, to 3.2 percent. But the owners of the bars, whose patrons were sometimes the men who were paid to enforce the laws, all understood the system.

"Everybody knew when a raid was coming," Ferguson said. "The police would notify 'em so the real booze would get cleared away, get put all under the bar; you had to make it look good for the citizens. So as soon as the sheriffs or the deputies or whoever would leave, well, they'd bring out the booze again. It was all payoffs back then, you know, everything got taken care of. There were a lot of bars around there."

Mutt used to load up the car with Mickey and his friends and take them to ball games too, to minor-league games up in Kansas and Missouri and sometimes, treat of treats, all the way up to St. Louis itself, to see the great Cardinals. On one of these trips, Mantle saw a young left-handed hitter in a Class C game. The hitter was an unknown player named Stan Musial, playing for a Cardinal farm team in Springfield. Mantle's father had his son watch the young hitter spray the field with line drive after line drive, and Mantle swears that he became a Cardinal fan thereafter and that Stan Musial became his idol. But Mantle may also have become a Cardinal fan because his father was one and because of those trips to the big city and to old Sportsman's Park.

"Every now and then, when he had saved up enough money and he could round up his companions," said Mantle, "my father and one or two of his brothers would schedule a pilgrimage to

St. Louis to watch the Cardinals in a Saturday night game and a Sunday doubleheader. To me, this was like a journey to the Big Rock Candy Mountain. It meant an early bath on Saturday, then getting into a clean T-shirt, clean blue jeans, and my beloved baseball cap."

Mantle wore a baseball cap all the time; the hat became part of his head the way feed caps seem permanently secured to the heads of farmers. Mantle bent and creased the bill of his cap over and over again until it made him look like an old grizzled veteran of the game's wars rather than one of its dreaming striplings. His old ball cap, Mantle said, "was one of my deepest vanities. . . . I would have worn that cap to bed, I believe, if my mother had let me, and I often put it on first thing in the morning."

Seventh grade marked a change in Mantle's life. It was a passage over an invisible boundary but a significant one, because in the 6–2–4 school system of the day, it meant moving on from grade school to junior high. His body was beginning to change, and his interests were widening.

Beginning in the seventh grade, said Bill Mosely, Mantle began playing basketball—for real. He threw himself wholeheartedly into what was virtually a new sport, played in a new way. Around the area and the country, the game in 1945 was very much station to station, played below the rim. A player who scored in double figures, ten or twelve points, was often a team's high scorer. Passing was a critical part of team strategy. The idea was to work the ball around from player to player until someone was open, usually for a standing, two-handed set shot. "Set-shot artists" could position themselves twenty, even thirty feet from the basket and, with a dip of the knees and a flick of the wrists, send the ball in a high accurate trajectory to the basket. Or if a team had a big man—a player who was six-four or six-five, say—the ball would be worked in to him, the player would spin left or right and with a long, sweeping motion, arc a hook shot off the backboard into the basket.

At Commerce, the game was taught a little differently. A coach named Frank Bruce wanted the players to scramble, to run whenever they got the ball, and to guard their opponents man to man rather than in the standard zone defense. Commerce was the first "fast-break" team in the area and, as far as anyone knows, one of the first schools anywhere to employ what has since become the standard for the game.

Mosely was a center on the team, "Little Mickey" was a ball-hawking guard and outside shooter who if anyone came up to challenge him would drive for the basket. Or he could use his speed to simply peel off with the ball, lead his team up court on a fast break, and look to drop the ball off or to go straight for the hole, playing exactly like a point guard decades before the term itself was invented.

"They called him Mr. Outside and me Mr. Inside," Bill Mosely said. "But that didn't mean exactly what you think, because we both played all over the court. Yeah, I had a good hook shot and we'd work the ball around and try to get it in to me and then if they dropped off, I'd get the ball back out to Mick who was open for that outside shot. But more times than not, Mick would drive for the basket, get double-teamed, and drop the ball off to me. We'd always be doing different things. One night I scored thirty-eight against Overton in the Northeastern Oklahoma School Tournament. Another time, Mick scored over thirty in a game."

Basketball was one thing, but soon Mickey began playing football. He went out for the team at Commerce High and made it and then was something of a star. He was fast, he had good hands, and he was fearless—all of which made Mutt Mantle understandably fearful. The idea of Mickey's wrecking his baseball chances on football was deeply disturbing. He tried to talk him into quitting football but could not bring himself to lay down the law. There was no look or lash attached to Mutt's misgivings, just as there were no doubts in Mickey's mind that the challenge of two, three, or even ten sports would ever reduce his love of playing baseball. Baseball was always a "commitment," a passion; those other sports were just play.

Commerce High was not a school that attracted anyone's attention outside the immediate area. There were no scouts or recruiters around, only vociferous, partisan fans—and cheerleaders. Mickey Mantle and Bill Mosely became, in the words of schoolmate and friend Ivan Shouse, "the two studs of Commerce" as they starred in three sports, but the distinction apparently never went to their heads. According to friends and by his own accounts, Mantle remained shy and withdrawn. Meanwhile, Bill Mosely met and began dating a childhood sweetheart who became his wife.

Mantle's biggest fan was his mother. Lovell Mantle had none of her husband's reservations about Mickey's playing other sports—or if she did, they never interfered with her lusty partisanship. Her passions, unlike her husband's, were always visible. She was the one, not Mutt, who administered physical punishment when it was called for, Mickey said, and her moods were never a secret. At heart, though, Ron Mantle believed, Lovell was really a softy when it came to her own.

"She was a jewel, she was just somethin' else," he said. "She'd get mad at the kids all right, but you have to take that as it comes. I remember one time Ray stayed out late one night. We were around nineteen or twenty then, I may still have been in high school. Anyway he had stayed out late and I was there in the morning and Lovell was in the kitchen rantin' and ravin'. 'He's gonna get up and he's gonna want me to fix him toast and bacon and eggs and coffee and I'm not gonna do it!' She just carried on and on. Pretty soon Ray came down, draggin' in there, and said, 'Mom, fix me some toast, bacon, eggs, and coffee,' and she just went right over to the stove and did it. No matter how much she let on, she just didn't have no meanness in her."

But at games, there was no need to back off. "I was no longer a peanut, though smaller than most of my teammates," Mickey said. "It didn't stop me from feeding Bill Mosely winning points at key games during the season. My folks were always involved. They loved every minute of it. And mom used to rant and rave at those games. . . . If she objected to a referee's decision, you could hear her voice travel across the gym: 'Where are your glasses, you bum!' Believe me, if the referee called anything against Commerce, she'd cuss him out like a sailor. It unnerved my father. He'd cover his head with his hands and sit a few rows behind her to get away from the shouting."

Football was the same. Once, during a game, Lovell came out of the stands to help out one of her sons in an on-field brawl. But football had a far more serious, far more extended affect on Mickey's life.

The Commerce football team, like the basketball team, was innovative. As the basketball team was one of the first to employ the fast break, the football team was one of the first in the area to use the T-formation. Mickey's size made it unlikely that he ever seriously thought about making football more than a way to pass time in high school, but his speed made him a natural running back, and his hands and feet made him something more.

"We had only about forty, forty-two guys on the football team," said Ivan Shouse. "Mickey was a runner and he could catch a ball. I remember reading in the local papers recently where Marshall Smith in Miami said he could have been a professional at anything he wanted, but one thing I'm sure of is that Mick could have kicked the football for anybody. Basically, I think he just liked to kick the football; whether he had his shoes on or off, he just could put his foot into it."

There was no platooning in football back then. Mantle played both ways, and because of the position he played and because he was also the team's kicker, he was involved in literally every play of every game. The team's coach, Alan Woolard, was apparently something of a backwoods Vince Lombardi. Woolard was the school's baseball coach as well; he brought no special flair to Mickey's favorite sport, but he was an ambitious and determined football coach. He was, in the words of one Commerce player, "too good for the school." He later went on to coach in bigger schools in Nowatte, Oklahoma, and Lawrence, Kansas. He eventually tutored some top-notch players, including the pro quarterback John Hadl.

Bill Mosely, who got a college football scholarship out of Commerce High, was the T-formation quarterback and remembers that it was in his and Mantle's freshman year that the new system was introduced. Mantle did well with his speed, both running and catching the ball, but he could also surprise opponents with a halfback dive through the line. Sometimes faking that play would allow Mantle to go out and become an open receiver. But also, Mosely remembered, Mantle was easily injured. In that freshman year, Mantle was kicked in the shin during a game. The injury led to the most celebrated case of osteomyelitis—a staph infection of the bone marrow—in sports history. It was the kind of injury that Mutt dreaded all along, and its psychic damages eventually exceeded any of the real physical ones involved.

The injury initially seemed more like a severe bruise or sprain. Mantle was staying at his aunt and uncle's house, a block from the school, and he went there following the game. He could barely walk. Soon afterward, Floy Norton remembered, Coach Woolard arrived. "Mickey was at my house when the coach came by and found him," she said. "His ankle was all swelled up and they took him to the hospital in Picher where he stayed for quite some time."

The only concern then, and for almost a year following, was whether or not Mickey would recover, and if he did in what shape he would be. In the hospital in Picher, Mantle was separated from his family for the first time. His mother visited him during the days, and his father came on some evenings, after he got off work. Nick Ferguson was a regular visitor, too. And on his visits, he noticed that his friend was usually despondent. "He was really sad, he was depressed. I think he was lonely because he had never been away from home before," Ferguson said. "He was always used to having his brothers and sister around. The people he saw most of the time were doctors and nurses, and he wasn't getting any better and he didn't know what was happening to him. He was scared and he didn't know what was going on."

After futile treatment in Picher, Mantle was transferred to the Crippled Children's Hospital in Oklahoma City. Doctors told the family that Mickey's leg would have to be amputated. Mutt Mantle's shock must have been enormous; it was Lovell, though, who ultimately took charge and saved her son. Credit the discovery of penicillin, too, but she was the one who intervened on behalf of the gods.

"When they took him to the hospital in Picher, they began giving him shots of penicillin, but they didn't work," said Max Mantle. "Penicillin was new and they were giving him shots every three hours and I think he had to have fifty-six shots. And at that time, I don't think he weighed 115 pounds. Then they took him to Oklahoma City, and it was there that they told him he was going to have to have his leg off. I don't know what his dad said, but his mom was the one who said no. His mom said there was no way in hell they were going to do that. She's the one who did that. She's a tough woman, yes she is. Said, 'Ain't a-gonna take that leg off.' And then after that, with all that penicillin, he had these boils all over him, had boils on his arms and legs and even his eyes. And they disappeared. And I don't know if it was the penicillin, or any other medicine but then he started growing, he just grew, shot right up in less than a year and it was all muscle. It had nothing to do with running and playing ball."

The suddenness with which he grew may or may not have been significant. Growth spurts are obviously common at that age. What was not so common, however, was how quickly he bulked up. Nick Ferguson recalled the time and the dramatic change in his friend's physical appearance.

"Mutt used to drive Mickey back and forth from Oklahoma City, to the Children's Hospital," he said. "They'd leave him there for awhile and then take him back. Mick was like 130 when this started, and then he lost weight to where he may have been a hundred pounds, I don't know, but then all that changed. I don't know what they were giving him. He thought maybe it was steroids, but I have no idea what it was, but he claimed that's what pumped him up to 160 pounds. When he came out of there he was 160 pounds, he looked totally different. I also happen to think that that's maybe what caused him trouble in his later years. His muscles didn't develop naturally maybe, and it caused a lot of pulls and everything. It was just kinda unusual the way he grew like that in one year."

Ferguson, over the years, saved many pictures and other memorabilia from his high school days when he, too, was one of the outstanding athletes of Commerce. About fifteen years ago, he gave most of his pictures and memorabilia to Mickey, but among the pictures he kept were a pair that showed Mantle the spring following his injury and then a year later when he was healed and he had grown. The photographs are sandlot team pictures from 1947 and 1948. "In the first one, [Mickey's] standing behind the bench because Leroy Bennett and I wanted him in the picture. Mick didn't think he should be in it, but we wanted him to be and you can see how ill he is. Then the next year he's all muscled up, 160 or 165 pounds."

Years later, Mantle was reminded of this period by the story of Terry Fox, a young man who set out to run across the country after he found out he was going to have a leg amputated. "When he found out they were going to take his leg off, he went berserk. I can imagine how he felt," Mickey said, "because I would rather have seen mine rot off than have somebody cut it off without at least trying to find an alternative."

The threatened loss of his leg confronted Mantle with all that he had been living for, all that he knew about who he was and what was expected of him. When he finally gained weight and strength, when he was at last able to put aside the crutches he had to use to get around, he threw himself into sports more fiercely than ever. By the time of the second photograph, Mickey's junior year of high school, he was playing ball full-time again. The practices with his father resumed with even more intensity. Mantle says he felt driven at this time. It was as though in the aftermath of seeing his own body nearly destroyed, his father's will and his own had merged. Mutt Mantle's enormous expectations were now fully reciprocated in Mickey's desire to please him. It was not his father's but his own obsession he was answering to now, his own determination to raise his sights beyond the black holes and cheerless towns that surrounded his life.

Chapter 4

The summer of 1947 was a momentous one for baseball, but it turned into a special one for Mickey Mantle as well. It was the summer when Jackie Robinson broke the color barrier, and from one stadium to another the look and feel of the game changed. Mickey had a summer job working in a cemetery, and he hung out in town with his friends, mainly playing pool. He was something of a pool shark; his game was eight ball, and his friends said he earned more than enough for pocket money. The summer stretched out with ball games to play, movies to catch over at the Coleman in Miami, and trips to take out to Spook Light—it was just like any other summer, until Uncle Tunney died. A short while later, in late August, Mutt loaded up his old LaSalle for one of those trips to St. Louis. Nick Ferguson went along on this one.

Ferguson remembers the good-natured banter between Mickey and Mutt as they made their way across Missouri. Mutt was a notoriously slow driver—a trait later picked up by Mickey. "This one time we left around midnight and we drove all night," Ferguson recalled, "and we got there about eight in the morning." When they got there, they were confronted by something they had never seen before at a major-league ballpark.

"The people were lined up—at eight o'clock in the morning—they were lined up all around Sportsman's Park, and they was all the blacks. They could only sit in the bleachers," said Ferguson, "but they were all there to see Jackie. I remember we saw that game. Jackie was playing first base that year. There was this play where he went after a foul pop-up and he ran full speed towards the dugout. He would have killed himself, but one of the Dodgers jumped up and saved him."

Ferguson said there was little talk about what they had seen. Mantle has elsewhere noted that coming from his area of the country, he was initially opposed to integration, but that his feelings were never strong and never persisted. Ferguson explained, perhaps more guardedly, "There were never any black people in our area, nobody ever discussed any of that, we never thought about it, really. There just was never any discussion."

The year was significant in a completely different way for Mickey Mantle. In that summer, people began to take notice of him playing in the Ban Johnson League. The league had originally been organized as the Junior Cardinal League for players up to eighteen, but it was expanded to include players up to twenty-one. College players as well as top amateurs were recruited to play. The league was clearly the best in the tristate region and had been the brainchild of an old miner-ballplayer named Barney Barnett. Barnett was committed to building baseball in the area, and he put some of his money into the operation, coaxing more out of local businesses. He fixed up a field at Baxter Springs, cutting out a real infield, installing bleachers, and even putting in lights for night games. He knew everybody who was anybody involved with baseball in the tristate area. All the miners and their teams knew him and, more important, so did major-league scouts. The scouts, it was said, rarely failed to stop off to catch a league game when they were traveling through.

Barnett was an obvious point of contact for Mutt Mantle. Through Barnett, Mutt had a practical outlet for pushing his son's career. Through Barnett, Mutt got to know and recognize some of the big-league scouts, and through Mutt, those scouts got to hear a little more about Mickey than they had gotten from Barnett.

In Mickey's junior and senior years, he played for a team in the B.J. League that Barnett organized and that had been named the "Whiz Kids," because the players were generally younger and better than those on other teams. "When old Barney came and talked to you about playing for him, it was just like you thought you were going to the big time," Nick Ferguson, an ex–Whiz Kid said. "Leroy [Bennett] and I were playing for a team up around Webb City that was in the same league, so when he came and asked us to play for the Whiz Kids, you bet we did. That was 1946 and we took Mick to all the games because he was still too sick to play that year, but then the following year he began playing regular." Mantle said, years later, that just getting a "real uniform" then made him feel like a major leaguer.

The team played its games midweek and weekends, traveling up into Missouri and as far south as Bentonville, Arkansas. On Fridays, Barnett often matched his Whiz Kids against miners' teams and other adult sandlot teams. For those nonleague games, the Whiz Kids were allowed to use a nonleague, adult pitcher. During the years that Mantle and Ferguson played, the Whiz Kids ran away with the league.

Barnett had all the while been talking to several scouts about different Whiz Kid players, among them Mickey Mantle, the team's erratic shortstop, sometime pitcher, and emerging slugger. It was at the sandlot park in Baxter Springs that Mickey Mantle ran headlong into his own myth. It was an innocent and, ironically, even troubling meeting, but given the great cost that Mantle paid for everything that was sweet in his life, this was just a minor flare-up on a lazy afternoon by a forgotten riverbank deep in Mark Twain country.

The park in Baxter Springs had a river that formed an outfield boundary, some five hundred feet from home plate in right field, cutting in a diagonal to about four hundred feet in center. The boundary had never been a factor because no player had the power to swat a ball into the river. The river was more challenging as a force of nature than as an outfield fence. In the spring when the rains were heavy and all the tributary creeks in the area became swollen with floodwaters, its steep gorge filled and spilled under and around the outfield boards, across the carefully manicured field, turning it into a swamp. On this one bright Sunday afternoon in 1948, the river was unusually high. It had not yet overrun its banks, but the spring rains had brought its level perilously close to the playing field.

That day, the Whiz Kids, representing the tiny town of Miami, were playing a league game at the park. There was a crowd of about 250 or 300. Mantle, in his new body, had been making local people take notice. He had hit some unusually long home runs that spring and early summer, and he had legged out some bunts from the left side of the plate where he seemed to reach first base even before the ball hit the ground. On this particular afternoon, Mantle hit three home runs, two from the left side and one from the right. The first time up, he launched a shot to right center field that carried far over the outfielders' heads and took one bounce into the stream. It was unclear whether the ball would have carried to the river in low tide or not. The next time up, same thing: an even longer one to right center. The third time up, he hit one that local people still believe was the longest home run they had ever seen, a ball that simply kept rising as it passed far over the center field riverbank, landing somewhere in the middle of the stream. So electrifying were these blasts that someone in the grandstand began passing around a straw hat to raise a collection for the boy who struck them. When the hat had made its way from one end of the bleachers to the other, there was a grand total of fifty-four dollars waiting for Mantle—more money, he said, than he had ever seen before at one time in his life. His mother and father, he said, made no attempt to have him give it back; it was all his.

The only problem was that when he returned to Commerce

High in the autumn, he discovered that he had been barred from taking part in school sports. Someone in the grandstand that Sunday afternoon, or someone later on who heard about what had happened, contacted the Oklahoma State Athletic Commission. The state commissioner, a man named Henderson, ruled that by accepting money for playing, Mantle had forfeited his amateur status.

If Mantle had spent the rest of the year sidelined and resumed playing baseball in the spring with the Whiz Kids, the chances are almost certain that his career would have unfolded exactly as it did. But no one then could foresee what would happen. Mutt Mantle, whether he believed his son's future was at stake or whether he simply found the ruling intolerable and unfair, made a determined effort to overturn it. He traveled to Oklahoma City to argue his son's case. The decision was ultimately reversed, and Mantle was allowed to retain his amateur standing as long as he returned the money that had been given to him.

Mantle says he worked at odd jobs to do it, but others in the area offer a laugh and a shrug of the shoulders at that suggestion. Bill Mosely said, "They worked out something where Mickey paid Barney back in some way in a check. It was one of those deals where Mickey got to keep the money, but it looked good on paper." In any case, the significance of that afternoon in Baxter Springs had little to do with paying back fifty-four dollars. The money was paper, but the home runs were gold.

Barney Barnett had by then included Mickey Mantle on his short list of players for scouts to look at when they passed through. It is unlikely that any were around that day because for a while longer, Mantle remained the area's Hope Diamond buried in chat. Several scouts had passed through and seen Mantle play and had apparently been unimpressed with him or, at best, only mildly interested. The Yankees' best scout, Tom Greenwade, was among those who came through to see some Ban Johnson players and saw Mantle as well. In a 1952 letter to J. G. Taylor Spink of *The Sporting News,* Greenwade outlined the way he had "discovered" Mantle. He had seen him first, he said, in the beginning of that season:

"This must have been in the early part of the 1948 season," he wrote, "for I went to Alba, Mo., about August 1948 to see Mantle and other players that I heard of on both clubs. Mantle, who at that time was referred to as 'Little Mickey Mantle,' was small and played shortstop. He pitched a couple of innings in this game. I wasn't overly impressed."

In his most recent autobiography, Mantle says that Greenwade first saw him at a Baxter Springs game, where he switch-hit a couple of home runs, and then during a rain delay Greenwade sat with him and Mutt and asked if he would like to play for the Yankees. Mantle said Greenwade then backed off by saying that he could not make an offer because Mickey was still in high school and could not make an offer until he graduated, but to make sure he kept the Yankees in mind, and that he would be back on graduation day.

There will forever hover around Mantle's life and career the wings and mirrors of fable so that what is remembered and what actually happened will always be in perilous tension. The discovery of Mickey Mantle by Tom Greenwade was, in David Halberstam's words, "a classic scene, straight out of Norman Rockwell. . . . The myth of Tom Greenwade, the greatest scout of his age, blended with Mantle's myth to create a classic illustration of the American Dream: for every American of talent, no matter how poor or simple his or her background, there is always a Tom Greenwade out there searching to discover that person and help him or her find a rightful place among the stars."

In all likelihood, it took awhile for the myth to jell; the mold provided by the gods may, in the end, have only teasingly resembled a cover of the *Saturday Evening Post.*

What is certain is that Mantle went back to school that year, glad to be able to play football and basketball again. Though he was sure he wanted to be a professional ballplayer, he had no real sense that he could be, no real belief that Tom Greenwade would call again. Nor did Mutt count on Greenwade or anyone then. He continued a strenuous and unabating campaign on behalf of his son in the hope that someone, somewhere would see that he was big-league material.

That fall or the following spring—the timing is uncertain—Mutt heard about a tryout camp being run by the St. Louis Browns in Lawrence, Kansas. He packed up his LaSalle and drove Mickey and Nick Ferguson there. As always, Mickey teased his father about his slow driving, urging him to get the car out of second. "He was on him all the way up there, just laughing, ragging on him, saying it was gonna take us a couple of hours to get there driving that slow," Ferguson said. By the time they arrived, heavy rain had canceled the tryout. It was not rescheduled. It seemed at the time like the cruelest of blows, but, as everyone knows, the rain gods were only playing. "It was just canceled," said Ferguson, "so I guess you could say if not for the rain, Mickey might have wound up playing for the St. Louis Browns not the New York Yankees."

There were other contacts, other disappointments. The St. Louis Cardinals at one point expressed an interest in signing Mantle. A scout named "Runt" Marr visited with Mutt and Mickey, talked with them, but apparently held off when a question of bonus money was raised. He said he would get back to the family. He never did.

Meanwhile, the school year passed like any other, except that the family had moved out of town, and it was harder to get to and from practices and games. The tiny Mantle home in Whitebird was seven miles away, and the bus that Mickey took from Commerce in the evenings let him off about a mile from home. The bus passed by the offices of the old Eagle-Picher Mining Company, but once the lights from the offices slipped by, the surrounding area was inky dark and frightening. Mantle says he worried about people being murdered, about "death in the dark," so that when he got off the bus, he ran the mile to his home in "less than four minutes."

But much of the time, Mantle stayed in town, either with his friend Bill Mosely or with his cousins Max and Ron. The 1949 school year was remarkable in still another way: He fell in love. As big an athlete as he was in school, he was still painfully shy. He had gone out before, nearly always on double or triple dates. Most of the time, he was unable to carry on a conversation, to enjoy something as simple as dancing. He was just too bashful, he said, plus he could not dance. There were Saturday night "teentown" dances, barn dances, proms, where his friends teased him and urged girls to ask him to dance, just to watch him squirm.

But then he met Jeanette Holmes, a best friend of Bill Mosely's girlfriend. Jeanette Holmes was one of the prettiest girls in school. She had short, curly blonde hair, freckles, and was a year younger than Mickey. Neva Mosely remembered that Holmes was "a real, nice person, but maybe a little spoiled." The Holmes family was better off than the Mantles and most other mining families, but Holmes—and her friend Neva Mosely—said that never was a factor in her relationship with Mantle. Holmes, Mosely said, "was sharp, funny, witty, she could make light of anything that was heavy, she could make the smartest cracks, she was very popular, she had a lot of friends, she was really something."

Most important, she was not overly impressed with Mantle's status as a big-time athlete. She was drawn to him because of his shyness, his sly humor. In his quiet and often dark moods, she found him puzzling—and lovable. She did his homework for him. He was her first love. She was Mantle's.

Their courtship, Holmes said, was very ordinary: Friday and Saturday night trips to the movies, dances where they left before the dancing began, and car rides when they could go park somewhere. Sometimes they double and triple dated, with two, four, or six others piling in with them. They took rides out to Spook Light, the most unusual tall-tale factory south of Calavaras County.

The attraction of the place was the strange lights that appeared there, lights that seemed to rise up from nowhere out of the woods and surrounding boulders and then circle around, move up and down, and then recede and fade completely. So far as anyone could tell, scientists included, the lights had nothing to do with swamp gas—there was no marshland around—or any other kind of measurable phenomenon. "Nobody ever figured out about them things," Ivan Shouse said. "*Ripley's Believe It or Not* has been here and they just can't figure it, no one can."

When Jeanette Holmes was asked if she remembered going out to Spook Light with her boyfriend, Mickey, she said, "Oh heavens, yes. We would load up eight or twenty in the car and go. We'd act real stupid. It was so crowded you couldn't do anything out there anyway, so we'd hang around and act silly and come home."

She never saw the lights, she said, though to this day "kids are still going out in carloads looking for the Spook Light." Ivan Shouse swears he saw the lights, but that the most peculiar thing about them was that if you emerged from your car and went out to meet them, they would disappear.

Bill Mosely, who occasionally went out to Spook Light with Mickey, also saw the lights. "It was a pretty long ways out there, sometimes we'd go out there and wait for the light to come and sometimes we'd miss it. But yeah, a light really would come up. It would only come up on certain days, certain nights; it would come up if it was damp or rainy, those nights it would really come out, it would come right up in front of the car, and boy it could scare the devil out of you. We'd start yellin' and everything and maybe somebody'd get out of the car and throw rocks at it or take a shotgun."

But Mick Charles—as Jeanette says Mantle called himself—by then was far more interested in his girlfriend than in shooting out mysterious lights. Holmes and others in the area who remember them acknowledge that the relationship they developed was serious. "We never exchanged anything, maybe a class ring, something like that, I don't remember, although I tell you this," Holmes said with a laugh, "I always wanted his baseball jacket. I would have liked to get that from him—but I could never ask for it. I'm a little bashful, too."

Holmes says that the only interests Mantle had then were centered around sports. "All ball, football, baseball, basketball, he was either at practice or gone to games, that was his life and his family backed him on it all the way and promoted him."

She was positive he was not a drinker then: "He drank some, yeah, but not around me," she said. She was most struck by how uncomfortable he was when it came to things like dancing. She went to his senior prom with him in the school gymnasium and remembered that they left after eating but before the music began. Then she remembered something else. "This is totally off the wall," she said. "One time we were at a gathering where we played Ping-Pong and I wound up beating him. It was a big mistake on my part. He wouldn't play anymore, that was it. That wasn't his thing, table games, he said. He got into this mood and he just wouldn't play anymore."

The relationship lasted a year and ended, Holmes said, because she got interested in someone else. There had been no marriage proposal, though she could not answer the question of Mantle's intentions. "Let's put it this way, I don't think his daddy would have approved." A marriage then would have gotten in the way of his career.

But that was something on Holmes's mind as well. She believed that when she broke off the relationship, no matter what Mantle felt, their lives were heading in totally different directions. The future for teenaged girls in Commerce, Oklahoma, in the '50s was as clear and limited as that faced by young women everywhere at that time.

"The guys had the pool hall and sports and had a lot of fun, you know," Neva Mosely said. "We silly girls just messed around. Jeanette and I spent a lot of time walking to and from each other's houses and being silly teenagers, but we knew what was out there for us, even then. We just kinda grew up thinking about getting married and having children and that was the extent of it. And where we came from it was so different you couldn't imagine. None of us were clothes horses, you couldn't get up and go and do, the future was just day to day and for us girls we knew how we had to fit into that."

Getting married and raising a family was just as much a calling for the men. The hope was always, for both the men and the women, that this inescapable summons would involve inescapable attraction, so that what was expected would somehow merge with what was truly desired. Given all that followed in his life, in the way he eventually made a family, this year in Mantle's life clearly marked a turning point for him. Jeanette Holmes remembered that sometime after they ended their relationship, she got a postcard from Mantle from Galena, Illinois. There was nothing on it other than his signature, Mick Charles. She assumed that the card was sent from a place where Mickey and his father had gone for summer jobs in the mines. She was wrong. Beginning in 1949, Mantle's summers for the next twenty years would be consumed by the unimaginable challenges and uncertainties of big-time, professional baseball.

Chapter 5

The almost legend of Mickey Mantle has its version of the steps that led to his signing with the Yankees and his going off to play minor-league ball. But the Yankees' actual signing of Mantle may have involved just a bit more than a great old scout's stumbling onto the find of a century hidden in a cornfield.

By the spring of 1949, the Yankees and other teams were well aware of Mantle. Barney Barnett and Mutt Mantle had kept up their active campaigning, and they now had every reason to believe that some team would take a chance in the not very distant future. Some chance: In the year since Mantle filled out, he had acquired a player's body—in the language of scouting, a "live" body—though he was still a boy. While it was clear that he just wasn't a shortstop, a pitcher, or a sometime catcher, his new-found strength enabled scouts to project ahead, to see Mantle not as a 165-pound kid but as a 200-pound man who, with all the raw skills he possessed as an adolescent, might mature into the sort of player any scout would have given his career to sign.

Tom Greenwade appeared again in early May to see Mantle play. "An umpire in the B.J. League, Kenny Magness, told me about a game the night before in which Mantle played, and he was very high on him," Greenwade said. Apparently, he made up his mind on the spur of the moment to get his second look. He caught a Whiz Kids game at Parsons, Oklahoma, and this time saw a lot more. First, he saw that "live" body, twenty pounds heavier, all of it muscle, distributed mainly in the forearms, chest, and shoulders. Mantle apparently still did not impress Greenwade with his hitting, but, he says, "I became interested in a hurry when I discovered he could really run." He says he asked Barney Barnett when Mantle's graduation from high school was, learned that it was to be the last Thursday in May, and then says he appeared the Friday following graduation.

Well, maybe. The flap over Mantle's amateur status had undoubtedly gotten around, and, surely, every scout in the area with any interest in Mantle must have been unusually alert to avoid doing anything that would cost them a chance to sign him. The rules were clear: Players could not be approached until they were out of high school. Contact before then meant a team would forfeit its negotiating rights.

The Yankees then were not only the most successful franchise in the majors, but also, along with the Brooklyn Dodgers, the most aggressive when it came to landing talent. Though racial attitudes at the top blocked them from pursuing black players, they were otherwise innovative and even daring when it came to finding and molding future Yankees.

Between the time Greenwade first saw Mantle way back when and his graduation at the end of May 1949, there was almost certainly contact between the scout and the family, contact that led to Mantle's decision to sign with the club. Sometime after Greenwade became impressed with Mantle, the Yankees invited Mickey to a tryout camp at Branson, Missouri. The camp was different from those of other teams, explained Lee MacPhail, who was the general manager of the Yankees' Triple A affiliate in Kansas City as well as being a farm director in the middle west for the parent team. "This was an invited tryout camp. Other teams all had tryout camps, but I think, I am almost sure, we were the first to do it by invitation only. We had them all over the country, and the one in Branson covered the middle west. So Greenwade brought Mantle in with his father."

Mantle apparently did not do that well. "I know Tom was a little disappointed in his showing there, but you could see all the tools that he had. Tom was a very good judge of talent, so it was only understandable that he hoped Mickey would do better, but he actually showed you everything you wanted to see, even though the great power didn't come till later. He was only seventeen then. I wouldn't say he was skinny but he got much bigger and stronger after that and he most assuredly developed more power. But still, for a high school boy, he had excellent power from both sides, great speed, and a great arm—and he was a shortstop. Eventually, we signed him—to a small bonus, something like five hundred dollars, something like that, it was less than a thousand dollars, which in those days added up to something. The question was where were we going to send him. We had two Class D teams, one in Macallister, Oklahoma, and one in Independence, Kansas. His father wanted him to go to Independence because it was closer to Commerce, so that was how he started. He was very close to his father."

The official story is a little different. In the version for the monuments, Tom Greenwade appears on graduation day and asks the principal to excuse Mickey from the school's graduation ceremonies that evening so he can play a Ban Johnson League game, sees Mantle hit two home runs in the game, is awed, and then immediately following the game, puts a contract in Mutt's hand, downplaying his son's talents so he can sign him on the cheap—four hundred dollars for the rest of the minor-league season at Independence—and then, after some caviling by Mutt, adding an eleven hundred dollar signing "bonus."

The real story, with the requisite amount of petty intrigue and finagling, is much more an American classic than the make-believe version. Greenwade, Mantle said, later told him he was the best prospect he had ever seen. And Greenwade told someone else that Mantle made him feel the way old Yankee scout Paul Kritchell must have felt when he first saw Lou Gehrig. There is no reason to doubt that. In the hard, grimy, underpaid world of scouting, where the best scouts are always invisible when they do their best work—even to their employers, who to this day pay them social security wages—the only real reward is the finding of talent. And for that rare scout who stumbles on a Mickey Mantle, no financial payoff can match the thrill of the discovery itself. In carefully understated language, Greenwade's account to Taylor Spink of the way he finally signed Mantle puts the legend in the shade:

> On Friday I drove to Commerce, and this is the first time the Mantles ever knew there was such a person as Tom Greenwade. I found out the graduation exercises had been postponed till that night for some reason. Since I had no desire to violate the H.S. tampering rule, I was careful not to mention contract or pro ball either, but had understood Mickey to play in Coffeyville that night and I wanted to see him play and I didn't mention that I had seen him play before. Well, they talked things over with the coach and superintendent and decided to pass on the exercises since Mickey already had his diploma and go to Coffeyville instead.
>
> Of course, I was there. Mickey looked better at bat, hitting left handed. I still don't know he switches since the only pitching I have seen him against is right-handed. After the game, Mr. Mantle tells me that Mickey will play Sunday in Baxter Springs. I told him I would be at his house Sunday morning and go to the game with them. I was there about 11 A.M. I was scared to death for fear some scout had been there Saturday. I asked Mr. Mantle if anyone had been there. He said "no." I was relieved.
>
> We all went to Baxter Springs, and for the first time I see Mickey hit right handed. Mickey racked the pitcher for four "clothes-lines," and I started looking around for scouts, but none were there.
>
> When the last out was made, Mr. Mantle, Mickey, and I got in

> my car behind the grandstand and in 15 minutes the contract was signed. We agreed on $1500.00 for the remainder of the season and the contract (Independence of the K.O.M.) was drawn calling for a salary of $140.00 per month. Mickey reported to Harry Craft at Independence. He was slow to get started and as late as July 10th was hitting only .225, but finished the season over .300. The following year at Joplin he hit .383 I believe. You know the rest.

Greenwade, the gentleman caller, was probably too mindful of the Mantles' feelings to say too much more here. But taken along with MacPhail's version, knowing that the Yankees had seen Mantle before and had not been impressed, the real story adds to our understanding of both Mutt and his son at the moment they committed to the Yankees.

"I asked Mutt what they wanted to sign," Greenwade told another reporter with whom he was friendly, "and I told him that the contract had to be with Independence of the K-O-M League." Mutt, according to Greenwade, replied, "Well, you'll have to give him as much as he'd make around here all summer, working in the mine and playing ball on Sunday. His pay in the mine is eighty-seven and a half cents an hour, and he can get fifteen dollars on a Sunday playing ball."

Greenwade then took out a pencil, did some figuring, and came up with a figure: "That's about $1,500, right?"

Mutt, said Greenwade, nodded in agreement. Then factoring in the monthly salary of $140 and the amount of time Mantle would play that season—three months—Greenwade said: "That's around four hundred dollars. Suppose we make up the difference and give you $1,100." Mutt, the agent for his son, agreed.

However excited Greenwade was, however close to the vest he had to play his hand, the impact of this moment on the Mantles was much less hidden. Suddenly the geography of their lives had been altered substantially. The main streets of the little towns that ran one to the other now pointed to unimagined distances. Whether the Mantles perceived it or not, this first professional contract, ridiculously paltry, turned out to be a passport to the world.

Mantle was terrified to leave home. His heart ached for what he was leaving behind rather than for the lights that beckoned to him from the new world ahead. He still was not over Jeanette Holmes. The thought of being without his friends and parents was unimaginable.

One day in June, his father packed him into his car and drove him the 170 miles that separated Commerce from Independence, Kansas. The Mantles pulled up at a hotel where the team's manager, Harry Craft, was staying. Craft met them at the door of his room, half undressed, in the middle of shaving. He struck Mickey as a hard, tough old-timer—something like his father. He said Craft had the same kind of stern dignity about him that his father had, although later, Mantle felt he was chilly and aloof. At that moment, however, Mantle transferred all the dependent feeling he had for his father to this total stranger. Or was that what he was instructed to do? Mantle remembers that Mutt told him, "From now on, Mr. Craft is your boss. I want you to do just as he tells you and pay attention to what he says, just as if I were saying it myself. And I want you to play this game just the way you would play it if I were here to watch you."

Mantle said he was struck nearly dumb with the solemnity of the occasion and that in the days following, he was painfully homesick. "I suppose small-town kids who go away for the first time still get homesick. But I have never met anyone who was any homesicker than I was my first days in Independence. . . . For a time I seriously thought I would give up the whole deal and go back to playing ball around Commerce."

The towns the team traveled to were strange and new to him: Carthage, Bartlesville, Chanute, Ponca City. The long bus rides and the cheap hotels made the players stir-crazy. They were all teenagers away from home, and they dealt with downtime and confined spaces as if they were extras in *Animal House*. They got into water bucket fights, flung chunks of watermelon at each other, and generally caused mayhem wherever they went. Mantle got into the swing of it because, he says, he found himself among other kids just like himself.

Harry Craft, it turned out, was hardly a surrogate father. The person Mantle looked to for guidance was a good deal less aloof than Craft and considerably less severe than Mutt. Lou Skizas, said Nick Ferguson, "was sort of like a poor man's Billy Martin." And Mickey followed him, leaning on Skizas's outgoing, gregarious nature to help him past his shyness and homesickness.

Skizas was not a drinker, though he was a ladies' man and an extrovert. Mantle marveled at the ease with which he seemed able to assert himself. The young players all boarded in private homes; Mantle and a couple of teammates lived quietly with an elderly couple on a tree-lined street not far from the ballpark, a typical minor-league park of the day with colorful local advertising plastered across the planks of the outfield fence. The players had a favorite hangout in town, a place to eat and watch the girls go by. Skizas had the easy swagger of a teenage confidence man. His derring-do got him into hot water with Harry Craft, who, Mickey said, was also something of a womanizer, only older and in a position of greater authority. When Skizas innocently made a pass at one of Craft's girlfriends, the manager called a team meeting and, without naming names or saying precisely what it was he meant, warned his players against violating his "sacred golden rule."

Slowly, under Skizas's good-natured and empty-headed tutelage, Mantle felt more comfortable and began enjoying himself. Skizas remembered Mantle from that time as a scared, shy, but very friendly kid, "just the most typical small-town boy you'd ever meet." Mickey wasn't wild or a drinker then, Skizas said, but he was fun-loving and laughed a lot.

Skizas kept Mantle and everyone else laughing on the field as well. He was the epitome of the superstitious ballplayer. He had one of the oddest batting stances anyone had ever seen. It was nearly one-handed because he carried a rabbit's foot in his back pocket at all times, and he would keep rubbing it as he stood waiting for a pitch to be delivered. Skizas's move of his hand from the rabbit's foot to the bat rivaled Pete Gray's maneuvers with ball, glove, and arm. Still, Skizas could hit. "He was a great hitter, and he was intelligent because he graduated from the University of Illinois with honors," said Steve Kraly, who roomed with Mantle at Independence and then the following year at Joplin.

Life in the minors was very different then, says Kraly. There were no Susan Sarandons around, and the days and nights, though hard, were as unexciting as most of the small towns they traveled through.

"We played cards a lot, poker, penny ante stuff; we'd sing on the bus, hang out in a sundry shop, there definitely weren't any places where you would go and see a bunch of girls and dance," Kraly said. What there was a lot of, he said, was baseball.

Harry Craft, according to Kraly, was not only a manager, but also a real teacher. "He actually was like a father to us because we were all so young, and he taught us what baseball was really like in the minors. He made us think about what to look forward to if we moved up, he made us think about the game, getting yourself prepared to play better baseball, moving up to better leagues, better traveling, better living."

Kraly and Mantle hung around with other teammates, talking baseball all the time. They thought of themselves as professionals, but they still talked about their heroes in the game: the Babe, Lou Gehrig, Lefty Gomez.

Mantle had two problems that first year, Kraly said. First, he had a hard time catching pop-ups. "He had difficulty throwing the ball from shortstop, but he had a harder time catching pop flies," Kraly said. "It was just one of those things. We'd tease him all the time, we used to tell him, 'Mick, on an infield fly, just get out of the way, let Muddy Waters come over and catch it.' And Mick loved to be teased, 'cause he teased right back.

"The other thing was, he was shy and it was tough for him to be away from home that first year—especially that first year." Mantle did a lot of singing on the team's bus trips. His favorite country performer then was Hank Williams, and his favorite song, according to many who knew him, was "Long Gone Lonesome Blues."

One of the team's road stops was Miami, the town Mantle had represented when he played on the Whiz Kids. When his team played there, he was, of course, surrounded by family and friends. The stops were too brief, and he tried in his way to extend them. He pleaded with his friends to visit him in Independence, suggesting that he might even try to arrange tryouts for them if they came. They were as good as the players he was playing with, he said, and he was sure that the manager would take a look at them if they came. Two Whiz Kid friends of his, Donny Dodd and Nick Ferguson, did get on a bus one day and travel up to Independence. They hung out with Mickey, saw where he lived, and met some of his teammates, but when the subject of a tryout came up again, Ferguson told Mickey he had forgotten his gear back in Commerce, and Donny Dodd said he wasn't really interested.

What mattered most was that Mantle was starting to play, raising his average from the low .200s to a respectable .313 by season's end. He had not yet convinced anyone, however, that he was ready for much more than the next rung up the long minor-league ladder. He made forty-seven errors that season.

But Mantle was already caught up in a world far larger than he had ever imagined. If the circuit around the K-O-M League was narrow, its connections to the wider world were not. The cold war was in full swing, and the fear of war had become part of the nation's life. Korea was still an unimagined peninsula somewhere, but the Russians were real, and preparation for war with them was a given. The fear of communism dominated national politics, and that fear trickled down into the smallest hamlets of the land, even into places like Commerce and Whitebird, Oklahoma.

In the fall of 1949, after the season ended, Mantle went to work in the mines with his father. By now, Mutt had worked his way up to the position of ground boss for Blue Goose Number One. His salary was up to seventy-five dollars a week, and that fall he was able to find something of a sinecure for his son with Eagle-Picher, doing odds and ends above ground. Mantle earned thirty-three dollars a week—about what he was earning playing ball—running errands and helping out around the electrician's shop.

But the job offered no protection at all from the military draft, which at the time could separate a player from a promising baseball career at the drop of a postcard. Mantle's draft notice arrived one day in November, instructing him to appear for a physical at his local draft board. Mutt and Mickey were both sure that this was it, that their baseball dreams were going to be put on hold at the worst possible moment.

But there was an ironic twist in his draft call: The injury that nearly cost him his leg now let him continue his baseball life. The draft board weighed his history of osteomyelitis, and following his November examination, he received a notice in December classifying him 4-F, removing him permanently from any further threat to his career. That was not the end of it by any means, as Mantle would soon discover, but for now he could continue playing baseball, and the future was as open as the Oklahoma sky.

That same autumn, Mantle began dating the woman he would later marry. Merlyn Johnson was a shy, attractive girl from Picher. She was a cheerleader and had met Mantle casually when he was in high school. Johnson's sister went out with one of Mantle's friends, Ivan Shouse, and it was Shouse who, at Mantle's urging, set up a triple date to Spook Light one night. Shouse was well aware of his friend's hurt over losing Jeanette and was also mindful of the unsuccessful dates he had arranged for him before. "First time was with Levanda Whitby," Shouse said. "We went out to Spook Light, but then he asked me to call Merlyn, whom he had seen before. He knew I went with her sister. After that they began seeing each other. There wasn't much more to it than that."

In the spring, Mantle reported to a Yankee minor-league facility in the Ozarks, the sprawling complex near Branson that he had seen once before when Tom Greenwade brought him in. Now he was on surer ground, surrounded by players he knew, players who had spent a season with him. The weeks at the camp were enormously successful; Mantle and several of his teammates from Independence were bumped up to the Class C Joplin Miners of the Western Association, and as the camp unfolded and Joplin began to play other Yankee minor-league teams, it became clear that a good team the year before was going to be quite a bit more in the year to come. During spring training, they beat everyone in sight, including squads of Triple A players.

Mantle enjoyed himself enormously. His teammates all were players the Yankees seemed interested in, players who shared a sense of mutual admiration and mutual skepticism that they would find themselves anytime soon playing in so august a place as Yankee Stadium. The players hung out together in camp and spent off hours fishing and fooling around. They went on nighttime frog hunts, where Mickey learned to shine a flashlight in their eyes and then snap them up from behind. The players lugged along ice chests of beer and food, sat around and ate and drank until they were like overfed frogs themselves. The days were idyllic, Mickey remembered: "It was one of the most fun times I ever had. Not a care in the world from the middle of March until mid-April"—until the baseball season began.

The Joplin Miners, Mantle's new team, tore apart the Western Association from day one. By midseason, they were ahead by more than twenty games, prompting league officials, wanting to maintain fan interest in the second half, to declare a split season,

In addition to his football and baseball exploits, Mickey Mantle was a star guard on the Commerce High School basketball team. Mantle is in the front row, far right. 1

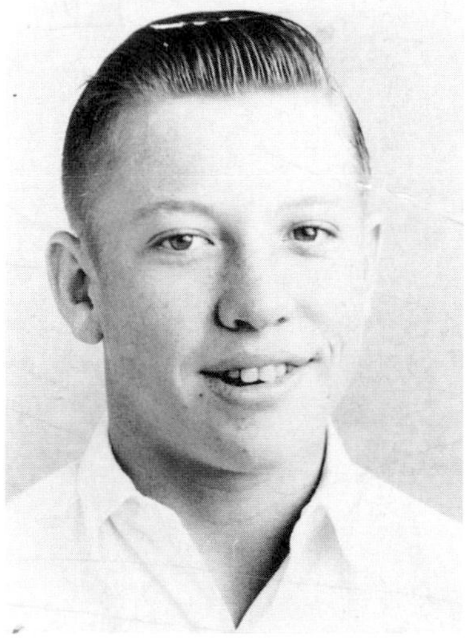

Mantle, in a high school photograph.

2

In 1947, Mantle (left, at center, in street clothes) missed playing with his sandlot team, the Whiz Kids, because of his football injury. In 1948, Mantle (below, far right) returned to the team, considerably more filled out in the shoulders and chest. (Mantle's friend Nick Ferguson is at left in the 1948 photo; team coach Barney Barnett, who also coached Mickey's father, is seated in the middle.)

3

4

Mantle, before an exhibition game in Dallas, Texas, on April 10, 1951, with his girlfriend, Merlyn Johnson, and his father, Mutt Mantle.

5

Mickey, with Mutt, outside the family's Miami, Oklahoma, home on April 12, 1951, awaiting word from his draft board about a possible reclassification from 4-F. Mantle's draft status was a cause of friction and controversy during the Korean War.

6

Young Mickey relaxes and reads his fan mail a month into his rookie season.

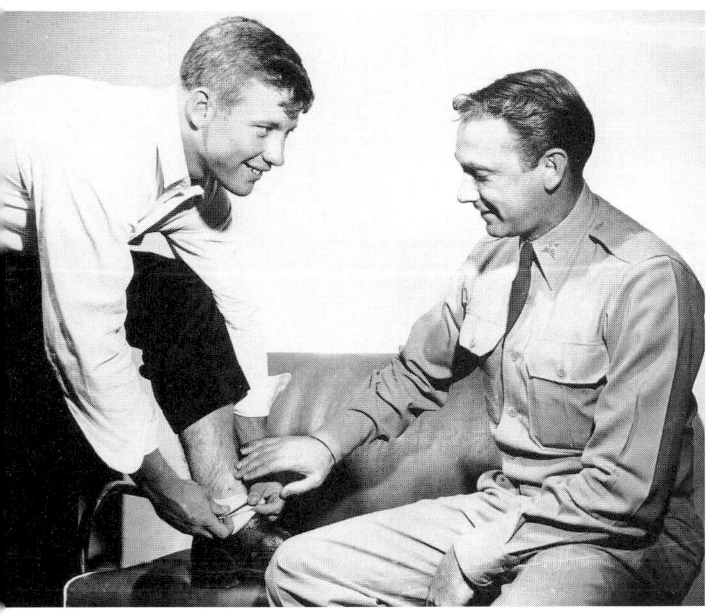

Captain George L. Farrell of the Army Medical Corps checks out Mantle's ailing leg once more before again reclassifying him 4-F in August 1951. Mantle's osteomyelitis required an automatic 4-F classification, no matter how much uproar it caused.

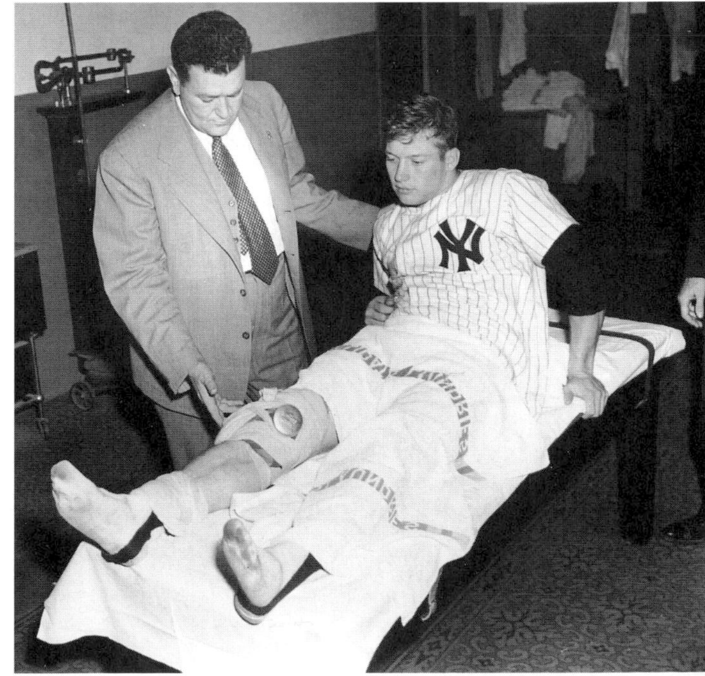

Another examination, this time by Dr. Sydney Gaynor in the Yankees dressing room after Mantle was carried off the field on a stretcher during Game 2 of the 1951 World Series.

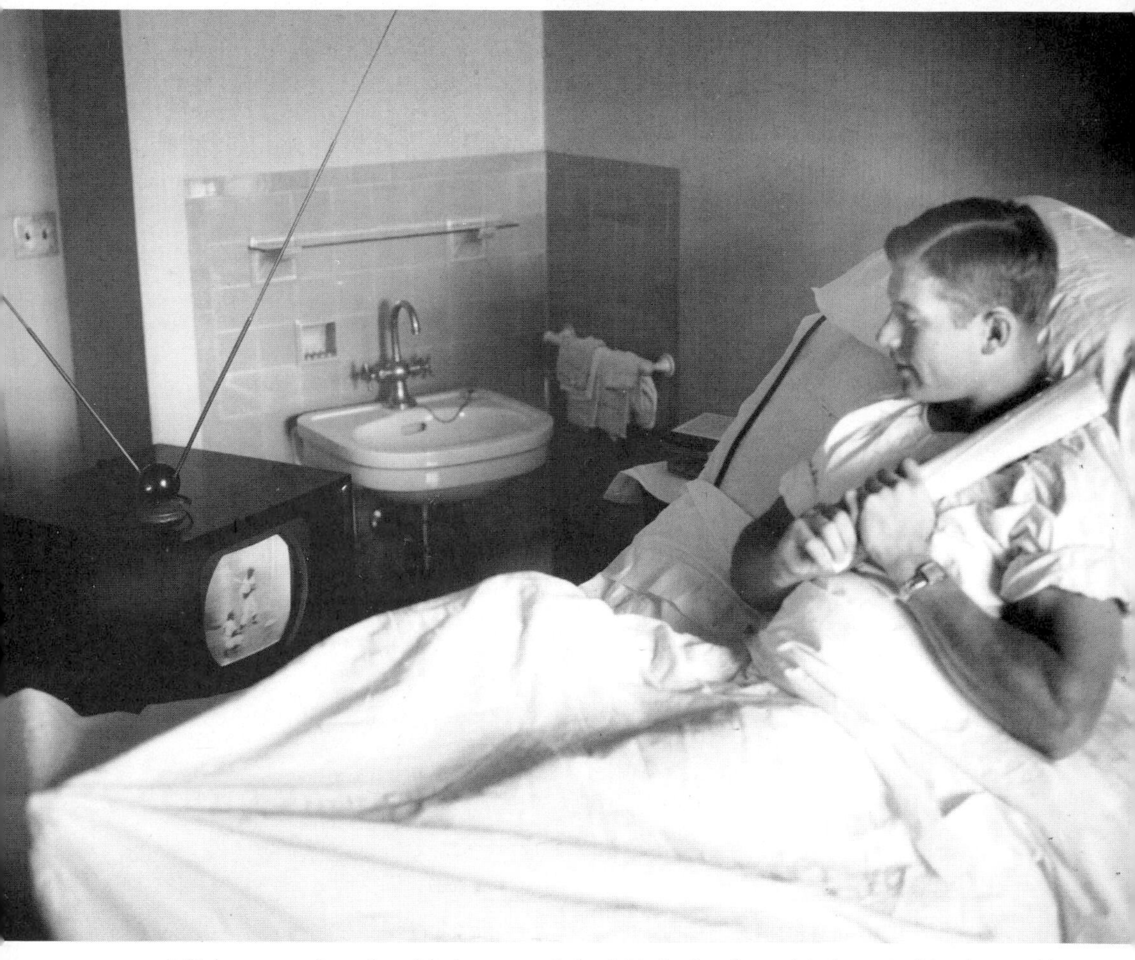

Mickey watches the third game of the '51 Series from his hospital bed, awaiting surgery. His father was in the next bed, and Mickey only then learned of the seriousness of Mutt's condition; neither knew that Mutt had seen Mickey play for the last time. 10

11

Mickey with his mother, Lovell, in Commerce in the fall of 1952.

12

Mickey talks with Mutt (left) and outfielder Cliff Mapes in Commerce.

13

Joe DiMaggio hangs up his glove after thirteen major-league seasons. From left: Casey Stengel, DiMaggio, and Yankees owners Dan Topping and Del Webb.

Mickey and Merlyn Mantle cut the cake after being married in the Johnson family home in Picher, Oklahoma, December 26, 1951.

14

something that has since become a feature of lower minor-league baseball everywhere. The splitting of the season meant little, however; Joplin picked up in the second half where it left off in the first. They were a Class C team with talent good enough for Double A and Triple A. They won again by a huge margin—only to lose, perhaps predictably, in the playoffs.

Mantle's roommates in Joplin that season were Carl Lombardi, Steve Kraly, and Bob Weisler. Lombardi was a middle infielder, only vaguely remembered by Lee MacPhail, the Yankee farm director. Mantle recalled him, though, as a second baseman who was on the receiving end of many of his poor throws from short and who always took them with a "good deal of patience" —as though Lombardi was the star putting up with the lesser player. Mantle's other roommates, though, were genuine prospects. Bob Weisler was a lefty pitcher who was then the best pitching prospect the Yankees had in their entire system—including Whitey Ford and all the others who became marquee players later on. Weisler stalled and dropped away at Triple A when he hurt his arm. Kraly made it all the way up through the system to appear in one Yankee season, 1953, by which time his old minor-league roomie had become a major-league star.

As memorable as the Miners' season was that year, Mantle's was even better. Steve Kraly remembered that when Mantle showed up that spring, he was different physically. "The year before he was like 160, 165; then at Joplin he was all filled out, the way everybody knew him later. And instead of hitting an occasional ball over the left field wall, he was hitting these things over the light towers."

The Miners' equipment manager that season told Mantle—and his teammates—that one of Mantle's homers was the longest he had seen since Babe Ruth hit one clear out of Sportsman's Park in the 1928 World Series.

Through much of the summer, Mantle's batting average hovered near .400, finally settling at .383 for the year. But Kraly also remembered that Mutt Mantle came to most of the Miners' home games and was Mickey's sternest critic. "After the ball game, we'd come out and he'd be sitting there waiting for us and we'd talk with him. Sometimes he'd give Mick a pretty good slashing, because, you know, sometimes he'd lose his temper even though he was hitting .380; or if a guy caught a long line drive he hit he'd get real mad, and his father would tell him, 'Hey, don't you ever do that again—you're not gonna succeed if you do that.' "

Still, despite such moments, it was a dream season, the sort any minor leaguer would pray to have and one that came to Mantle as easily as a season in Baxter Springs. With his pals, Mantle enjoyed the social life of Joplin as though it was the center of civilization. There were parties to go to, hangouts where it was easy to waste money on beer, burgers, and pinball. Mantle's home run hitting even helped him eat well that year; a local eatery sponsored a free steak giveaway for every Joplin Miner home run, and Mantle hit for a ton of beef.

There were other, less pleasant forms of attention. One night Mantle went to a party in town. There apparently had been some drinking, and among the drinkers was someone who either harbored some sort of resentment for Mantle or simply thought it would be fun to surprise him, really surprise him. Years later, Mantle told friends that when he went to this party, he opened the door, stepped inside, and simultaneously received a punch in the face, breaking his nose. Call it the first of his baseball injuries or the first episode in another, darker part of the legend, but in any case, it left him staggering in pain even as his season continued without anyone but his closest friends knowing what had happened.

If the season ended anticlimactically for the Miners, it was something else for Mantle. He was ordered to report to the big team the day after Joplin's season ended. Mantle says he received the news from Harry Craft aboard the team bus, and that Craft also told him he would be the manager next season at Beaumont, and he hoped to have him play for him there. Mantle could scarcely believe what he heard. He was actually going up, was going to dress elbow to elbow in the same locker room with players who until then were only make-believe stars in Broomball games. He was going to New York, Chicago, Detroit, St. Louis —that's where the team would be the day after the Miners' season ended. St. Louis—Sportsman's Park, the dream palace he had seen with his own child's eyes. The big-league players he saw there in the past he only saw from a distance; Mutt had never allowed him to approach a big leaguer then, no autographs, no pestering words at the gates to the ballpark or in the dining rooms. Mutt had always insisted that he never disturb a big-league player from the right to his own well-earned private life. But now he was going up; *he* was going to the big leagues.

Mantle remembers the day—September 17, 1950—and the feeling in the pit of his stomach as he joined the big team. He said that it was impossible to imagine anyone more frightened and awed than he was. The sight of the New York Yankees on the field was dazzling, blinding. He remembered Phil Rizzuto first —and why not? Mantle was a shortstop, and Rizzuto was the team's star at that position. And though Rizzuto later would make funny remarks about his uneasiness at seeing his new young rival in camp—rather in the manner of one of those old violinists who gathered at Carnegie Hall to hear the debut of a child prodigy, saying "it's warm in here," while a great pianist answered, "Only for violinists"—Rizzuto, on seeing Mantle standing near a batting cage, was asked by a reporter what he thought of the Yankees' new find. He said, with a wink, "A little big for a shortstop, don't you think?"

Mantle noticed Rizzuto's range and ease during infield practice, and he too was painfully aware that he wasn't the player to take his position. He watched the players in the locker room talking with the press, handling them with the same ease Rizzuto showed in fielding ground balls. And then there was DiMaggio, who came and went like royalty. Impeccably dressed, reserved to the point of frightening even old teammates away from him, he was a figure of awe and terror to Mantle. Years later, Mantle recalled one of the first times he was sent in to pinch hit. "I yanked off my jacket in two quick moves, flung it behind me, and grabbed a bat from the rack," he said. "But there was a smothered yell from the bench. . . . I had tossed my jacket right in Joe's face and he was wearing it like a hood."

With DiMaggio—and everyone else on the team—Mantle remained hopelessly unable to speak unless spoken to first. The joy he felt at being there was mixed with this unabating sense of personal discomfort, one more keenly felt because he was on his own, clueless, leaderless. Mutt wasn't around, nor was his minor-league pal Lou Skizas. There was no one until the team arrived in Chicago, where another rookie player, Bill "Moose" Skowron, was added to the roster.

Skowron was a genuine "bonus baby," a player out of college whom the Yankees had paid big money for—twenty-five thousand dollars. He was as lost as any other rookie, but he was from Chicago and far more self-assured than Mantle. He was friendly and open, and Mantle reached out to him. He and Mickey roomed together on the road and then back in the Bronx for the season's final few weeks. In Chicago, where Skowron was on his home turf, he was able to show his new friend the Loop and other familiar downtown sights. While they were on the road, the roommates reported to the ballpark, took their batting practice, watched the game, and then afterward saw one movie after another in their free time. In New York, it was a little different. Both of them were lost.

"He was eighteen and I was nineteen years old," said Skowron, today a sixty-four-year old who recently had double bypass surgery. "We didn't know anything about New York. It was funny. We didn't have much pocket money, so we'd usually go eat pizza somewhere—'cause I liked pizza and Mickey had never even heard of it before—and we used to write everything we spent down and then we handed it to the traveling secretary, Frank Scott. I remember the look Scott gave us. He laughed and said, 'Hey, you guys are Yankees, you get *spending* money.' We had just put down what we spent, that was all."

In New York, the two rookies roomed at the Concourse Plaza Hotel, where many of the players put up. The hotel was just a couple of blocks from the Stadium, easy walking, in an area that was then solidly middle class and where personal safety was just a thought in hygiene class. Skowron and Mantle worked out in the mornings, taking batting and fielding practice. During the games, they sat in the stands watching. Then, afterward, when the Stadium had emptied, there was another practice round, led by the team's coaches, Frank Crosetti and Johnny Neun. When they finished, Skowron said, they sometimes ventured out into the big city.

"We'd go downtown to eat, look around. We'd get lost on the subways sometimes—that was fun. We'd never know where we'd wind up, only that sooner or later we'd find our way back."

Skowron remembered how painfully shy Mantle was in those first days, but that beneath the shyness there was genuine sweetness and good humor. "He was such a quiet, shy guy, I mean he didn't bother with anybody. But he had so much God-given talent and you could see it right away, I mean, he could play. And it was like he never understood it. He'd get on me for being a 'bonus baby,' he'd just agitate me, real funny, he'd say, 'I got $500 and you got $25,000'—did it right up to this year," Skowron said in 1995.

Teasing, "agitating," was the way the two players learned to be accepted among their new teammates. "The guys used to agitate us all the time. Jackie Jensen was another one who'd tease me about being a bonus baby," Skowron said, "and he was a bonus baby himself. But all the guys were great to us, Allie Reynolds and Ed Lopat, we were scared shit and they made it easier for us."

No one made them more welcome than Hank Bauer, the tough young marine then in his second full season in the Yankee outfield. Skowron remembered that Bauer was the first Yankee to take him under his wing. "We were working out with the Yankees at Sox Park in Chicago and I was looking around . . . and he says, 'What are you lookin' for?' and I said a bat, I don't want to use any regulars' bats because if I break one I'll be in trouble. He says, 'Use mine.' Just that way. I never forgot that."

Later, after Skowron was shipped down to the minors where he stayed for several seasons before returning to the big club, it was Bauer who stood in and helped Mantle get through his rookie days.

When the season ended, it was as though Mantle had literally wakened from a dream and found himself in the room he had always known, back in Oklahoma. Though he had tasted pizza in New York, there was another taste waiting for him in Whitebird.

The details of that winter are now shrouded by the varying accounts Mantle has given of them. It is clear that Mickey worked in the mines, though at what it is less certain. In his early autobiography he says he worked above ground as a sort of roustabout. In his later book, *The Mick,* the work is both above and below ground, and murderously hard. "I was a miner, no different than the rest. We would drill holes and install motors to pull fresh air into the shaft. . . . I'd have to go down there, cleaning, fixing, and sometimes taking them out altogether for an overhaul. I'd slowly ride up in one of those cans, 300 feet or more to the surface with a hoisterman controlling the hook, the speed and smoothness, depending on his touch. . . . One time [the hoisterman] let go of the controls and I plunged half way to the bottom before he caught me."

Whatever he did, and however he embellished it later, the fall began late for Mantle that year. He did not immediately go home but instead went to Phoenix, where the Yankees held an instructional camp for their best prospects. The camp was unique; it was formed by the organization to provide the sort of learning opportunity that bench-warming at the end of a big-league season could not. The Yankees hoped by this camp to give their young players a chance to play in competitive situations and to have the organization's best instructors there to guide them as they worked. Eventually, the Yankees worked out an arrangement with the St. Louis Cardinals to run a similar camp with them in Florida. This first Yankee instructional camp, said Lee MacPhail, who was one of its organizers, "was the beginning of the winter instructional leagues." He is the only one on record to acknowledge this brief fall workout.

Why Mantle would have made no mention of this brief trip to Arizona is not clear. Perhaps it merged in his mind with the prespring training camp, held in late January, which the team's top prospects also attended. Perhaps it was because there were more serious things happening in his life.

Mantle became aware that fall that his father was not well. There was nothing specific, just a sense that his father was without his usual energy, that he seemed fatigued most of the time, that sitting up in the living room after dinner seemed to be a chore.

There was also the renewed question of the draft. Mickey Mantle was not yet a name in the nation, but he was in Commerce. When he got home, the town papers were full of the great news that a native son was a New York Yankee. Mutt Mantle took every opportunity to point out to his friends, to anyone who stopped over at his house or whom he ran into around town, that Mickey had worn the famous Yankee uniform, that he knew Joe DiMaggio and had actually talked with him, "personally."

But the great news was countered by those who wondered aloud why Mickey Mantle, if his legs had carried him all the way to New York was not also healthy enough for a couple of years' service in the U.S. military. Things had changed since Mantle's 4-F classification the year before. In June, war had erupted in Korea.

All through the summer, the war dominated headlines in the United States and around the world. At the outset, South Korean and UN forces had been pushed all the way back south on the peninsula, only to launch a massive counteroffensive, replete with a World War II–style seaborn invasion behind enemy lines.

By the fall, the allies were pushing north to the Chinese border and then, ignoring Chinese warnings, undertook a "final offensive" to end the war that only provoked a wider, far deadlier conflict when hundreds of thousands of Chinese troops streamed across the Manchurian border, throwing the war into a prolonged and bloody stalemate.

Because the cold war had turned hot, with each day's battlefield reports containing the sobering news of casualties and deaths, the question of who served and who did not became far more touchy. The sons of miners automatically served, while the sons of the privileged somehow slipped away. And suddenly Mickey Mantle, a miner's son, who was healthy enough to hit baseballs out of sight and to run faster than the wind, was looked at not just as a New York Yankee but as a common draft dodger.

The talk was barely more than a whisper at first. Mantle says he remained unaware of it for some time. But it was insidious and ultimately became part of that mixture of resentment and hostility that awaited him in New York when he arrived there, heralded as next in line to Ruth, Gehrig, and DiMaggio. It also awaited him in his hometown each year when he returned from the baseball wars.

But the worst of that was still in the future. In that late fall and winter of '50 and '51, there was only the memory of a great season past and the almost unendurable anticipation of a better season to come. New York was now a real place to him, full of excitement and possibility.

Mutt Mantle, who had never seen New York but who had his small-town fears about its temptations, was full of concern as well as anticipation. He wanted his son to get his life in order so he would be able to focus entirely on baseball when he got there. The girl he was going out with, Merlyn Johnson, with her simple homespun ways, would make a perfect wife for him, would make sure he kept his mind on the game and his life down to earth. He urged Mickey to marry her. Mantle thought about it but wasn't ready to commit himself. He had other things on his mind. The

Yankees had ordered him to report to Phoenix again, but now, because he had to get there on his own, he did not have the money to pay the fare. The Yankees thought he might be holding out. They ordered him to report immediately—but also wired the money for his train ticket, astonished that in his naiveté he was unaware that travel costs were always reimbursed.

Leaving home this time really meant leaving home. Spring camp was fifteen hundred miles away, and then, after that, what? Beaumont, Texas, or Binghamton, New York? In either case, the upcoming journey he was about to make, he knew, was unlike any he had made before. There would be no friends within reach; the look and feel of his life would be beyond anything he had known. When his father and mother drove him halfway across Oklahoma to catch the express train for Phoenix, Mantle says he felt overwhelmed.

"In the station, I kept swallowing hard and drinking more water than I ever needed before," he said. "I turned at the steps to the train, took my suitcase in my hand, and tried to say good-bye to my mother and father. I was just about able to speak. I got on the train, looked for a seat by the window where I could see my parents, and tried forlornly to wave up at them as they waved up at me. The train began to roll at last and then the sobs rose up and choked me. For a whole hour I sat with my fist pressed tight to my mouth and my swimming eyes fastened unseeing on the blurred country outside as I tried to keep from weeping aloud. Tears kept welling up in spite of me. . . . What a jerk I felt like!"

But what a rookie! Frightened and withdrawn, he entered the game and also the minds of those who grew up during his career like no other athlete since. He was about to make his mark on a decade that would be forever associated with James Dean, Marilyn Monroe—and Mickey Mantle.

Chapter 6

The Yankees were in Phoenix in 1951 rather than in Florida because they had swapped training sites for a year with the New York Giants, who went that season to St. Petersburg. When the Yankees assembled in Phoenix for their early spring "instructional" camp, there were forty top rookies present, including Gil McDougald, Andy Carey, Bob Cerv, Tom Sturdivant, Skowron, and Mantle. Among them, without question, Mantle was the one everyone was talking about.

Casey Stengel was starting his third year with the team and, having won World Championships in the two previous seasons, was, said the author Robert Creamer, in a "new position of strength." His hold on the team had been questionable through his first two seasons. He was not yet the professor of doublespeak and indecipherable riddles so beloved by the media when they were otherwise scratching for copy. In '49, when Stengel won his first championship, he did so with a team that had no reason to look to him for leadership. He was resented by older players, DiMaggio and Rizutto among them, and that resentment seemed compounded by Stengel's uncertainty about his own position in the organization. Stengel was blamed by Joe Page, the great relief pitcher who faded badly that year; Page felt Stengel overused him, although it is not clear that that was the case. Page appeared in a few more games that year than he had the year before and had almost certainly been asked to warm up without being used more times than he had in the past, but his total of innings pitched matched those of previous seasons.

If Stengel had been uncharacteristically reticent and even tentative in 1949, in 1950 he became so sure and full of himself and what he had accomplished in winning the pennant that he became overbearing to his players. Rizzuto told Creamer that "we'd have clubhouse meetings that would last an hour, an hour and a half. . . . and he'd talk the whole time. If you listened carefully there'd be something useful for everyone in there, but he confused a lot of players. Especially the younger ones."

But winning gave Stengel the authority to do what he most wanted, which was to teach. Stengel faced an organizational problem for which he was going to be held principally accountable. The Yankees of 1949 and 1950 were an aging team in transition; the great farm system that had been developed over the years was about to provide the club with the players it needed. Stengel's job was to keep winning while the team turned over.

DiMaggio, Rizzuto, Johnny Mize, and Tommy Henrich, the nucleus of the '49 and '50 championship teams, were all reaching the end of the line. There was no guarantee that those coming up behind them would ever be able to take their places.

The rookies had to be taught. So the staff, the best teachers in the organization, were assembled to make sure the young players got the crash course they required. Jim Turner trained the pitchers, Bill Dickey the catchers, Frank Crosetti worked with the middle infielders on the fine points of turning double plays and with the rest of the squad on base running; it was essential, he preached, for players to learn to think for themselves in determining when they could take an extra base, move from first to third on a single. Stengel himself took the outfielders. He gave lectures on the seven ways a player could slide into a base, illustrating what he said by talking about DiMaggio, the best base runner he had ever seen.

Above all, in working with outfielders, Stengel came nose to nose with Mickey Mantle. There had long been pressure from within the organization to change Mickey from an infielder to an outfielder. Mutt Mantle, who had seen all of Joplin's home games the previous season, had bent the ears of the Miners' manager Harry Craft with that idea. Craft, who was a shrewd enough judge of talent on his own, submitted a manager's report at the end of the season in which he urged that Mickey be shifted "to 3B or the O.F." Craft noted that as a shortstop, Mantle had "a fine arm and a good pair of hands. Lets the ball play him too much." But the most significant words in Craft's report were ones that said what Stengel and many others in the organization already knew about Mantle: "He has everything to make a great ballplayer." Craft was also present in camp as a teacher, one of Stengel's assistants.

For Stengel, Mantle was the sort of player who came along once in a lifetime. If he could make him over into *his* player, Mantle would be to him what Ruth and Gehrig had been to Miller Huggins, what DiMaggio had been to Joe McCarthy, and what Mel Ott had been to John McGraw. In the dry desert air, the raw power of the young player was astonishing. With his wild tomahawk swing from the right, and his uppercut from the left, he hit balls out of sight, farther than Stengel had seen anyone hit before. He was Jimmie Foxx from the right side, Babe Ruth from the left.

Part of the regular routine of the camp involved sprinting drills. Trios of players lined up to run fifty-yard heats. Invariably Mantle won these, no matter whom he was matched against, by ten or more yards. The first time this happened, Stengel thought his eyes had betrayed him, that the other players racing Mantle might have stumbled or started too slowly. He ran Mantle against the same group and then against everyone in camp, and the result was always the same. No one had ever seen a player with this kind of speed.

But Stengel had a problem. Because his great prize was an inadequate shortstop, he had to make him over quickly if he wanted to keep him. George Weiss, the team's GM, was already on record with the belief that Mantle needed at least another season or two in the minors before he would be ready. But Stengel thought the way around that was to go ahead and convert him to the outfield. But this, too, was risky. Where to place him? Center field was still occupied by DiMaggio. Left field was a possibility, though Gene Woodling, a twenty-eight year old traded for a year earlier, had been solid there. Also, left field in the Stadium was just too treacherous. It was vast, and late in the season it became blinding anytime a ball was hit above the roof of the ballpark. The sunfield in Yankee Stadium was the most notorious in the league. Right field, then, was the spot, although there were other, more experienced outfielders already on the squad.

The Yankee right fielder since anyone could remember had been Tommy Henrich, who had just retired—but who was back in camp, helping out. Stengel turned the job of tutoring Mantle over to Henrich.

Every day, the player they called "Old Reliable," who for so many seasons had been one of the best right fielders in the game, went with Mantle out to a corner of the field and worked. The principal thing Henrich tried to teach was how to come in under a fly ball, catch it, and then as quickly as possible unload a throw. The maneuver, seemingly easy, was tricky. The ball had to be caught at a point where the transfer to the throwing hand would be easiest. Then the footwork had to be just right, so the fielder's momentum would be carrying him into the throw as he was catching the ball. An extra step, an extra split second often meant the difference between making or not making a play.

"The very first time I saw him, I didn't know how good a ballplayer he was going to be," Henrich said. "You mighta said there was raw potential, but a lotta guys come up to the big leagues with potential, it's the easiest word in the book to use. He was a nice kid, very quiet, did everything that was ever asked of him—very, very dedicated."

Henrich positioned Mickey about twenty or thirty feet from him and then began making easy, pop-fly throws. "I'd lob the ball up in the air to him, that was all I had him doing," Henrich said, "so he could get his footwork right. He was practicing just this one thing: that as the ball came down, he had to prepare himself, he had to be ahead of the play. Start the action as the ball's coming down, learn the best way to transfer the ball from your glove to your throwing hand, and at the same time your body's in motion—gotta happen with it, like it's all part of the same move or you don't make the play."

There were other aspects peculiar to the position, like fielding balls that were slicing away as they hit the turf, or making throws from the corner where, for a right-handed thrower like Mantle, a pivot was required. Henrich and other coaches fungoed ball after ball to Mantle to give him the proper feel for what it was he had to do. "You can't do it any other way, you can talk all you want but you have to do it. It's like teaching a guy to play the piano," Henrich said. "You can't really teach anything until he puts his fingers on the keys."

And then the games began. Henrich, like a lot of Yankee veterans, simply did not know what to expect from Mantle. He saw that he could hit, but he wasn't sure he'd hit big-league pitching. "I didn't know whether he was going to be a good hitter or not. But the most obvious thing was the power."

Whether it was batting practice or in the games themselves, Mantle's power hitting impressed Henrich as it had Stengel and the Yankee coaching staff. But Henrich was an old pro who had forgotten the names of so many would-be sluggers who never stuck. "I just didn't know how good a hitter he was going to be. You think of guys like Dave Kingman—he comes to mind—and Bill 'Swish' Nicholson. You don't know whether it's going to be

Mickey 'Swish' Mantle or not. These guys get up against a Warren Spahn or a Whitey Ford who can make 'em look awful bad. You just don't know."

But Henrich noted that Mantle could field, that he could make plays from the outfield that could never be altered by what clever pitchers did. "I started seeing he was doing it right. He was perfect. I don't know if he's gonna do that all the time, but the point is he did it so right. And then there was this one game. . . ." In telling the story, Henrich's voice seemed to soften, as though the recollection of what he had seen forty-five years ago brought back his original sense of incredulity.

"I remember the play exactly. We were playing the White Sox in a spring training game, and the play involved Jim Busby. Look him up, he's there in the book, he was with the White Sox then, and he could really run. He's on third base, there's one out, they hit a fly ball to Mickey and I'm thinking, 'Okay, Mickey, now let's see what you can do.' And I wanna tell you he did it perfect, the whole routine perfect. He got his momentum started, and when the ball came down he got it transferred so fast you could barely see him do it—and he was in motion as he was catching the ball. He doesn't take a single wasted step and he throws this bullet all the way in the air to the catcher and Busby is out by so much that he actually turned around and tried to go back to third base! It was the greatest throw I ever saw anyone make on a baseball field."

And still the great raw power was on display every day. Before anyone in the media began fitting him into Babe Ruth's uniform, Mantle's peers were the ones who were doing it. The hard-bitten old pros, it turned out, were the first to be awed by him.

"Yeah, I remember his first spring training out there in Phoenix," said Tommy Byrne, the veteran left-handed pitcher. "He was hitting the ball so damn far. It was unique back then to see someone hit the ball like that where it not only went over the fence but it was still going up when it went out. He actually got the attention of opponents. You could see them all come forward in the dugout to watch him when he came up, even in batting practice, just to watch his swings. You'd see guys sitting out in the bullpen standing up to get a look at him."

Some of the players, like some reporters, wondered whether the thin desert air made the home runs go farther than they normally would. Gene Woodling, worried about playing time in an outfield that was becoming too crowded, asked the same questions and came to his own conclusions: "Oh, I remember that first spring all right. Here comes this kid and BOOM he's hitting balls out of all those ballparks. Well, everybody's a home run hitter out in that area. But he hit his so far you just had to take notice. You know, they soon started comparing him to Babe Ruth. But I'll tell ya', and this is no knock on the Babe, they'd tell you that Ruth hit one here and hit one there, but with Mickey it was like he hit thirty from each side of the plate. There's nobody who will ever hit home runs the way he did, with the power and with the consistency."

The Yankees played a series of exhibition games on the West Coast. The games drew big crowds, invariably excited by the big-name Yankee players and by their spectacular rookie, who hit over .400 on the trip, including some memorable home runs. The home runs had press and fans openly talking about him as DiMaggio's successor. At one game, played on the USC campus, Mantle hit two homers, a triple, and a single. One of the home runs was believed by some of his teammates to be the longest he hit anywhere against anyone. It is a nearly forgotten home run now, but at the time it was a building block in the mythical stature he was already assuming. Mantle himself recalled that there was "absolute bedlam" following the USC game, that students and fans tore at his clothing, shoved scraps of paper at him, pleading for his autograph.

Mantle all the while believed people were making an undue fuss. He enjoyed the attention he was getting but basically shrugged it off.

"I was dressing alongside Mantle all that spring," said Johnny Hopp, who was soon to be Mickey's roommate in New York, "and I told him you're going to make a million dollars out of this game, the Lord behold. Well, he just laughed, he thought that was real funny because he didn't think anything he did was so great. For a long time I called him 'The Champ.' He just did everything you'd ever want to see on a ballfield. The home runs were only part of it. Casey said one time that the kid runs so fast he doesn't even bend the grass when he steps on it."

But Mantle was a Class C player, and the Yankees were the world champions. No matter what his manager said, he believed the front office wanted him to gain more experience in the minors, and he accepted that. He may have played with more ease and self-assurance because he knew that when the spring ended, he would be heading somewhere other than Yankee Stadium.

Mickey's buddy from home, Nick Ferguson, had moved to the West Coast by then, and Mantle invited him to spend time with him at the Phoenix camp. It turned out that a roommate of Mantle's at the team hotel was called for National Guard duty, so Ferguson wound up living with him for about a week. "Instead of getting another room, I stayed with him," Ferguson said. "Next door was a connect room and the two guys there were Ernie Nevel and Clint Courtney—remember him, 'Scrap Iron'? Those guys were wild, used to throw water balloons out of the hotel windows, stuff like that."

Courtney, Mantle's next-door roomie got into it that spring with a little-known second baseman on the team, Billy Martin. "They were practicing run-downs one day and Courtney tagged him a little hard, I remember," Ferguson said. Billy undoubtedly remembered the tag, too; after Courtney was traded to the Browns, he got into one of the bloodiest on-field fights of the era with him.

In the week he was there, Ferguson's impression was that Mantle was enjoying himself enormously, that what pressure he might have been under from all the attention coming his way was more than balanced by his sense that he would soon be playing in the minors.

"I don't think he was confident at all that he was going to be with the Yankees when the season started. I remember calling him up then and pretending that I was the general manager from Beaumont and that he had to come and report to Beaumont," Ferguson said, "and he just said, 'Yessir, yessir.'

"He was having fun just being himself, I think. He had this dry, playful sense of humor when he's happy and you could see that then. He used to practice all day long and then we'd go out to eat, me and him and Courtney and Nevel. At this restaurant they signed the checks, signed them because the Yankees paid for them. So I told them I wanted to pay for mine and Mickey tells me, 'You sign Joe DiMaggio.' He wanted me to sign Joe D's name on the bill, but, naw, I wouldn't do it, couldn't. I paid—and they laughed."

Ferguson also had a chance to observe Mantle with and around his team. He accompanied Mantle to and from the park on the team bus, recalling that DiMaggio always traveled by cab, never with the others. Ferguson remembered Casey Stengel. "I'd come in and out of the hotel with Mickey, and Stengel would always seem to be sitting there in the lobby just looking and staring at us when we went past. I guess he wondered who was this guy hanging out with Mickey. I wasn't any ballplayer he knew, and there I was with this player he had all these plans for."

And Stengel surely did have big plans. As the spring wound down, the time was drawing near when roster moves had to be made. Stengel's earlier judgment that he wanted Mantle on the big club had been more than reinforced by what his young star had produced on the field. But the time was at hand when there was no more politicking to be done.

There has been a great deal written about how difficult it was for Yankee brass to make the final decision. The standard version is that the original division of opinion between Stengel and General Manager George Weiss remained and that Stengel simply wore down Weiss with his insistence that Mantle join the club. From a distance of nearly half a century, Lee MacPhail, Weiss's assistant then who was present when the okay was given to bring Mantle up, says the differences between Weiss and Stengel have been exaggerated. "Once we made an outfielder out of him, the decision to jump him to the Yankees was really simple."

Mantle was an even greater prize to the front office than to Stengel. Mantle was potentially the best player anyone in the Yankee organization—from the dugout to the executive suites—had seen since DiMaggio, and he had been demonstrating what he was capable of all spring.

"No one knew what would happen on a major-league field, but Mantle had more ability than Gehrig, Ruth, anybody," Lee MacPhail said. "He could hit with Ruth's power and Ruth could never run like Mantle. Ruth had a great arm but so did Mantle. Oh, he was just outstanding. I can remember a funny thing: You know, at that time we were struggling to fill some holes on the Yankees and I was commuting then from Scarsdale, taking the train in every day, and somewhere near the 125th Street station there was a building and on it said, 'Mantle Engineering Company.' I'd see it every day and I'd say to myself, he's the guy who's gonna be the solution for us—and he just about was. We all believed that."

The closer the Yankees came to opening day and the more obvious it was that Mantle had made the team, the more troublesome Mantle's other big problem, the draft, became. It was one thing for a young obscure player at the time of the Korean War to be disqualified for an obscure medical condition; it was another for a deferment to be given to the game's most talked about rookie, a symbol of robust health if ever there was one. Mantle began to receive hate mail regularly. Complaints were voiced locally and nationally that the draft board's decision had been unfair, unjust, even unpatriotic. To short-circuit the criticism, the Yankees themselves intervened to ask the Oklahoma draft board that had earlier rejected him to reexamine Mantle. Thus, just when the team was completing its spring schedule with games in New York against the Dodgers, suddenly it was as uncertain of

Mantle's future as he had been. But the results of the physical were the same. He had been disqualified not because he would have been unable to kick anyone in Korea, as one sarcastic columnist suggested, but because his condition was chronic, covered by regulations. Contrary to popular belief, the draft board had no choice but to disqualify Mantle. Osteomyelitis, even in an arrested state, was automatic grounds for disqualification. But there was no way, short of serving in the military, that Mantle could have quieted the talk. Even after his deferment, the pressure remained for his case to be reviewed, and twice more in the next few years he underwent new physicals.

In any case, Mickey rejoined his team in time for opening day, which that season was in Washington. On the train ride down, Stengel escorted him back to one of the cars where the team executives were gathered. The meeting was something of a charade, ostensibly about whether or not Mantle was going to be on the roster or be shipped out. Mantle says Stengel gave him a wink and a nod as they went into the meeting with George Weiss and team owners Dan Topping and Del Webb. The results of the meeting were, predictably, that an official okay was given for him to join the club. He signed his first Yankee contract for a little more than the minimum (which was then five thousand dollars), and that may, in fact, have been the point of the charade—to make him feel so grateful for being promoted that he would overlook the fact that his employers were signing him on the cheap.

It is certainly true, however, that the man who most eagerly wanted him was Stengel. Stengel was so sure Mantle was ready that he had already penciled him into the starting lineup for the foreseeable future. Never mind that Mantle was still a teenager and was so unsure of himself that no one could tell what might happen.

Arthur Richman, then a baseball writer for the New York *Daily Mirror,* who got to know Mantle well, believed that Mickey's greenness may initially have been a blessing in disguise. "I don't think the pressure affected Mickey then like it would a normal person. Mickey was a small-town boy from a farm, what did he know about a place like New York? You know what pressure is, you go into a big city and you have to get a job in order to survive, that's real pressure. What he knew was he had to go up and swing the bat, that was it. He could run like hell and he could throw and he had all the natural instincts of a great player."

The picture of a naive country boy packing a straw suitcase and the talent of a god is so enduring that it seems almost trite now to recall how this real-life Roy Hobbs confronted the bright lights of the gaudiest, naughtiest, nastiest city in America. But Mantle's own teammates were the ones who were most touched by all that was fabulous and storylike in his emergence. They, better than anyone else, could see how ill prepared he was to take on life in New York.

When the team's initial games were rained out in Washington, the Yankees returned to New York to open the season. Emerging from the train at Penn Station, Hank Bauer got his first real look at Mantle beyond what he had seen on the ball field.

"I knew Mickey was a young kid not earning that much money," Bauer said, "and I noticed him when we got off the train in New York because we didn't fly in them days. I saw he had a pair of pants on that looked kinda funny. They were something like tan jeans and they were rolled up at the bottom, and he was wearing white socks and he had his puppies on. In those days we had to wear a shirt and tie, and I guess he had something on that looked like a tweed sports coat, and he had a tie that was about six or seven inches wide that had a picture of a peacock on it. So I got a hold of him and said, 'Mick, you can't wear them kind of clothes in New York. I tell you what, tomorrow morning I'll take you to a place and get you a couple of suits.' So he says, 'That sounds pretty good.' So we got up real early and went to Eisenberg & Eisenberg, where a lot of us went for our clothes. I bought him two sharkskin suits. I think they were about thirty-five bucks apiece, and I don't remember if I got him a shirt and tie or not."

Bauer turned out to be even more helpful to Mantle throughout the rest of his rookie season. Mantle started out hitting well and for power. He played daily in right field, alongside Joe DiMaggio. The press stories comparing him with DiMaggio may or may not have made an impression, but he could surely hear the frequent boos that greeted him whenever he struck out or failed to produce in situations where the great DiMaggio would almost certainly have come through. Bauer, without knowing anything about Mantle's feelings, took it on himself to tell him not to worry about the hype and criticism, that he was going to have his good days and bad days. "In New York," he told Mantle, "most of the fans here are DiMaggio fans, so you're surely gonna get booed for being the guy who's gonna take his place. It's just a New York thing."

Another "New York thing" was getting fleeced by unscrupulous agents and entrepreneurs always on the lookout for new arrivals with fat wallets. Though he was down near the bottom of the salary barrel, Mantle was still a Yankee and fair game. In these early weeks, he signed himself over to a Broadway sharpie named Alan Savitt. Savitt actually had Mantle sign two contracts: one, a two-year deal covering endorsements, personal appearances, and testimonials; the other, a personal services contract covering all earnings outside baseball for ten years. The agent's cut on the first deal was an unbelievable 50 percent, on the second a standard 10 percent. Then, as if that was not enough, Mantle got involved with a showgirl who, when she came up for air the morning after one of those nights before, had a piece of paper in hand saying she had the rights to another 25 percent of him.

When Bauer got wind of the mess Mantle was making for himself, he interceded. At Bauer's prodding, Mantle got the Yankees involved on his behalf. Yankee officials soon began pursuing Savitt, trying to get him to put aside his contracts with Mantle.

Then Bauer steered Mickey to an agent, Frank Scott, a former team official, who he knew was reliable. With Bauer's help, Mantle extricated himself, though a lawsuit followed. "I don't remember the details exactly, but I was working with Frank Scott who then was out on his own," said Bauer. "We were renting the apartment from Scotty and he was working with about five of us then. I told Mickey about him and asked Scotty if there wasn't something he could do to get them cockroaches offa him, 'cause they were taking him to the cleaners. So Scotty did, that's all."

Then there was the city itself, a dream island for a Pinocchio from Oklahoma. "Those Broadway lights, the neon glowing, hamburgers sizzling behind plate-glass windows, a carnival atmosphere, with Dixieland sounds floating up from basement steps on 52nd Street," Mantle remembered. "I couldn't avoid the newsstand dailies. Big black headlines, grisly headlines, a murder a day. This is how it looked to a nineteen-year-old kid from Oklahoma. But I was starting to like the excitement of the big city."

Bauer says with a laugh that he was the one who has been wrongfully accused of teaching Mickey Mantle to drink. In that first season, Mantle began rooming with Bauer and the veteran first baseman and pinch hitter, Johnny Hopp. The three had an apartment over the Stage Delicatessen in midtown, where, Mantle says, he was a "gofer" for his two roommates. Bauer says that Mantle and he and lots of other players often stopped to have a few beers after a game, it was part of the routine, but more important, living over the Stage Deli, was all that food. "Mickey musta put on a good thirty pounds that season eatin' all that deli food. If I sent him down there all the time and he ate like that, okay, I'll accept my share of the blame."

But the pressures of New York were intense, and they soon affected what Mantle did on the field. In May, his batting average was up near .320, and he was among the league leaders in home runs and RBIs, but by the end of June, it had sunk to the .260s.

Whether it was because the league's pitchers had finally gotten a "book" on him, learning that he was vulnerable to high fastballs when he was hitting right-handed and to low outside breaking pitches from the left side or because he had simply begun pressing too much, Mantle began striking out with alarming frequency.

More often than not, the strikeouts were accompanied by ferocious explosions of anger. Bats got flung or broken, water coolers got kicked; he was laughingly teased by teammates for being the King of Water Coolers. After one doubleheader in which he struck out five times, he wept openly in the dugout. Yogi Berra asked him one day if he was nervous. When Mantle replied that he was not, Berra deadpanned, "Then how come you're wearing your jockstrap outside your uniform?"

Stengel, who even more than the team's executives was counting on Mantle's emergence as a superstar, ordered him to keep the bat on his shoulder whenever pitchers fell behind him. It was an ego-shaking, confidence-rattling move, but one that made sense: Mantle had been swinging at everything, at pitches over his head, in the dirt, far wide of the plate. Allie Reynolds, the half-Creek Indian pitcher from Oklahoma, once told Mantle why he thought Stengel was putting on the take sign in those obvious hitting situations: "If you can stand up there and swing at good pitches, hitting them isn't the point. You're going to miss some because you swing so hard, and you go for the long ball. But you have to swing at good pitches, and if the count is two and oh and you swing at a pitch over your head, the pitcher has an advantage, and Casey has to take the advantage away from him."

Mantle's friend and protector, Hank Bauer, saw what was happening as surely as anyone but was just as powerless to do anything about it. Bauer said that, "Me and everyone else, all the players, were one hundred percent behind Mickey when he started striking out so much and getting down on himself like that. I know I felt sorry for him and I think most of the players did." But they could not ignore the obvious. Mantle was not yet ready for the majors. Like so many phenoms before him, he had come into the game full of early accomplishment only to run afoul of his own inexperience at the hands of opposing pitchers who soon enough understood what they had to do to get him out. In just a few months' time, Mantle lost all belief in himself. He said later that, more than anything, he was scared and there was no way he could then overcome it. Just like that, he had gone from being DiMaggio's heir apparent to just another rookie with a hair shirt. On July 15, while the team was in Detroit, Stengel got the word from Weiss and called Mantle in to give him the news: He was being sent down to Kansas City "for a few weeks" until he started hitting again, cutting down on those damn strikeouts, doing what he had been doing all that spring. Stengel assured him that he would be back up in no time.

The news was devastating. Even if it was only Triple A, even if ordinary common sense dictated that this was the usual way for rookies who finally made it—making the jump, being sent down, coming back up again—it did not matter. Mantle assumed that his career was over, that his dream, his father's dream, was finished.

Mantle was much too distraught at first to play at Kansas City. If he had been sent all the way back to the K-O-M League, the chances are he would have done just as poorly as he did in those first games in Triple A. He could not hit. His rhythm, timing, temperament, everything was off. He went after pitches out of the strike zone just as wildly as he had in his last weeks with the Yankees. Over his first twenty-three at bats, he had one hit—a bunt single. And that hit had prompted his manager, George Selkirk, to take him aside and tell him the sole purpose for his being back in the minors was to *hit,* not to bunt.

After a week or ten days of this, Mantle says he wanted to quit. This much visited turning point in his career remains stark and a little mysterious. The story has been told so many times, the embellishments and decorations so numerous as to wipe away all traces of nuanced feeling that occurred through these next critical hours.

Mantle called his father and told him he was finished. He says that when he spoke to his father, he could hear that Mutt was fatigued just from the way he said hello and then, when he told him the news, he picked up from the sound of his voice that his father's body had tensed. Mutt muttered something like "Hell you can't play!" got the name of the hotel where his son was staying, and then hung up.

After "what seemed like years," Mantle said, his father was at the door, eyes blazing, looking worn and rumpled from the long drive from Commerce. The look he had in his eyes was the one Mantle had always feared as a child, the one that had always been an adequate substitute for fists or belts. When Mantle told him again that he wanted to quit, he said his father told him to shut up, that he didn't want to hear any whining.

"I thought I raised a man, not a coward!" Mutt Mantle said.

And then when Mickey tried to protest, Mutt told him to pack his bags, he would take him home where he could go to work in the mines, "same as me."

Over time, because of his deep and complex love for his father, a love that had as much fear as affection in it, Mantle has blurred his own story so that in its waving lines it is possible to confuse flesh and blood with fable. Mantle says this moment confronted him with his inability to be a man. But it is just as likely that what it most sharply put before him was the reality of actually having to spend the rest of his life owing his soul to the Eagle-Picher company store.

How was this moment resolved?

Whether Mantle is telling the story early in his career or near the end of his life, the turning point moment remains distinct. He asked for another chance, and his father gave it. Sometimes, in telling it, Mantle provides dialogue; other times, the dialogue is different, or there are no words exchanged at all. How did the imploring, how did the yielding shape themselves? Did Mantle draw from the give-and-take of the moment the spark of something Promethean and empowering, or did he derive from the stark view of an intolerable future the sense that he had no choice but to go on, that he had to go back to the field, and that survival for him—a life outside the mines—meant becoming the next DiMaggio, Ruth, or Gehrig? Or did he just go out and happen to hit the hell out of the ball that night? The moment is a tease, except for the reality of the two colossal home runs he hit that evening—with his father watching—and for what followed.

In the next month, Mantle staged a protracted assault on Triple A pitching. In forty games, he hit .361, with 9 doubles, 3 triples, 11 homers, and 50 runs batted in. What more could he have done to win back his father's approval—or Casey Stengel's? He had done all that a superstar in the wings could conceivably do. All that remained was for those watching from afar to tap him on the shoulder and invite him to return.

This was finally done: by the New York Yankees, but unfortunately also by the United States government. Just at the moment when the Yankees recalled him for the team's stretch drive for the pennant, Washington recalled him for another round with the draft board. Before Mantle could return to Yankee Stadium, he was ordered to report to Fort Sill, Oklahoma.

Once again, the fanfares that might have accompanied him to a place of honor sounded off-key and a little sour. He again was rejected by the board, but he turned up in the Bronx with the newspapers full of stories about his relationship with the military rather than his relationship with the Yankees.

Another remaining problem was Joe DiMaggio. During the summer, the great star had clearly begun to fade. His average dipped, and even his usually smooth and graceful ways in the field seemed off. Stengel, in one notorious instance, replaced him in midgame because he had botched a play in the field. Because DiMaggio did not realize that he had been replaced, he took the field again after the Yankees batted. Only then, when another player came out to center field and told him he had been replaced, did he realize what had happened. He had to leave the field in full view of everyone in Yankee Stadium. When Mantle returned, the "Next DiMaggio" tag was more onerous—and more demanding—than ever.

But the Yankees won again, their third straight pennant, and Mantle, though far from playing like DiMaggio, played regularly until the last week of the season when, with the pennant on the line, Stengel chose to load his lineup with veterans. Mickey finished the season hitting .267, with 13 homers and 65 RBI in 96 games. Not bad but not nearly up to the Rookie-of-the-Year season turned in by Gil McDougald. Still, he was back in New York, glittery, eye-opening, and open all night. It was a championship year once more, and a chance to play in the World Series, to show the nation—and his father, who made the trip from Oklahoma—that he was up to all the challenges that anyone could ask of a young baseball player.

The Giants had won the pennant in the National League—on that Bobby Thomson home run—so the all–New York series coming up was unusually charged with excitement and expectation. Mutt had gone to the deciding Dodger-Giant game at the Polo Grounds and seen for himself what all the hoopla was about.

Mickey, on the other hand, saw something else. Between the time he saw him in Kansas City in July and the start of the Series in October, Mutt had lost almost thirty pounds. Normally a straight-bodied, vigorous man, he looked wasted and worn. His clothes hung from his body. Mantle says that he ignored what he saw, that he put off to old age—Mutt was all of thirty-nine—what he might have seen as illness. Mantle saw his own excitement in Mutt. His father had made the trip to New York with two friends, and the men, loose in New York, were agog. Mantle remembers that his father mistook the statue of Atlas at Rockefeller Center for the Statue of Liberty. Mutt and his friends got drunk, rode the subways like lost children enjoying themselves. It was easy not to see how sick he was.

When the Series began, Mantle was incredulous that he had actually been placed in the starting lineup—leading off, playing right field. His first World Series game, as it happens, was also that of the Giants' own rookie sensation, Willie Mays.

The Giants seemed still to be on the high that carried them to their miracle finish. Behind lefty Dave Koslo, they easily won the first game, 5–1. Mantle went hitless but was walked twice, a sign of the Giants' respect and also of Mantle's newly acquired patience at the plate. Over the years, Mantle's strikeouts would become as much a part of the legend as his home runs; but forgotten in the boom-or-bust numbers, Mantle's real secret, always, was that as hard as he swung, he was a *hitter*. The most bitter disappointment in his career, he said after he finished with a couple of nosedive seasons, was that his lifetime batting average fell just below .300. In his career, Mantle walked 1,734 times, fifth on the all-time list. In World Series play, he was first in homers, walks, runs scored, and RBIs—as well as in strikeouts.

But this Series ended quickly for Mantle. The outcome, the Yanks winning their third straight World Championship in five games, had nothing to do with him. In the fifth inning of the second game, with the Yankees leading 2–0, Willie Mays lofted a fly to medium right center-field. It was an easy play for Mantle, who had been told by Stengel before the Series began to cover any fly balls in the gap because "the Big Dago can't get there anymore." When Mantle went for the ball, though, he looked up at the last minute and saw DiMaggio camped under it. "I got it," DiMaggio said, and Mantle, trying to get out of the way, caught his spikes on the rubber cover of a sprinkler fixture. The sound of ligaments ripping in his knee, Mantle said, was like the sound of a tire blowing. He fell heavily to the turf, in agony. A stretcher was called for. The Series, the season, and who knew what else, was over for him.

Mantle always blamed himself for not being more alert on the play. He always took pains to point out that DiMaggio called for the ball and that if there was anything unexpected in the play, it was that DiMaggio indeed could cover the ground Stengel said he could not. But there was another factor in this play.

DiMaggio, quiet in the clubhouse, was also quiet in the field. When he called for a ball, it was often hard to hear him because his voice was thin and soft. Charlie Keller, who played left field alongside DiMaggio for years, maintained that as great as DiMaggio was, it was always risky playing alongside him because "You never could hear him call for a ball until the last minute." Mantle did not hear DiMaggio calling until he was on top of him, needing then to twist out of the way to avoid a collision.

With his knee swollen to almost twice its size, able to walk only with crutches, Mantle, accompanied by Mutt, was sent along to Lenox Hill Hospital to be examined. It was then, Mickey said, that he finally understood something was seriously wrong with his father. At the hospital, Mantle said, "He got out of the cab first . . . and then I got out. I was on crutches and I couldn't put any weight on the leg that was hurt, so as I got out of the cab, I grabbed my father's shoulder to steady myself. He was a very strong man and I didn't think anything at all about putting my weight on him that way. . . . But he crumpled to the sidewalk."

Father and son occupied the same hospital room, watching the rest of the World Series on television. Mickey's knee was operated on, while Mutt was put through a battery of tests. Then, Mantle says, he got the news: Doctors came to him and confided that his father had cancer and that it was incurable, that all he could do was take him home and let him live out the rest of his life.

It is not clear that Mutt knew how sick he was. The doctors told Mantle but not his father about his condition. Yet Mantle believed his father already knew. He later said his father was "the bravest man in the world" because he would never let anyone close to him see a flicker of emotion concerning his own death.

The news was devastating to Mantle. He was not yet twenty years old, and his father was the emotional pillar of his life and career. He could not accept that Mutt would die. He hung on his father as never before, as though Mutt still had much more to give. Mutt, in turn, had his own agenda for the time he had left.

Whatever he knew about himself, he had seen during those days he spent in New York that he needed to do more for his son, to safeguard the victories already won. He had seen—because Mickey had unabashedly shown him—what a good life there was in the biggest of America's big-league cities. Mickey had introduced him to his showgirl friend, Holly, and he had tried to win his father's approval not just for the success he had on the field but for the new life he had found off it. Mutt was anything but impressed. He told Mickey before they left for home what he now had to do. When they got home, he said, he wanted him "to do the right thing" and marry his hometown sweetheart, Merlyn Johnson. Mutt, as always, did not have to raise his voice. There was no challenge, no threat—just that look and his son's certain understanding that he would not resist his father. When Mutt told him he wanted him to marry Merlyn, Mickey said, "I half turned from him, nodding silently. There was nothing more to discuss."

Mantle returned to Oklahoma to get married. His father went home to die.

Chapter 7

The wedding and honeymoon were something of a fiasco. The ceremony took place at Merlyn's parents' home in Picher a couple of days before Christmas, with only the immediate families and a best friend of Mutt's present. Mutt's friend served as Mickey's best man. Afterward, Mantle says, he and his bride spent their first married night together in "a dumpy little motel" not far from home. Mantle asked his friends, the Moselys, to join him for the honeymoon. He had a deal, he said, all expenses paid at a resort up in Arkansas. The Moselys agreed to go along, but they each had very different recollections of what followed.

Bill Mosely remembered that "we were gonna go somewhere around Little Rock where Mickey knew this guy that owned the place, a baseball player or something, some good pitcher, and everything was gonna be on that guy. So when Mick said come on along, I said sure. Me and Neva had been recently married and we hadn't gone on a honeymoon because we couldn't afford it, so we went. We kinda felt out of place at first, but you can't feel out of place for long with Mickey. It was nice. We all knew each other, of course. We fooled around Hot Springs for a couple of days, the guy owned a bar and everything, I can't really recall what we did, but that was really a honeymoon for Neva and me, too."

Neva Mosely was willing to forget about it entirely. "It was kind of like a nightmare, a bad dream," she said. "Oh, Mickey had all these plans for us, you know, and being Mickey we thought we'd go in and everything would be taken care of. The guy who was supposed to own the place was Johnny Sain, I think. He had come to the Yankees that year. Well, Bill and I were so happy because he was home from the army for a little while and so we weren't using our heads either, we thought, like Mickey, oh, this will be some kind of trip. Well, we never did find Johnny Sain. So we ended up in a motel and then going out to a nightclub, very snazzy, like nothing we have here at home, where the music was loud and they had a lotta drinks but all we did was wind up coming home the next day. I was sorry we went because it was at Christmastime and I really didn't want to go away from my folks then, but we did—and that was that."

That winter was anything but joyous for Mantle. He and his new wife drove his father up to the Mayo Clinic in Rochester, Minnesota, for further evaluation. The doctors corroborated the diagnosis of terminal cancer—Hodgkin's disease—given in New York.

The choice of the Mayo Clinic, so far from home, was at first glance a logical one: The facility was one of the nation's top medical institutions, and it was also the one used by the Yankees for players who needed special attention. Mantle at the time needed to check his surgically repaired knee. But unknown to the public, there was another, more serious problem: Mantle's drinking, which he says got out of hand later on, was already causing enough concern that doctors were asked to intercede. During the previous spring training, before Mantle had even made the team, there was an incident where a Yankee official had had to haul him semiconscious and disheveled into a local hospital in the middle of the night for treatment. As his drinking continued through the season, the matter was closely watched.

No particular steps were taken, but it was emphasized to him that he needed to cut back if he wanted to maintain himself in top physical condition.

In the spring, with his leg healed, even though he had ignored the rehab program of exercises he had been given in New York, Mantle returned to the life he left. Mutt Mantle, saying he had heard about a center that might be able to help him, left his family and traveled to Denver, where he died alone one month into the new baseball season.

Mantle was informed by Stengel of Mutt's death on May 6, before a game with the Cleveland Indians. He got the news by telephone in his hotel room, and his reaction, he said, was an explosion of fury, grief, and guilt. Why had his father been taken so young—he was thirty-nine? Why hadn't he paid more attention to his father's condition? Why hadn't he been able to tell his father, ever, that he loved him? Why had all this happened? Mantle smashed a fist against a wall of his room. His new wife looked on in amazement.

Mantle was given time off to go home. He went by himself, leaving Merlyn behind in New York. His father's funeral was spare and simple. He was buried in a miners' cemetery next to Tunney and Grandpa Charles. The few mourners who came to the graveside stood there through the burial and then left, but Mantle says he stayed on alone for a while. When he thought about his father's final trip to Denver, he realized he had gone there not for a cure but to die alone so those close to him would be spared the sight of him wasting away. Mantle says the thought of his father being taken that way made him wonder about the nature of God.

When he returned to New York, in a real sense he was returning to a new and different life, one that would forever be without the stern and certain hand that had guided him for so long. His childhood was over, he said, but what now faced him was the more formidable task not only of adulthood but of baseball stardom.

Joe DiMaggio had retired that winter. That also marked a major change in Mantle's life because now, whether he wanted it that way or not, he was no longer someone in the wings waiting for his cue.

At first, he did not become the team's center fielder. Because Mantle's leg was still weak, Stengel tried other players in there. During the spring, he tried Bob Cerv, a burly, bright player from Nebraska who was also a home run hitter. Cerv supplied some power but could not keep up in the field.

Stengel switched to another young player, Jackie Jensen, who had played for Stengel in the minors. He was a "golden boy," or at least one whose substantial bonus money translated into high expectations and clubhouse jokes. But Jensen didn't work out either, and with the season still in its early stages, he was traded to Washington along with another player for outfielder Irv Noren, who was next up. Noren was not the answer, either. There was really only one player for the job, no matter how uncertain his future, no matter how unwelcome the pressure.

Writers who covered the Yankees, even when they were trying to praise the boy king, could not help but compare him in unflattering ways with his more regal predecessor. Such comparisons should have been irrelevant; Mantle was as different from DiMaggio as DiMaggio was from Ruth. Joe Trimble was typical of many who acknowledged Mantle's enormous skills but who could not allow him to simply be the player he was.

"It is only natural to compare Mantle with DiMaggio," he wrote in 1953. "There are points of difference and others of similarity. Both are brooders. When in a slump, DiMaggio was a surly, unhappy human being. He would walk the streets at night by himself, eat alone, refuse company and, in general, make himself miserable.

"Mantle lacks the high professional pride which Joe possessed, but the kid does show similar reactions to tough going. . . . DiMaggio tried to analyze his trouble and lick it with a scientific approach. Mantle, bewildered and hurt, finds no solution but the physical relief of going up to bat until he finally gets the fat of his bat on the ball and can smile again. . . .

"DiMaggio gloried in being a celebrity and, in a harmless way, 'went Broadway.' The former fisherman's apprentice from San Francisco loved the gaiety of the clubs and the good restaurants and the company of glamour girls. He didn't dissipate, however. With DiMaggio, baseball came first."

DiMaggio's presence was even more haunting in the clubhouse, where teammates pulled for Mantle and sympathized with him for the enormous load he was being asked to carry. But DiMaggio, to the elders on the squad and to fans and writers alike, was Yankee tradition itself. And being a Yankee had a meaning that carried far beyond the members of the team.

"See, for most us who grew up in that period," said Jerry Coleman, who shared second base with Billy Martin through the '50s, "the Yankees were the epitome of success. It wasn't your job so much as your religion. We just thought it, ate it, dreamed it. And nobody *ever* said 'trade me' if he was on the Yankees. You would eat dirt on the end of the bench before you would ask to be traded from the Yankees."

Coleman had come up a couple of years before Mantle and saw DiMaggio before he faded. He, like so many of his teammates, understood far more than any writer who DiMaggio was and why he was so special, both before and after he left the team.

"DiMaggio never talked about it because he just didn't talk much," Coleman said, "but he exuded Yankee tradition, he had this tremendous class, aloofness, his presence on the field and in the locker room was just unbelievable. When he walked into a room it was like he was all by himself. I remember once being at a Graziano-Zale fight in Newark, I forget which one, but here you have Frank Sinatra and Walter Winchell and then DiMaggio comes in and they all start screaming. They didn't care about any of those others. When Joe came in, he stopped traffic. In the spring of 1950, we stopped in Los Angeles, Ft. Worth, New Orleans, and finally Tampa–St. Pete, and every place we stopped he walked out—and this was before television—and people just went crazy.

"The way that rubbed off on the rest of the players on the team was interesting. You see, as a Yankee player you're carrying the banner for them. You always say, 'I'm gonna do my part.' And when you get nine guys on the field who are thinking that way, you're never going to lose. If you go out there and say, 'I'm gonna get five hits today,' that's the wrong approach. The approach was always, 'I don't want it to be me if this thing goes sour.' Every player had a stake in Yankee tradition, and Joe was the guy who carried that banner highest of all."

Mantle could not live up to the comparisons because nearly all of them were unfair and impossible. His special skills were no more like DiMaggio's than his build, temperament, or lifestyle. But Mantle, far more than DiMaggio ever could have been, was a teammate and a buddy. He took shelter in the team and in its identity. He was, different though he was, a Yankee in Jerry Coleman's sense if ever there was one.

But the pressure to produce went beyond the ball field. He was expected to live up to DiMaggio's "aura," his class, his regal celebrity status, when there was no way he could ever do that. His draft deferment continued to clank behind him like a ball and chain wherever he went—as adulation had accompanied DiMaggio. Mantle was booed, taunted, derided—and cheered only when he produced.

Dick Young recalled that in these early years the hate mail, the snide whispering, even the occasional death threat were nothing compared with what he faced in the ballpark. Drunken military personnel on leave would often taunt him from the stands, sometimes from box seats that protruded out onto the field with a close-up view of the Yankee bench. One of Mantle's teammates, Young reported, "could not understand how Mickey refrained from jumping into the stands after those guys."

Then there was the pressure that came from Stengel. It was different from the kind he put on other players. Stengel was dedicated to winning; he didn't care how or with whom, as long as the result was there. Players constantly resented him because he unceremoniously benched them, moved them around, and platooned them.

"Stengel alienated most of his players," said Jerry Coleman, "just by the way he handled them: impersonal and cold. Bauer and Woodling wanted to kill him every day because of the platoon situation. The pitchers would moan and groan . . . if you were just a spear carrier he would move you around like a pawn."

But that was never his approach to DiMaggio—or to Mickey Mantle. DiMaggio, Coleman said, "was the only player I ever saw him really shy away from because of his stature—and even then he alienated Joe by hitting him fifth one day without telling him." Stengel not only refrained from shying away from Mantle, but also embraced him to the point of nearly smothering him. Of all the players on the Yankees during the fifties, the two who most clearly affected Stengel in a personal way—and for very different reasons—were Billy Martin and Mickey Mantle. Billy probably reminded Stengel of himself when he was a player, someone with limited talent but limitless desire and baseball savvy. Billy was nursed as a "pet," encouraged to take charge when he was on the field.

"With Mantle," said Jerry Coleman, "he didn't see him as a player. When he looked at him he saw everything he had wanted to be as a player. Casey never had any children, so if he had a son, that's his son, and he wanted him to be perfect."

But if Stengel and Mantle had a father-son relationship, said Robert Creamer, it was that of "an angry father and a stubborn son." From the time he first saw him and was determined to mold him into his team's defining player, Stengel failed in almost every attempt to budge Mantle from what seemed, increasingly, like pig-headed resistance. Mantle simply did things his own way. When Stengel wanted him to cut down on his swing, to go at the ball like "a butcher boy," Mantle listened politely as the exact technical adjustments were explained to him and then continued hitting as he always had.

When Stengel tried to teach him the refinements of outfield play, he was met with the same stolid obtuseness. The first time Mantle saw Ebbets Field, Stengel walked him out to the wall in right field with its peculiar concave shape. He told Mantle about what he had learned playing there years before. Mantle looked at him in astonishment, as though Stengel had been old all his life. "You *played* here?" he said.

Robert Creamer said that with someone like Martin, Stengel "could talk and teach and yell, and if Martin objected to something Billy would yell back and curse." Stengel was able to tease and play with Martin. After enraging him by removing him from a game for a pinch hitter, he openly teased him, "Widdie Biddie mad at me?" He could not do that with Mantle. Jerry Coleman recalled an instance where Stengel removed Mantle from a game for failing to run out a ground ball—something Mantle did often. "I saw Casey yank him right from the game, took him right out, and then when Mantle left the dugout he went running after him. They were yelling and screaming at each other in the runway." Stengel had no way to defuse things for himself or for Mantle. Stengel was frozen by love—and, even more, by his impossible expectations. His name for Mantle was "Ignats," which Mantle hated. It was Stengelese for a comic strip character and, translated into English, probably referred to Mantle's stubbornness.

But of all the pressures Mantle faced, none were so deep, persistent, or consuming as those he placed upon himself. For no matter what Stengel or any writer thought, Mantle was a Yankee heart and soul. He was exactly the kind of player who thought of his place on the Yankees not as a job but as a religion. Personal goals were real for any Yankee, but winning was everything. Mantle's moods kept Stengel from seeing that. If he destroyed water coolers, it wasn't because he was thinking too much of himself but because he was too much into the game—to a point where failure, anytime, in any situation, was intolerable.

Mantle knew how to be a teammate; that part was easy. But he did not know how to separate himself from the sense that when he failed, the team failed. He lashed himself with that admonition not to let it be he who was responsible for letting things go sour. But what he asked of himself was impossible; he lacked the temperament to bring it off. He was not DiMaggio, with fire that was really ice, with a magisterial aloofness. Mantle's failures—like his successes—were always out in the open, plainly visible. He was as present in his misery, his insensitivity, and his childishness as he ever was in his success. Mantle was, from day one with the Yankees, like a condemned man who was also his own executioner.

Many of Mantle's friends and relatives believe that had his father lived long enough, he might have provided the sort of steadying hand Mickey was really looking for. At the very least, Mutt could have assured him that his dream was fulfilled by Mickey's best efforts, that all he needed was patience and discipline. Regardless, the person he reached out to then, more than anyone else, was Billy Martin.

At first glance, Billy seemed to be exactly the sort of person Mantle would shy away from. Fast talking, street-smart, a hustler, an uninhibited extrovert from a big city—Oakland and the Bay Area—he was an in-your-face dead-end kid, rough edged and cocksure. He reminded others in the Yankee organization of an earlier Yankee: Leo Durocher, a Yankee who never fit and was ultimately shipped out.

But just as Mantle had leaned on friends back home and in the minors to help him past his own shyness, Billy was a friend in need and one he secretly admired because he was so outward, so unafraid of anyone or any situation. While even veteran players, for example, feared DiMaggio and kept a respectful distance, Billy hounded him like a puppy dog. "Hey, Dage, let's go to dinner," he'd yap at him. On one notorious occasion, he went up to DiMaggio in the clubhouse as he was getting out of his street clothes; DiMaggio was wearing an expensive silk shirt and

Billy, flourishing a fountain pen, somehow managed to stumble and splatter ink on it. Of course, it was invisible ink, and the stain dissolved with the joke.

Another time, Billy went after Johnny Mize. Mize, said Jerry Coleman, "used to talk a lot, you know, if you asked him how he felt he'd tell you—for a long time, too, maybe twenty minutes. Well, one day, Billy gets on the team bus and says, 'Okay, John, give us a few thousand words, tell us how you feel.' 'Oh my God,' we all go. John looked at him with daggers. But it was all in fun."

On an earlier occasion, respected Yankee coach Frank Crosetti was working with a group of middle infielders, including the rookie shortstop, Mickey Mantle, showing them how to make double plays. "That's not the way I learned to make a double play," Billy piped up—and then proceeded to demonstrate for Crosetti and everyone else how to do it.

To many of his teammates, Billy was generous and fun to be around. To Mantle, he was all that and more. Billy was a friend and even something of a mentor. Unlike Casey, Billy could talk to him about what he was doing on the field. But more than anything, unlike the older players whom Mantle had run errands for, Billy was someone he could simply run with.

Mickey and Billy reduced the pressures of playing in New York to child's play—literally. They went at each other in the clubhouse with water pistols, soaking towels, shaving cream, anything. At the hotel they were staying in with their wives, they tried to spy on each other through open doors or lighted windows. On the road, when they roomed with each other, the horseplay could get as seriously out of hand as the drinking, which both of them did with increasing regularity. One night in Detroit, after they had gotten thoroughly plastered, they both crawled out on the twenty-second-story ledge of the hotel they were staying at and followed each other on their hands and knees around the entire building because they could not back up to the open window they had come through. On another, even more notorious occasion at the Hotel Shoreham in Washington, Mantle was dangled upside down from a window by Billy, possibly with the help of a few other Yankee party goers.

Mantle found much more than horseplay and booze in all this. Pat Summerall, who knew Billy and Mickey and had occasionally run with them over the years, believed that Billy was important to Mickey because he enabled him to be just one of the boys. "Billy attracted people who wanted to be around him," Summerall said. Billy was a guide to the bright lights and big city in ways that older players like Hank Bauer could not be. Mickey increasingly was drawn to all that was available to him downtown as the most celebrated young player on baseball's most celebrated team. "Hell, we drank up a storm and didn't go to bed until we were ready to *fall* into bed," Mickey said. Living it up opened him up.

Mel Duezabou, an old West Coast friend of Martin's, had dinner with Billy and Mickey one night at the swank Harwyn Club. "The night I was there, Grace Kelly and Prince Ranier were there," Duezabou said. "It was a big place. Jeez, all those celebs —and they loved hanging around them. We had dinner with Rocky Marciano. Can you believe that? He sat right next to me. . . . Before he got there, Mantle was there with some contractor, supposed to be some friend of his, and he had one of those whoopee cushions—he blows this thing up and he slips it under the contractor's seat before the guy gets there and . . . then after that, after dinner, we were going to this cocktail party. We go to this real fancy place, like on the twentieth floor, and there are only about ten people there, and I look and here's Teresa Brewer sitting there. Billy told me after she kinda liked Mickey a little bit."

Mantle never thought that he was wasting himself. "I never used to have hangovers," he said. "I had an incredible tolerance for alcohol and I'd always look and feel great in the morning."

The question of why he drank so much was one he simply did not ask then. But his drinking might have been protecting him from what he faced every day at his job.

His rages at failure were as unbroken as the booing and criticism. He was as helpless to ward off his mood swings as he was to push away that next drink. Reporters covering the team took it for granted not to approach him after a poor game or a tough loss. But sometimes how well or how poorly he had done had nothing to do with it. George Vecsey, who was a young beat writer for *Newsday* toward the end of the '50s, remembers that Mantle could be charming, had a sly and genuine sense of humor, "but that too often he was unapproachable or worse. Reporters would walk towards his locker and you'd see him sort of cock his head to the side, roll his eyes upwards and say, 'FUUUCCCK' —and then burp. It wasn't much fun covering him; you didn't really want to be around the guy any more than he wanted you to be around him. You know, you wind up covering other more important national stories, and you just finally get turned off by that behavior." Whitey Ford put it another way: "Mickey could always let a reporter know that he had asked his last question."

Who knows what might have happened if Mantle had had a steadier relationship with the media then? The question is as unanswerable now as the one Mantle himself raised about how much greater he might have been if he had not so abused his body.

What is not open to question is what he did on the field. Mantle in '52, '53, '54, and '55 slowly, inexorably, consistently established himself as the most dominant player on the game's most dominant team. In '52, the Yankees went down to the final weeks of the season with the barest of leads over the Cleveland Indians, but Mantle hit .362 down the stretch, .311 overall, to help the team to its fourth straight pennant. Injuries and home runs seemed to define him; the knee he had injured in the series the previous year was flaring up again, but he played through the season, till a second operation could be performed. His twenty-three home runs were second on the club to Yogi Berra's thirty. But Mantle's homers seemed to have stardust and magic sprinkled all over them.

"I remember a day game in Cleveland," Hank Bauer said. "I

think Bob Lemon was pitching against us and Joe Collins could hit Lemon pretty good and he hit one in the upper deck just to the right of the scoreboard and he came in and said something to Mickey like, 'Hey, lemme see you top that one.' Well, Mickey got up and hit it way further, to the left of the scoreboard. He came in the dugout laughing, and he says, 'Well, whaddaya think about that one, Joe?' I remember another time Mickey got jammed on a pitch, broke his bat and threw it down because he was so disgusted, you know. Well the goddamn ball went halfway up in the right-center-field bleachers in Yankee Stadium."

The Yanks took the Dodgers in seven games in the series in '52, another in the ongoing stretch of all–New York postseason pageants that marked the game then (in a twelve-year period, New York teams appeared in ten World Series; in seven of those seasons, both World Series teams were from New York). Mantle hit .345 in the series and hit his first postseason homers. His eighth-inning home run in the sixth game was the difference in a 3–2 Yankee victory; his home run in the series clincher preserved a 4–2 win.

In '53, Mantle again had good but not great numbers, played through well-publicized injuries, and was instrumental in another Yankee world championship, the team's fifth straight—a record unparalleled then, now, and probably forever. The most distressing part of the season for Mantle and the team was again an injury. At midseason, Mantle sprained his left knee and fluid accumulated on the kneecap. He continued to play, but because he favored his "healthy" leg, it, too, gave way. Setting up to throw on a play in the outfield, he tore ligaments in his right knee—the one that had twice before been surgically repaired—and then proceeded, against all common sense and Stengel's wish to keep him out of the lineup, to return to action wearing a heavy brace, in time to finish the season.

Again, the home runs somehow eclipsed everything else. Though Berra again hit more, Mantle's somehow got hoisted out of the realm of counting altogether. In a game on April 17, he hit one out of the park in left center field off Chuck Stobbs in Washington's Griffith Stadium. The homer, some said, was the longest ever hit in the majors. It cleared the back of the bleacher wall some sixty feet above the playing field, grazed the corner of a large scoreboard, and came to rest in the backyard of a private home a block away. The Yankees' publicity director, Arthur "Red" Patterson, announced that he had tracked down the ball, paid five dollars to the kid who retrieved it, and had the distance of the blow measured, thus creating the term *tape-measure home run.* The ball traveled 565 feet, he said. (Mantle said that years later Patterson confessed that he had actually never left the park —he just announced that he had after jotting down the name and address of the youngster who returned the ball.) The mammoth home run covered the back pages of newspapers in and out of New York and eclipsed what Mantle did in his very next game. After a day of travel, in St. Louis against the Browns, Mantle hit another monster shot, but it was ignored in the wash of print, photography, and broken-arrowed charts from Griffith Stadium.

"He did the first one in Washington, which was never done before," said Gene Woodling. "I was there when he hit it so I know how long it went. But you know, we went to St. Louis the next night, and you know the old Sportsman's Park, how long left field was. Bleachers, about 380, huge scoreboard. He hit one outta there that night even better, but they publicized the one in Washington so much that they had to lay quiet on that one."

In the World Series that year against the Dodgers, Mantle had a couple of home runs. Neither of them were tape-measure shots, but both of them were as important as any he had hit till then in his career.

Mantle went into that series feeling more pressure than he ever had. Early in the season, Merlyn had given birth to their first child, Mickey Junior, and Mantle was acutely aware that he was now the sole support for both his immediate family and his widowed mother. He did not feel that his place on the team was secure yet; Stengel had been all over him for months to cut down on his swing, and he had resisted. The home runs could not have come at a better time.

The series happened to mark the fiftieth anniversary of the first World Series, the 1903 games between Pittsburgh and Boston. For the occasion, the first ball was thrown out by Cy Young. Mantle was more than aware of the moment. "I don't care how cool a ballplayer tried to act," he said, "I've never known one who wasn't impressed to be in the same ballpark as a Ty Cobb or a Cy Young. It's like watching statues come to life."

Throughout the series, Mantle seemed unable to get untracked. He wound up hitting .208 and striking out eight times in twenty-four at bats—but the two home runs he hit were probably the difference between winning and losing a championship. In the second game, played at Yankee Stadium, Preacher Roe and Eddie Lopat, both smart veteran pitchers, pitched tight, stingy games. The Dodgers took a 2–1 lead into the seventh inning, but the Yankees tied it. Then, in the Yankee eighth, with two out and a man on first, Mantle hit a "short-porch" homer into the right-field seats to give his team the lead, 4–2, and the game. In the fifth game at Ebbets Field, Mantle came up with the bases loaded, two out, and the Yanks leading 2–1 in the third inning. Russ Meyer, a right-handed pitcher, had just been brought into the game especially to face Mantle and to force him to hit from the left side. Mantle then became only the fourth player in World Series history to hit a grand slam home run. It was an opposite field homer, landing in the upper deck in left, and it provided the Yankees with the winning margin in an 11–7 slugfest.

"The grand slam was a big moment in my life," recalled Mantle, "because baseball wasn't a game to me as the spectator understands it. It was my job and my living and all I knew. Without it, I was going to be digging fence posts back in Commerce or carrying a pick down to the zinc mines."

• • •

In '54, the Yankees finally missed the postseason, even though they won 103 games. The Indians happened to win 111 (and then lost in four straight to the Giants in the World Series). Mantle had another .300 year and, for the first time, drove in more than 100 runs. His 27 homers finally led the team. In 1955 he hit 37, with 99 RBIs and a .306 batting average. In that same year he became the first player in American League history to hit home runs from both sides of the plate in the same game. In fact, he hit three out in that May game against the Detroit Tigers at Yankee Stadium, all three homers—two from the left side, one from the right—traveling into the middle of the right-center-field bleachers. And then, in a perfect postscript to the day, Mantle told reporters that the three home runs were all hit with borrowed bats, the first two from Enos Slaughter, the last from his old rookie buddy, Moose Skowron.

In both '54 and '55, he played in almost all his team's games and proved to anyone who cared to notice that he was able to play through serious injury and that he was a complete player: not Joe D, not the Babe, but at just twenty-four years old, one of the true stars of the game. In New York, it was becoming fashionable now to argue about Willie, Mickey, and the Duke as though center field in New York was one of the world's most prestigious royal addresses.

It was still just as fashionable to withhold from Mantle the sort of unalloyed approval that he might have gained if he had played away from the greedy eyes of the guardians of Yankee tradition. In New York, in Yankee Stadium, he was DiMaggio's successor but still was not DiMaggio. His exploits off the field, rather than raising comparisons with the Babe, only raised the eyebrows of those who insisted that Yankee pinstripes and Yankee history were not well represented in bars and after-hours clubs.

In '53, after the team won its fifth straight pennant, Mickey, Whitey, and Billy had a night on the town. At New York's Latin Quarter, the merry trio piled up a huge bill for food and drinks, and then when the check came, Mantle signed the name of the Yanks owner, Dan Topping. "Billy and Whitey," Mickey said, "signed the others. After the tab was paid, there was hell to pay."

The next morning George Weiss summoned the players to his office. Mickey and Billy showed; Whitey, who lived out on Long Island, avoided the dragnet. Mantle said that he and Martin literally were roused from bed and arrived at Weiss's offices, buttoning their shirts and adjusting their ties.

Topping made an appearance, too. The players were told they had committed forgery and could go to jail for it. They were each—Ford included—fined five hundred dollars. The fines stuck only until the Yankees won the World Series, and then, at the party afterward, they were forgiven. "At the World Series party," Mickey told a reporter, "Topping and Webb sent for us, one at a time. He told me and Whitey that we wouldn't have to pay the fine. But Billy wouldn't even go to see them. He said, 'The hell with them.' "

By now all of this had become part of a too-familiar pattern. There was just something about this great new star that seemed to be missing, that permanently kept him from fulfilling his enormous potential. It was as though the very process of maturation with him had been reversed, so that with experience he seemed to grow more, not less, childish.

One spring training, Stengel, in exasperation, railed to reporters that Mantle was simply stupid. He was hardly alone in believing that it was intelligence that stood in his way. An article in *Look* during that period asked its readers to ponder the question, "Is He a Rockhead as Some Claim?"

Of course, Mantle was hardly unique among ballplayers in cutting up or living it up. He was also not unique in taking his time to become the player he was expected to be. But if anyone cared to look at his first several seasons not for what was missing but for what was there, they might have been less concerned. In his first five seasons with the club, he was a .300-plus hitter who had driven in 345 runs and hit 141 home runs. By any yardstick, he was already a formidable and impressive ballplayer—and one whose best years were still clearly ahead.

But those critics who wanted still more from him were about to get the surprise of their lives. He was only twenty-four years old when he put together one of the greatest individual seasons in baseball history. Mantle answered his critics the only way he could—with an explosion of talent and effort. It should have been enough to quiet Stengel, the Yankee brass, or anyone else overly concerned with Mantle's I.Q. or his baseball future. It was not. Even then, it turned out, Mantle had much more to prove before he would finally be accepted for what he was.

Chapter 8

In 1956, in the middle of a year in which Mickey Mantle became only the twelfth player in baseball history to win the Triple Crown, leading the league with 52 home runs, 130 RBIs, and a .353 batting average, Casey Stengel filled reporters' ears one afternoon with this:

> Sure the feller is not a finished center fielder. Mays and Snider could have an edge, but the feller is getting so he can catch them as good as anybody with his tremendous arm, although he still throws to the wrong base now and then. But it takes time for a feller to learn how to play the outfield if he never played it before until he got into the big leagues. . . .
>
> Never put his foot into the outfield until I told Hendrix [Tommy Henrich] to see how he looks in right field. . . . Now wait a minute and listen to me. So now he's my center fielder. But he didn't become my center fielder, that is when he wasn't crippled, until 1952 after DiMaggio quit.
>
> You might say his shifting from right to center forced him to start all over again and learn how to execute. I know because I played in all the fields. And he's catching on as a center fielder just as he is at the plate, waiting for the good pitch. All he's got

> to do is meet the ball and it will leave any park. If you'd cut most of his drives in two they'd still be homers but, unfortunately, they only count as one. No, he's not at all slow in learning to wait for a good pitch. What most people fail to consider is that he must learn how to hit two ways instead of one.

From a distance of almost forty years, Stengel's goofy gab reads like lighthearted needling. What more could any manager want from a player than Mantle was providing in that special year?

From the opening day of the season, it was clear that Stengel's Ignats was in the best playing shape of his career. For the first time in seven springs, Mantle could concentrate on baseball rather than on his aches and pains. On opening day, in Griffith Stadium, he hit a home run, out of the park to dead center field off the Senators' right-hander, Camilo Pascual. The ball disappeared over the fence into a clump of trees 465 feet away. The only other player known to have hit one out at that spot was the Babe. Later in the same game, with dignitaries in full attendance, including President Eisenhower and House Speaker Joseph Martin (Billy told Mickey, "That's my uncle," and Mickey, country innocent as ever, believed him), Mantle hit another home run, this one into the center field bleachers.

By the end of April, he had hit nine home runs in sixteen games. It had taken Ruth, in his sixty-homer season, twenty-nine games to hit that many, and writers were already working the math into their game stories. The home runs continued to fly in May, including the Memorial Day blast off the stadium facade against Pedro Ramos; through almost one-third of the season, Mantle was hitting .425, with 50 RBIs and 20 homers. Yet Stengel continued to believe he could do more.

Though nearly as young as a rookie—over the previous five years only one of the ten Rookies of the Year was younger than Mantle—he had clearly played through his green time; he was as focused, as concentrated as he would ever be. And Stengel could now legitimately compare him with the game's greatest players. "He's a tree-mendous player," he told Arthur Daley one day. "Don't matter what park he's in, either. See that last exit in the upper deck. . . . Look, way up there, almost over the bullpen. They say that no one ever hit one outta the Yankee Stadium. But if the stands hadn't a gotten in the way, Mantle's would have gone over the wall because it was still climbin'. . . . Or you take the Pittsburgh park which nobody hit outta till Ruth did it and so did Mantle [in a '53 exhibition game] which don't get many opportunities to hit there on account of his age.

"Mantle is the fastest slugger I ever saw," Stengel rambled on. "Ty Cobb was the fastest on the bases for that sensational stuff, but he don't hit the long ball. Max Carey was fast and so was Frank Frisch. But they couldn't clout like my feller. Rogers Hornsby was fast goin' down to first and he was also a slugger which didn't hit as far as Mantle but more often."

If Mantle could just calm his temper, choose his pitches, and, above all, change his swing, "meet the ball" in order to send it out of the park, Stengel believed, he would be a .400 hitter with more power than the Babe.

Mantle was used to this from Stengel, but now, despite his great success, others were chiming in, including his old childhood hero, Ted Williams. Williams insisted that if he would just cut down his swing, it would mean twenty points in his lifetime average while maintaining plenty of power.

Williams's opinion meant more to Mantle than Stengel's because he still regarded Ted as the game's greatest hitter. And Williams, unlike Stengel, wanted nothing from Mantle; he was a competitor, a rival, but he was also clearly an admirer.

"As far as I can see," he told reporters in the spring of '56, "Mickey has improved every year and he'll continue to improve. My guess is that he's now definitely heading for his peak. Why shouldn't he be great? He has good speed, good swing, good power. There's no reason in the world why he can't be a .340 hitter and a forty-homer slugger—or maybe better. I'll tell you one thing: He's the only guy in this league who has a chance of breaking Babe Ruth's home run record."

But Williams studied hitting like no other player before or since, and at all-star games or around batting cages, he invariably got into discussions with Mantle that focused on the ways he might further improve.

"I used to love to talk to Williams about hitting—or rather listen," Mantle said. "He could talk about it for hours—and he usually did. All the technical stuff that I didn't understand."

Williams questioned Mantle about which hand he used to guide the bat, which was his "power hand," and so forth. As with Stengel, there was no way Mantle could—or would—take it all in. But that year it didn't matter; the hits kept coming. Mantle's all-out swing always had behind it the intention of hitting a baseball as far as possible, yet everything in that swing went first to making hard contact, same as a singles hitter. Because he now knew the pitchers he faced, he was simply a better hitter. Though he talked about it very little, Mantle studied, too —not the "technical stuff," but how pitchers threw, what their moves and idiosyncracies were. He used his time in the on-deck circle as a part of an at bat. (Years later, when he served as a springtime coach for the Yankees, that was his standing advice to young players: Watch the pitcher from the moment you step out on the field.) In 1956, Mantle was a far more experienced hitter than in his early years—and a far smarter one than his critics imagined.

The Yanks took the American League by nine games over Cleveland that year, but Mantle's pursuit of the Triple Crown came down to the final games. He had the home run title locked up; he had slumped after the all-star game and slipped behind Ruth's pace, but he still wound up with fifty-two home runs, twenty more than his nearest rival, Vic Wertz. Going into the final weekend of the season, he led Ted Williams by a few points for the batting championship and was barely ahead of Al Kaline for the RBI title.

The Yankees and Red Sox just happened to close out the season with each other in a three-game set at Yankee Stadium. Going into that showdown weekend, Mantle was hitting .354, Williams, .350. Williams not only needed to add points to his average, but at bats as well: He was nine at bats shy of qualifying for the title when the games began. In Detroit, meanwhile, Kaline had 124 RBIs going into the final weekend; Mantle had 127.

Mantle urged Stengel, who wanted to rest him for the postseason, to play him. Mantle started the first game of the series and went one for four, a solo home run. Williams went oh for three, grounding out to Billy Martin three straight times, walking once. At the end of the day, the lead was .353 to .348 over Williams and 128 to 124 over Kaline.

Mantle was held out of the lineup for the second game of the series. But with the bases loaded in the eighth, Stengel had him pinch hit. Mantle walked—one RBI, no change in his batting average. Williams went one for six in a thirteen-inning game, qualifying for the title but falling too far behind to catch Mantle in the one remaining game. Kaline, though, stayed in the hunt by picking up two RBIs. He trailed Mantle 126 to 129, close enough to add a little Triple Crown suspense to the season's last day.

Williams did not play in the finale. Stengel held Mantle out of the lineup, again using him as a late-inning pinch hitter. Mantle got an RBI on a ninth-inning ground out. An hour or so later, word came from Detroit that Kaline had picked up 2 RBIs in his game, hiking his total to 128, two short of the title. Mantle had become the twelfth Triple Crown winner in baseball history.

Afterward, responding to a reporter's question about how he felt losing a batting title to Mantle, Williams growled, "If I could run like that son of a bitch, I'd hit .400 every year." Mantle, gracious and modest, probably rubbed salt in open wounds when he agreed with Williams: "I don't know how many bunt hits and leg hits I got that season," he said later, "but it must have been at least twenty. I know it was enough to give me my eight-point margin over Williams."

The Triple Crown season established Mantle at the top of his profession. But a more subtle change was taking place. Mantle was being looked at as more than a mere baseball player. He had a way of polarizing people; for every one who hated him and downplayed his accomplishments, there were more now who felt an almost cultish adoration for him, as though he was a movie star or a pop singer rather than a ballplayer. There was something about him that set him apart from other players, from other sports celebrities entirely. Perhaps it was the way he looked, so blond and blue-eyed, so perfectly middle American; perhaps it was his lack of sophistication and his obvious reticence, the qualities writers and even his own manager mistook for limited intelligence. Maybe it was his magical name with its built-in diminutive, a name that is hard to say without smiling. Whatever it was, he was a great ballplayer who happened to come into his own at exactly the time television was beginning to replace radio as the principal transmitter of baseball games to the nation.

That autumn, Mantle agreed to appear at a book signing on Long Island. The first of his autobiographies, *The Mickey Mantle Story,* had recently been published, and New York police, fearful of a mob scene, had talked the publisher into moving his appearance out to the suburbs where the problem of crowd control would not be a factor. But when Mantle showed up, according to a *Newsday* dispatch, "the joint was jumping. The mob was beating at the door. Pretty teenage girls were squealing and swooning for a glimpse of the Yankee slugger." The bookstore owner had boarded the windows of his shop, hoping to minimize property damage. Mantle was hustled in and out of the place. "1000 fanatics ranging from 8-year old little leaguers to pretty bobby-soxers to their mothers, fathers, grandfathers, and grandmothers," reached out to touch him and tore at his clothing. "It wasn't Elvis (The Pelvis) Presley," said the *Newsday* reporter, "it was Mickey (The Bomber) Mantle."

The book signing was only an hour in a single afternoon, but it reflected the uproar he would have to contend with for the rest of his life. He had become, whether he wanted it or not, someone on whom people projected their dreams, hopes, frustrations, resentments, and hatreds—more accessible than the aloof DiMaggio, and thanks to television, even more available than the gregarious Ruth. The only comparison in sports might be with Michael Jordan today, but since baseball was the only sport that mattered then, he was a star virtually without rival.

On the field, the challenges were at least confined to familiar boundaries. The Yankees met the Dodgers in the World Series again. The year before, the Dodgers had won in seven games. It was, Mantle said, one of the most disappointing moments in his career—not as wounding or as lasting as the defeat in the '60 World Series to the Pittsburgh Pirates, when the better team lost, but painful, nevertheless, because it was the first time he had experienced a World Series defeat. "They deserved to win," Mantle admitted, acknowledging that in a corner of his soul he even felt a twinge of happiness for the Dodgers. But, he noted, "The Yankees of my era looked on the World Series as a kind of birthright." It was not one he was ever willing to give up.

Mantle followed his magnificent regular season with what was, for him, a mediocre Series. He hit .250 but also hit three home runs, including one in the fourth inning of Don Larsen's perfect game. Mantle also helped save Larsen by outrunning what looked like a sure triple to left center field by Gil Hodges, thrusting out his glove at the last second to make the saving catch. Larsen, one of the hardest drinkers in the history of the game and who Mantle says reeked of alcohol when he showed up at the park that day, kidded Mantle in the dugout after the catch by mentioning the unmentionable, that he had a perfect game going. (Arthur Richman, who says he spent the entire evening before the game with Larsen, insists that he was cold sober for his date with history.)

Mantle was the unanimous choice for MVP that year, and he followed his Triple Crown year with another that was close enough: In 1957, he hit .365, with 34 homers and 94 RBIs, not good enough to win an unprecedented back-to-back Triple Crown, but enough to repeat as MVP. The vote this time was controversial because Ted Williams, at age thirty-nine, hit .383 along with 38 homers, teasing the baseball world through much of the summer with the unlikely prospect of his once more hitting .400.

The summer of '57 highlighted an even sharper *mano a mano* between Williams and Mantle. For most of the summer, though Mantle was slowed again by injury, he stayed neck and neck with Williams in the batting race. When the Yankees went to Fenway for a three-game series in mid-August, Williams was hitting .387, with Mantle right behind at .379. The games were billed in both Boston and New York not for their importance in the standings (the Yanks were comfortably in first, the Red Sox far back in the middle of the pack), but for their importance to the fans of the two stars. And those fans were very different.

Ted Williams had not captured the imaginations of bobby-soxers, but he had the baseball traditionalists. He was the lingering star, the link to the past, to the game's greater days. In much the same way that fans across the country had pulled for DiMaggio when he made his spectacular midsummer comeback after heel surgery in 1949, longtime fans far beyond Boston and New York rooted for Williams in his showdown with Mantle.

The showdown turned out to be Hollywood perfect. "Mantle Good, Ted Sensation in Swat Duel," proclaimed the *Sporting News* after the three games were played. The story line was simple: "Batting .625 in the three-game set, Ted raised his average to .393 for the season," the paper reported. "Mantle had a .444 average for the series and finished it with a .380 mark, giving Ted a lead of thirteen points with forty-one games remaining to be played."

When the Baseball Writers of America (BBWA) named Mantle —and not Williams—as the American League's MVP at the end of the season, there was a huge outcry. In twelve fewer games, Williams had more home runs and nearly as many RBIs, and he led the league not only in batting average, but in slugging and on-base average as well. Still, Mantle's team won the pennant, while Williams's finished sixteen games back. How much that mattered is unclear. Williams finished only slightly ahead of Washington slugger Roy Sievers in the voting, and Washington finished dead last.

The Sporting News, which named Williams Player of the Year in '57, as it had named Mantle in '56, was inundated with angry complaints directed at the baseball writers. A fan from Forest Hills wrote, "There is something absolutely wrong with baseball if a thing can happen as the undeserved selection of Mickey Mantle in preference to Ted Williams. . . . Baseball has degraded itself." Another fan said, "How could anything but personality influence the picking of Mickey Mantle ahead of Williams? Somehow, the writers must be convinced that it is the player's ability, not his disposition, that is the basis of making the award." Several sports editors and writers not belonging to the BBWA chimed in, calling for voting in the future to be done openly rather than by secret ballot. Underneath all the criticism was the unspoken assumption that Mantle somehow did not measure up to players like Williams—and to baseball's cherished past.

There was no way Mantle—or anyone—could answer such an amorphous charge, any more than he could justify the wild adulation he received. Whether it was Casey Stengel, Ted Williams, the Baseball Writers of America, or fans who mobbed him or jeered him, he was caught and could not escape. Gay Talese watched Mantle haters during this period and tried to make sense of them:

> Ever since Roman spectators jammed arenas to watch lions devour Christians, certain sports followers have tried to perpetuate this grand old sadistic tradition. They burn coaches in effigy, mob athletes and occasionally bounce beer bottles off the heads of great outfielders.

> Such un-Chesterfieldian courtesy towards professional gladiators is not stylish in this generation, but when it occurs it is generally said to be "part of the game. . . ."
>
> Eddie Waitkus of the Phillies tried to be understanding in 1949 when one of his devoted female fans got a pistol and shot him. . . .
>
> And now the Yankees' Mickey Mantle is trying to be understanding.
>
> Every time he drives up to Yankee Stadium he is mobbed by a pack of young baseball fanatics. If he does not stop to sign autographs, some teenagers squirt ink into his clothing.
>
> On Friday, before a doubleheader with Washington, a girl of thirteen jumped at Mantle as he got out of his cab. She punched him, began to pull his short, blond hair, and slapped him until he swatted her off and bulldozed his way towards the Stadium's player entrance.

Wisecracking that there was a shortage of psychiatrists at the Stadium, Talese said he simply listened, notepad in hand, to the alternating mix of booing and wild cheering for Mantle, to the words of hate and praise that ranged from Mantle's old problems with the draft to his having to measure up to Ruth, Gehrig, and DiMaggio.

One baseball writer told Talese, "Ruth was booed but never maliciously. DiMaggio was not booed much, either. They don't boo Berra, because he's a great politician, the greatest baby-kisser in baseball today. Somehow the name 'Yogi Berra' is warm. He's so ugly you can't help loving him."

Red Barber told Talese that he believed Babe Ruth was responsible for the booing Mantle got. The Babe was freewheeling on and away from the field. DiMaggio and especially Mantle did not have that kind of showmanship in them. The fans expected it, though, from Mantle.

"Now Mantle is great," Barber said, "but when he does not hit a home run people are mad. There's only one way to answer the fan. And that's with your bat. Should Mantle get hot for two weeks or so, then the booing will be over."

Not necessarily so. The adulation and the booing followed Mantle wherever he went. And troubles in his life away from the field could not be settled with a hitting streak—even when baseball was the subject.

Mantle discovered, for example, that when he went into contract negotiations with the Yankees, his record had little to do with what the team was willing to pay him. Until his MVP seasons, Mantle had never bothered much about salary; his '56 salary was $32,500, more than many players made but certainly not what the game's best earned.

In '57, he asked for sixty-five thousand dollars and was summoned to meet with Yankee boss George Weiss. Weiss told Mantle flat out that he would not get that kind of raise, that he was young—twenty-five—and Weiss asked what would happen if he kept doubling Mantle's salary like that for ten years, till whenever it was he retired. This time, instead of reluctantly caving in, Mantle resisted. He pointed out to Weiss that other players—Williams, Willie Mays, Musial—all made around one hundred thousand dollars and that he had had a better year than any of them.

Weiss was not about to budge. Instead—according to Mickey—he removed a manila folder from his desk and showed it to him.

"He pats the folder, leans back in his chair, and twiddles his thumbs," said Mantle. The folder contained reports compiled by private detectives ordered to follow players to and from their hotels while the team was on the road.

"I'm looking at the detective reports. I'm reading, 'Mickey Mantle and Billy Martin left the St. Moritz hotel at 6:00 P.M. Came in at 3:47 A.M.' and so forth." Mantle said Weiss told him that the reports could hurt his image and, worse, that "he wouldn't want this to get into Merlyn's hands."

Weiss was never asked in his lifetime about whether or not he used such reports as blackmail, but there is no question that the Yankees in that period had private eyes shadowing their players.

In one notorious incident a few years later, detectives followed Tony Kubek and Bobby Richardson from the team hotel to a local YMCA, where the two, kidded by teammates for being the "Milkshake Twins," spent the evening playing Ping-Pong.

Billy, Whitey, almost all the Yankees in those years remember that there were private detectives around. Hank Bauer laughed as he recalled an incident involving the relief pitcher, Joe Page: "They didn't bother me, but I remember Joe Page, I think it was in Chicago, we had a lady detective on us and he tried to make her on the beach. I don't know what happened, but Joe said it turned up in the report."

Lee MacPhail, who believed that Weiss was always a decent man and a good boss, said that he was unaware of any blackmail episode involving Mantle. Eventually, Yankee owner Del Webb personally intervened to offer Mantle the contract he wanted. But MacPhail remembers that the following year, after Mantle hit .365 and won the MVP but not the Triple Crown, Weiss wanted to cut his pay.

"Weiss insisted on cutting him, or at least not giving him any raise. That was the one time in my dealing with him that I ever had any problems with Mickey. We talked a lot and I finally said to him, 'Mickey, I'll argue it out with Weiss, but you'll have to settle it with him, too.' I think it got settled again in spring training by Webb and Topping. He got a token raise."

The contract negotiations in these two seasons were only part of a discontent that went far beyond money. The Yankees, and Weiss in particular, were very much concerned about Mantle's after-hours behavior. His increasing drinking and womanizing were part of it; so was his seeming indifference to physical conditioning in the off-season. Mantle embarrassed the team in '55 by concocting an excuse to get out of a postseason tour of Japan—a move that cost him five thousand dollars. There were countless episodes of behavior where Mantle seemed to thumb his nose at both common sense and self-preservation. In George Weiss's mind, and perhaps those of other Yankee executives as well, the simplest cause of this growing threat to a great career was Billy Martin. Scratch Billy, and Mickey might have a chance.

Even back home in Oklahoma, his drinking was out of control. Billy came down to spend part of one winter with him, and their time was spent almost exclusively on boozing. "I fell into the routine of getting out of the house by saying we were going fishing. Instead, we would go into Joplin, have a few drinks, and before I knew it I was drunk. I wouldn't even think about going home," he said. One time he left home and didn't return for days. When he finally turned up, he plopped down a couple of fish on a kitchen counter, thinking his wife would be happy with what he brought home. She was so unhappy that later that winter she left him. Mantle arrived home late one night and found himself locked out. He smashed a pane of glass, cutting his hand, to open a door. Inside, he found the house deserted, the family gone, closets and refrigerator emptied. Believing that Merlyn had gone to her parents' home, he went there, saw his car parked out front, and pounded on the door until Merlyn's father answered. Mantle demanded and got the keys to his car, went to it, opened the doors, and then hurled the contents, including Merlyn's and the children's clothing and bags of groceries, all over her family's front yard.

If he had lost control of himself, he had also lost touch with the life he had always known, one that had sustained him until he became a professional ballplayer. Mickey, to his hometown friends, was the same person, but his life had changed. His fame, his celebrity status—his notoriety—clung to him even as he wanted to pound them from his clothes like an accumulation of so much alkali dust.

Some of Mickey's friends did not like Billy. Bill Mosely met him, knew him, and shrugged him off. "I didn't think too much of him. Little bit too fast for Mick," he said, in the same to-the-point manner Mantle once had. "I mean, that's only my opinion. He meant well, but he was a little bit too fast."

Max Mantle, however, thought Billy was a good and loyal

friend. "He wasn't no bad influence. He and Whitey both—they were good friends to him. Yeah, one of 'em was from California, the other from New York. Whitey had a little more common sense than Billy, Billy just didn't back off from nobody, that's just the way he was and that's the way he made the major leagues."

Mickey and his family increasingly felt singled out in the place where they used to feel at home. Max Mantle believed that fame inevitably changed his cousin and probably caused the growing sense of alienation he felt in his hometown. "When he made it like that, he suddenly had all kinds of friends," Max said. "Everybody knew him, wanted to be around him, talk to him. And it changed him, yeah. See, he just didn't want all that. . . . he was used to being friends with everybody, but not when they started wanting things from him all the time."

Max's description of those fishing trips was somewhat different from his cousin's. "We'd go fishing and go off and try to get away from everybody; we'd go huntin' and try to get away from everybody; when we played golf we'd try to be away from everybody. He just didn't want to be around the people as much."

There was a division in the town between those who wanted to mob Mantle and those who resented him—just like in New York. But in Oklahoma, it was up close and really personal, and anyone named Mantle was a target. During the off-seasons, Mantle coached a pickup basketball team that toured the area. But the games were anything but fun, and Mantle soon gave them up.

"We'd go play ball in high school and everybody was wantin' to beat us real bad," Max remembered. "One time we come out on the basketball court and the fans threw balls at us and a fight broke out. This one guy hit a guy on our team, and the people came out of the stands wantin' to kill us. Because he had a couple of Mantles there, they hated us. They hated the Mantles. They threw basketballs, Coke bottles, everything. . . . You know, a lot of people didn't like us. Even people in the town where we grew up didn't like Mickey because their sons had to go into the service and he was 4-F because of the leg. That's stayed to this day. There's people who've been proud of him and others who weren't. Maybe it was all because of jealousy, I don't know, but there sure was a lot of that."

Whatever it was, Mantle increasingly found himself unable to feel at home when he was home. Where he had once wished to play ball around Commerce for the rest of his life, he reached a point where he no longer felt as though he belonged anywhere. He was the father of three young children with whom he rarely spent any time. For several years, Merlyn and the children had stayed with him in New York, but that had not worked out. Merlyn hated flying and did not particularly like New York. For a while, the family lived in suburban New Jersey during the season, but with Mantle away most of the time, Merlyn felt isolated and even frightened. During a loud thunderstorm one evening, she was upstairs in the house, feeding her youngest son, David, when a noise or sound of some kind downstairs startled her. She thought burglars had broken in. With her baby in her arms, she took a loaded pistol she kept in the house at all times and went downstairs with it. No one was there. But either in panic or because she slipped, she fired her revolver, sending a wild shot through one of the walls. At the end of the '58 season, Mantle moved his family to Dallas because, he said, it was near an airport, easy to get in, easy to get out.

At the same time, outside interests were consuming more and more of his attention. Since his Triple Crown year, Mantle had welcomed the chance to earn some outside income. He made television commercials and personal appearances and endorsed all types of products. He helped his friend Teresa Brewer cut a record, "I Love Mickey."

But if he had the urge, he surely did not have the skill or even the stick-to-itiveness when it came to marketing his name and image. For years, really until the last decade of his life, he seemed to have a special capacity to be taken when it came to business schemes.

In one venture, he made a sizable investment in an insurance company that turned out to be nonexistent. In another deal, he and Whitey Ford each invested ten thousand dollars in a phony bomb shelter program. A more carefully investigated deal was a stock purchase—at five cents a share—in a Holiday Inn with Mantle's name on it. The pitch to the public was that the motel had a "Mickey Mantle Suite" where travelers could spend the night in a bed Mickey Mantle slept in. The innkeepers advertising the places where George Washington slept probably did about as well.

In Dallas, a group of wealthy friends talked Mantle into opening a bowling alley that would also bear his name. For a while, there were high hopes for profits—and some fun. Mantle was attracted to the idea because two of his teammates, Phil Rizzuto and Yogi Berra, had recently opened a bowling alley in New Jersey that seemed to be doing well.

Mantle scheduled the opening of the lanes for late winter, before spring training, and he invited his own bowling team, the Yankees, to join him for the occasion. The party goers traipsed down to Dallas to enjoy themselves for a few days, and they, and most especially Mantle, did not have business on their minds.

Ryne Duren, the relief pitcher who had severe alcohol problems of his own, remembered those few days well. "Billy was down there, Dorothy Malone made an appearance for the opening, and it was quite an affair, quite a bowling alley," he said. "Mickey had invited a bunch of his ballplaying buddies—Yogi, Whitey, Billy. Mickey had an acquaintance who had a whole bunch of new apartments that hadn't been leased yet, so each of us got one of those. We had a helluva time. I guess I was there four or five days, and then when I flew on to San Antonio the airport was fogged in and the plane flew right back to Dallas. I called Mickey and said, 'I'm back.' He said, 'Oh no.' So I played golf with him and Billy. I can't play golf worth shit—who cared? —but we had a lot of laughs. I was so much a part of it then."

But Mickey Mantle Lanes, like all his other ventures outside baseball, flopped. The business went bankrupt and closed within a few years.

The one place where he truly felt at home was on his team, among his teammates. Whitey and Billy remained his team within a team, his drinking buddies, the all-out Yankees. But even on this most secure turf, the ground was shifting out from under him.

The Yankees for some time had been contemplating changes. Losing the World Series in '55, after five straight championships, was a shot across the bow. The organization understood the need to keep securing and promoting the best young players. But from the mid-'50s on, the challenge was to make sure the team would be strong enough to keep winning championships in the coming decade.

In George Weiss's mind, in the minds of all the top Yankee brass, the blueprint still started with Mantle. There was no foundation without him. But changes had to be made.

For years the Yankees had a sort of cozy relationship with the Kansas City Athletics that raised snickers in the media and something more from other clubs. The A's owner, Arnold Johnson, had been a good friend of Yankee owner Dan Topping for years. Their general manager had once run the Yankees' Triple A farm team in Newark.

The Yankees frequently turned to Kansas City for reinforcements in these years. In February 1957, they sent a carload of second-line players, including pitchers Tom Morgan, Rip Coleman, and Mickey McDermott, along with Billy Hunter and Irv Noren, for three important KC players: veteran pitchers Bobby Shantz and Art Ditmar and rookie third baseman Clete Boyer.

But the deal that hit Mantle the hardest came in late June of that year. For years, Weiss had been aching to get rid of Billy Martin. Billy, in return, despised Weiss, but as long as Stengel defended him, as long as the team had needed him at second, he could not be gotten rid of. But the team managed without him in '54 and '55 when he was in the army, and when they promoted second baseman Bobby Richardson to the majors in the beginning of '57, he became expendable.

While Weiss was already guiding Martin toward the exit, Billy himself gave the door a big push in mid-May. A group of Yankee players, including Mantle, had decided to throw a birthday party for Martin. The party spread out all over New York's fanciest supper clubs—and then got splashed onto the front pages of the papers when one of the Yankee players, said to be Hank Bauer (who has always denied it), knocked someone out cold in a brawl at the Copacabana.

The investigation into the incident by the police and the Yankees was a farce. All that anyone was able to prove was that a group of noisy, probably drunken, patrons began badgering the Yankee group that included Mantle, Billy, Whitey, Johnny Kucks, Bauer, and a few of the players' wives.

Bauer's most recent version of what really happened goes like this:

After rounds of drinking and eating at other clubs, the Yankee group arrived at the Copa in the early hours because they wanted to see a performance by Sammy Davis Jr. "We got a great big round table and all of us are sittin' around it and we're having coffee and an after-dinner drink," said Bauer, "and this big fat guy walks by me and he says somethin' like, 'Don't test your luck too far tonight, Yankee,' and I just looked up and said, 'Go fuck yourself.' You know. So now he goes down to the other end, the fat guy and his friends are gettin' pretty loud and somebody tries to quiet 'em, and I looked up and he looked up and pretty soon his cousin goes back to the men's room. Well, Billy and Mickey followed him back there. So Joanie Ford says to me, 'Hank, you better go back there and see what's happenin',' and my wife says, 'It's none of your business,' and I say, 'Oh yes it is.' So I go back there and what do I see? Nuthin' but tuxedos, bouncers all over the place. You know. So what happens? This big fat guy, the guy that started everything, makes a move and I think it was either Whitey and Yogi or Johnny Kucks grabs me and says get the hell out of here, so I did an about-face, walked down the steps, my wife's waitin' for me, we get a cab, it's about two, two-thirty in the morning and we get back to the hotel. About four-thirty the goddamn phone rings, it's a writer who tells me, 'Hank, whaddaya gonna do about this?' I say, 'What?' He says, 'The guy at the Copa says that you hit him.' I said I didn't hit anybody. So the next day when I'm leavin', one of the bellboys says, 'Hank, don't go out the lobby, it's full of writers and cameramen, TV guys, the works.' So I go out the side and go to the ballpark and I explained to Casey what happened and he says, 'I don't see nuthin' wrong except you broke curfew.' Then Topping comes down, gets us all in Casey's office, closes the door, and says, 'I warned you sons of bitches.' So I says to myself, 'I don't remember getting a warning.' He says, 'Mickey, Billy, Whitey, it'll cost you a thousand dollars.' . . . So when I went out I went over to Mickey and I said, 'What the hell did he mean by warning?' He says, 'Oh, you weren't there.' I says, 'What the hell happened?' He told me he and Whitey and Billy and Dwayne Pollette and Andy Carey, about seven of the guys went to this place to eat and ran up a tab of $700 or somethin' and then signed Dan Topping's name to it."

When the Yankee players were eventually hauled before a grand jury investigating the incident, Mantle, to the horror of his bosses, was summoned to testify. He had nothing to say, although his jaws kept working ceaselessly. The court finally asked: "Are you chewing gum, Mr. Mantle?"

"Yes," replied Mickey.

The judge ordered him to remove the wad. He did so, placing it beneath the chair he was sitting in. That was it—that is, until June 15, when George Weiss used the incident as a pretext to trade Billy Martin, along with two others, for Ryne Duren and a pair of extra bodies.

The trade caught everyone—except Billy—by surprise. When it was announced, the team within a team spent all night commiserating and drinking. The three players all had their own George Weiss horror stories to share, and they made a pact with one another, something that would preserve their bond the next day when they no longer would be teammates. "If I happen to throw you a curve ball tomorrow," said Whitey, who was scheduled to pitch the next day in Kansas City, where the trade had been announced, "I don't want you hitting one out off me."

"That's just what I'll do!" Billy said.

Ford left them around one in the morning to get some sleep. Mickey and Billy stayed on, drinking till dawn. Billy hit one out the next day, when Ford, with the game won, signaled the pitch that was coming.

All along, Mantle understood what the trade of his friend meant. An era was over. The trade marked a dividing line for Mantle: Before it, he was a boy; from that point on, he was expected to be a man.

"We were like family, the Yankees were like family," he said. "I know people say that about sports teams, but it's very different today than it was then. I mean, when I joined the Yankees it was like I was the little brother. Hank Bauer, Gene Woodling, Allie Reynolds, Vic Raschi, those were the big brothers. Whitey and Billy were like my best friends, but they were still like my brothers."

What was in the works for Mantle was just what George Weiss had been planning all along: a different team, one that would see Mantle as its leader, not as a follower.

For a time, it was not at all clear that the changes that ensued would be for the better. It would be years before it became clear that this was not just the end of an era, but the beginning of a glorious new one.

Chapter 9

When the Yankees avenged their World Series loss to Milwaukee in 1957 by beating the Braves in 1958, it looked like Weiss's plans were perfect. The team won with youth. Mantle was a veteran at twenty-seven. Surrounding him were Tony Kubek, the starting shortstop, who was twenty-two; Bobby Richardson, who divided his playing time with Gil McDougald at second, also was twenty-two; McDougald was an old-timer at just thirty. Jerry Lumpe was twenty-five, as were Marv Throneberry and Norm Siebern. Andy Carey was twenty-seven, Moose Skowron twenty-eight, and Elston Howard twenty-nine. Yogi Berra was the old man at thirty-three.

The Yankees ripped apart the American League in 1958, getting out to a big, early lead, fading toward the end of the summer, but still retaining enough to win the pennant by a full ten games over the Chicago White Sox.

Mantle started slowly, finished strongly through the last months of the season, and played in all but four of his team's games. He wound up hitting .304, knocking in 97 runs, hitting 42 home runs. But perhaps because his numbers were off from his Triple Crown peak—or just because it had become fashionable—he was booed frequently at home as well as on the road, where hating the Yankees and their insufferable success had become one of the habitual pleasures of a baseball season.

But the look and feel of things were already different for Mantle. It was becoming clear Casey Stengel was near the end of the line as a manager. It wasn't apparent so much in his moves as in his moods; he was frequently sour, cantankerous, and impatient. He lashed out at his players, particularly the younger ones, to a point where he was resented and even feared. Standing at the batting cage one day, watching infielder Jerry Lumpe, he told reporters, "He looks like the best player in the world until you put him into the lineup." Lumpe was close enough to hear what Stengel said, and if he missed it, it was there, in print, the next day. Another time, he chided a player during batting practice for hitting a ball into the seats. He asked the player loudly, enough to be overheard by reporters standing nearby, if he had a bonus clause in his contract for hitting forty batting practice homers. When the player said no, Stengel suggested he might get one if he got forty base hits during games.

Mantle once more played through injury—to his right shoulder—and suffered for it. The volume of booing he received at home seemed in direct proportion to his inability to produce when he was hurt.

During the years when Billy was a Yankee, Mantle said that he leaned on him for help with his own mistakes and shortcomings. "We didn't talk much away from the field. Only if I messed up," Mickey said. "The first thing he'd do before we got to drinking too much is he'd say, 'You know, I got to tell you something—you remember that ball you caught in right center, the one you threw over my head? From now on you better to be sure to hit the cutoff man.' Hell, he could tell me stuff like that anytime. Like I told you, it was like he was my big brother. See, I was never known for being very smart as a baseball player. . . . I could run and throw and hit. But I didn't know the game. He did. He taught me a lot about baseball, yeah. He'd even tell me when to steal sometime, like if Casey didn't give the signal to steal second. . . . If it was like the eighth or ninth inning and we were one run behind or tied or something, Billy'd give me the go-ahead. He'd tell me to go ahead and steal and I would."

On the Billy-less Yankees, Mantle still had players who helped out. One player was Bob Turley, the veteran pitcher. Because Turley was so good at picking up what opposing pitchers were throwing, he had a set of signals worked out with Mantle to let him know what was coming when he was batting. Like some—but not all—hitters, Mantle felt more comfortable if he had signs flashed to him. The system, Turley said, was based on whistling.

"Mickey Mantle said I called about 25 percent of his home runs," Turley told Tony Kubek. "During most of the game, I'd sit in the bull pen. But when it was Mickey's turn to hit, I'd run down to the dugout and we'd go to work."

The signaling worked by assuming the pitcher was always going to throw a curve. "If I didn't whistle," Turley said, "Mickey knew it was a breaking pitch. If I did, he got set for a fastball. If I missed a signal, Mickey would touch his cap, and I'd know. If he couldn't hear me, Mickey would touch his stomach."

Turley said he began picking up his ability to steal signals, almost as a matter of survival, when he was with the St. Louis Browns in 1951 and 1952. When he came to the Yankees, Stengel began exploiting Turley's ability by hooking him up with different hitters. With some, the signals were no help. A hitter like Moose Skowron, for example, would swing at pitches that bounced five feet in front of the plate if he knew what was coming. Mantle, though, thrived. "Mickey was the one who really liked to know what was coming. He'd tell me to guess, even if I wasn't sure," said Turley. "Mickey once said, 'Bob, you know more about pitching than I do, so tell me what you think is coming, and you'll still be right at least 70 percent of the time.' "

Mantle's closest friend on the team now was Whitey. Almost as a reflex, he had drawn closer to him without Billy around. "Whitey," said Tony Kubek, "had always loved being Whitey

Ford," and that was probably what endeared him most to Mantle. He had great pride without great ego. He was a craftsman who thought nothing about putting his craft aside to win a game. If he needed to cut a baseball to make it move, he'd cut it. He not only threw "mudballs," but he had theories about the differing aerodynamics of flight of a baseball smudged with mud on the top or smeared with it below. In all his years with the Yankees, he was the team's money pitcher, but somehow he had never won twenty games—not because of the way he pitched, but because of the way he was used. Stengel liked to rest Ford, saying that he wanted to preserve his arm; Ford made more than thirty starts in a season just once under Stengel. He was "rested" enough throughout the seasons to keep him from winning twenty until Ralph Houk took over in 1961. But Ford never complained. It wasn't in his makeup. Winning was—and having fun. And that combination was particularly irresistible for Mantle.

On the field, Whitey was the sort of player Mantle would throw himself on a sword for. If Mantle felt he was somehow responsible for losing a game for Ford, he was inconsolable afterward. In the last game of the 1956 season, Ford was going for his first twenty-win season. "He got beat 1–0," Mickey recalled, "when I dropped a fly in center field. Then I ended the game with a man on third. I popped up to the second baseman. I didn't want to go into the clubhouse. Whitey was my best friend, and he could finally have won twenty games, and I blew the damn thing. If there had been a trap door on the field, I would have used it. I finally went into the clubhouse, and Whitey saw how bad I felt. He came up to me and said, 'Ah, Mick, the heck with it. We'll get 'em.' And Whitey meant it; that's why the players loved him. They always used to say that 'as Mantle goes, so go the Yankees.' I guess I thought I was an inspirational leader and all that crap, but we all knew that the real leader of the Yankees was Whitey. Line up all the pitchers in the world in front of me, and give me first choice, I'd pick Whitey."

Away from the field, Whitey could always make Mickey laugh.

He was good company, in bars and on the road. The two men roomed together, invariably taking a suite in the team's hotels, each man with his own room, with one room in the middle (called an "escape room" by some reporters who were convinced that the turnover rate of women visiting the two players was so high that an escape route was not only a matter of convenience, but also of practical necessity).

It was all part of the system Mickey had grown up with on the Yankees. But now the system was changing. Players like Billy were no longer needed, or they got older; the center was the team, but the center was no longer holding. The game itself was changing. There was a different atmosphere around the ball club. By the end of the decade, players were spending less time together as team travel changed from rail to air. Until the mid-'50s, transportation in both leagues involved long train rides between cities, which gave players hours to spend with one another playing cards, talking baseball, horsing around, drinking, generally building a bond that became far more tenuous in the age of jet travel.

The Yankees were one of the last teams to give up the railroad. "All the trains had a club car, and guys could go in there and sit around together for as long as they wanted. You could play cards, drink, anything you wanted," said Bob Cerv, a teetotaler then and now. "Heck, it wasn't just Mantle who drank, back then they always said they could pitch and drink and carouse so much. It went right back to Ruth. Everybody used to smoke cigars, cigarettes. You watch these nostalgia movies, and I swear three quarters of the time the heroes are standing around with a cigarette and a drink in their hand. After '55 I think we flew to Detroit, Cleveland, and Chicago, but we still used the train up and down the East Coast, to Baltimore, Washington, Boston—only at the very end did we start using shuttles. And yeah, I think players after that didn't get to know each other as well."

Mantle saw his team changing out from under him. In '59, the Yankees nose-dived. Injures decimated the squad through the early part of the season. Mantle reinjured his right shoulder throwing from the outfield, then broke an index finger one day during batting practice. Other key players—McDougald, Skowron, Andy Carey—also got hurt. In June, the team was in last place, the first time a Yankee team had been there since anyone could remember.

Mantle played through his injuries—foolishly, because he could do little to lift his team and in exchange was thunderously booed for his efforts. In one losing game, he hit a home run off the Tigers' Frank Lary, an old Yankee-killer. As Mantle circled the bases in his usual head-down trot, he was still greeted with hoots of derision when he crossed the plate and headed back to the dugout.

Mantle responded to the booing and to the team's misfortunes by sullenly withdrawing himself from the press and sometimes venting his rage on the field, this time not just by kicking water coolers or smashing his fists into dugout walls but by obscenely gesturing to the fans who were tormenting him.

Stengel more than ever appeared to be losing control. Jackie Robinson, who despised Stengel because he believed he was a racist, told reporters that season that he heard from Yankee players that Stengel sometimes took naps on the bench during games. It was just the kind of remark that was sure to spur controversy, raising questions about Stengel's age, his health, and his hold on the team.

The front office believed that he had served his time. A Yankee official who did not want to identify himself told a national newsweekly that with another manager, the Yankees in all likelihood would win the pennant, but that Stengel wasn't about to quit and "we are not going to win." Reporters became aware through the season that Dan Topping had become dissatisfied not just with Stengel but with George Weiss, too. Weiss, he felt, had let the farm system, the lifeline to all those championships, run down. It was not true, and other, more personal factors may have been involved, but Topping was unhappy enough to let some of his lieutenants tell the press that changes were needed at the top.

There was no way to salvage the '59 season. No matter the unusual number of injuries, the team that had so dominated the decade finished third, thirteen games behind the White Sox, who were then defeated by the Dodgers in the World Series. The aftermath was not pretty. Topping began shopping for a new manager, sounding out the White Sox's Al Lopez, who turned down the offer because Stengel was a friend. When the owner then decided to stay with Casey, he perhaps set an example for future Yankee owners by firing the pitching coach, Jim Turner. He next pressured Weiss to make some moves that would count.

Weiss did just that. He once again turned to the warehouse in Kansas City to make his biggest deal ever, a deal that turned out to be significant for Mickey Mantle in ways that were both surprising and surprisingly obvious.

In exchange for Hank Bauer, who was then thirty-seven; Don Larsen, sore-armed and ineffective; and first baseman Norm Siebern, a young player who had never recovered from a Stengel tongue-lashing years before, the Yanks picked up a couple of utility infielders and outfielder Roger Maris. Maris had only been in the majors for three seasons and had been moved from the Indians to the A's the year before, but he was a player with enormous potential who had already established himself as a genuine home run hitter. In '58, when he played 150 games, he hit 28 home runs, and it was said by almost any knowledgeable person who had seen him play that his compact, dead-pull swing was perfect for the Stadium. (Bill Veeck bitterly criticized the Indians' general manager Frank Lane, believing that trading the talented Maris to Kansas City was tantamount to sending him a one-way ticket to New York.) Though no one could predict just how spectacularly the trade would work, there was no question that it was the heist of the decade.

The immediate effect of having a player like Maris in the middle of the lineup was to make life tougher for anyone having to pitch to Mantle. The choice of where the men hit in the order did not seem important at the moment, but having two sluggers back-to-back in the lineup that also featured other home run hitters like Skowron and Berra kicked the powerful Yankee offense into an entirely new gear.

The Yankees again started slowly. Mantle had a difficult and slow spring. He had had contract problems with Weiss again, who wanted to cut him $17,000. Mickey held out for a while, finally agreeing to sign at $65,000, a $7,000 cut from the year before. During the spring, he and Ford and a handful of other players were involved in an embarrassing and near-disastrous boating accident, when a yacht they were partying on caught fire, burned, and sank. The players were fished naked from the waters of Tampa Bay. Mantle, who could not swim, was simply thankful to be alive.

In the early months of the season, the Yanks again trailed in the standings when, at the end of May, Stengel complained of chest pains and was hospitalized. Ralph Houk, the first-base coach who was rumored to be the team's next manager, took over.

Stengel's problems turned out not to be serious. He joked with reporters when he returned, "They examined all my organs. Some of them are quite remarkable and others are not so good. A lot of museums are bidding for them."

Stengel's return seemed to rejuvenate both him and the team. Beginning in early June, the Yanks climbed back into the race, reaching first place and then holding off a surprisingly stubborn run by the Orioles the rest of the way.

While the pitching was spotty, the Yankees' home run power simply demolished other teams. The Yanks wound up hitting 193 homers that year, 43 more than second-best Detroit in the American League, 23 better than the powerful Milwaukee Braves in the National League. With Maris batting third and Mantle fourth, pitchers could not work around the Yankees' new lefty slugger; Maris, on his way to an MVP season, hit 39 home runs, while Mantle, who might just as easily have been the MVP, hit 40.

Mantle's relations with the fans and the media remained thorny. In that initial season with Maris alongside him, the booing never let up—and Mantle seemed only to make things worse for himself with his moods and general surliness around those who crowded him for favors or words. (Perhaps in that he was a star ahead of his time.) He dealt with autograph seekers, even very young ones, sometimes generously, but sometimes with almost stupefying crudeness and hostility. He dealt with writers no better, singling out for favor those he knew were friendly, and turning his back on others he didn't know or didn't like. Often, he would retreat sulking into the off-limits trainer's room after games, like Achilles withdrawing into his tent, waiting there until the last reporter was gone.

But Mantle's teammates had a different perspective. Whatever anger he directed at others, he went at himself even more pitilessly. "He was our big guy, without him we were nothing," explained Moose Skowron. "What helped him was when Roger Maris joined the club and that eventually took the pressure off of him. But not right away. They just expected too much outta the guy, and he expected too much out of himself. You could see it every day."

In mid-August, with the team sagging through a doubleheader loss to the Washington Senators that dropped them into a first-place tie with the Orioles, Mantle hit a double-play ground ball in the midst of a tight game and refused to run it out. Infuriated at himself, he stood still in the batter's box, glaring hatefully at what he had just done. To make matters worse, the runner on first was Maris, who went all out into second base and wound up pulling a muscle in his rib cage—an injury that sidelined him for weeks.

The booing came down on Mantle like a mountain of refuse. Everyone in the park, including his teammates, understood that he had violated one of the game's sacred codes: run out *every-*

thing. Players, good ones, failed at bat seven out of ten times, but any player could run down to first ten out of ten times. A player's value to a team was, in part, measured by this intangible show of determination. All anyone could see in that moment was that it was missing from Mantle, that he was thinking of himself first and his team and teammates second. The fact that he had, once again, been playing injured—there was more ligament damage to his right knee—had no bearing now whatever. He was caught as naked as he had been in the waters of Tampa Bay—and with less excuse. As the teams changed sides and he walked out toward first base, waiting for a teammate to bring him his glove, Stengel sent in another player to take his position.

Afterward, Stengel, who was as angry as any fan, tried to contain himself. "It didn't look very good, us trying to win when the man hits the ball to second or third and doesn't run it out," he said. "That's not the first time he's done that. If he can't run, he should tell me. If he wants to come out, all he has to do is tell me. Who the hell does he think he is, Superman?"

In the game following, against the Orioles, the booing that greeted Mantle the first time he came to the plate was off the charts, louder and longer, said Peter Golenbock, than had ever been heard at the Stadium before. Mantle grounded out to more booing, but then with the Orioles leading 2–0, he homered with a man on to tie the score in the fourth inning. The Orioles then took the lead back, 3–2, and in the eighth inning, with knuckleballing reliever Hoyt Wilhelm pitching, Mantle again came up with a man on. He lifted a foul pop-up behind the plate that should have gotten the Orioles out of the inning, but it was dropped. With another life, Mantle hit his second homer, and the Yankees won 4–3. The booing turned to wild cheering, but in Mantle's mind what mattered was that he had won a game for his team, just when they needed it most. "I wanted to be good tonight more than I ever wanted to be good in my life," he said. "I don't know what I would have done if I had another day like yesterday."

He had not forgotten the booing by any means, nor what he had done to deserve it. So deep was his recognition of the baseball code he had violated that months later, long after the game and the season was history, when Casey Stengel was fired as the team's manager, Mantle still had the play on his mind. Following Stengel's farewell press conference, Mantle said how sorry he was to see him leave, then added, "About the other thing, Case, I'm sorry."

Stengel's firing came on the heels of the Yankees' loss to the Pirates in the 1960 World Series, a loss that was almost unendurable for everyone from the front office to the last player on the bench. Mantle wept openly afterward, calling the defeat the most painful episode in his entire career. The reasons can be read in the line scores. The Pirates won the first game in Pittsburgh, 6–4. The Yankees took the next, 16–3, with Mantle hitting two homers and tying a series record with five runs batted in. The Yanks won game three by 10–0 (Mantle hit another), but the Pirates took the fourth and fifth games, 3–2 and 5–2. Then the Yanks annihilated Pittsburgh in game six, 12–0. The seventh game turned on a bad hop double-play grounder that struck shortstop Tony Kubek in the throat in the eighth inning, opening the way for the Pirates to score five runs. Facing the end, the Yankees rallied to tie the game with two runs in the ninth, Mantle driving in the first of the two with an RBI single, but the game and the Series were finally settled on a leadoff homer by Bill Mazeroski in the bottom of the inning.

Stengel's firing after the Series was followed within months by George Weiss's resignation. The team's new general manager was Roy Hamey, who had been running the Yankee farm club in Richmond for the past several seasons; and the new bench manager was Ralph Houk, who had spent eight seasons with the Yankees before becoming a coach after his playing days ended in 1954.

Houk was a "player's manager," tough but fair, always willing to support his troops and unlikely to criticize anyone except behind closed doors, away from the press. "Mickey loved him as a gentleman and a great baseball man," said Bill Kane, the longtime Yankee publicist, statistician, and road secretary who became close to Mantle after he began working for the team that first year, 1961.

Kane recalled that one of Houk's first moves that spring was to approach Mantle and let him know that he wanted him, unofficially, to be the team's leader. But this was far more than a gesture, Kane said; Houk knew Mantle was not a talker, nor was he someone who would welcome the spotlight. He understood as well as anyone that Mantle would rather follow than lead, but he also knew that no one had his heart more invested in the team and no one was more important to its future. Houk was also, in Kane's words, "a lifetime Yankee, as Mickey was," so they both knew something about Yankee history.

The only player till then who had ever officially been designated as team captain was Lou Gehrig. There was no captain's designation for Mantle. "But when Ralph approached Mick in '61," Kane said, "he came out and told the club that Mantle would be the leader without being a pep talk guy, but would just lead by example. He said just the right thing, because Mickey could never be a rah rah guy, but he cared so much and he would always go out of his way to help guys on the team. I think he welcomed the responsibility even if he didn't want the limelight."

And what a year 1961 was. There is still debate in the baseball world whether that team or the 1927 Yankees was the greatest in the history of the game. For what it's worth, the '27 Yankees won 110 games and won the pennant by 19 games and the World Series in 4 straight. They hit 158 homers, had a good but not great pitching staff led by Waite Hoyt who won 22 games, and they had Ruth and Gehrig who, between them, hit 107 of those 158 homers. The supporting cast featured .300 hitters like Earle Combs, Bob Meusel, and Tony Lazzeri; the team had adequate defense but was questionable at best up the middle (Mark Koenig, the shortstop, committed more errors—forty-seven—than any other shortstop in the league), and was thin when it came to reserve players.

The '61 Yankees won the pennant by only eight games—but they won 109 games (the second place Tigers won 101 that season) and took the World Series in five games. Sixty-one, of course, was the year Maris broke the Babe's record by hitting 61 homers while Mantle hit 54, a combined total of 115. But if ever a team was a "Murderer's Row," it was this one. The Yankees hit a major-league record 240 homers. Seven players had 10 or more; Skowron had 28, Berra and Howard 22 each, and Johnny Blanchard, the backup catcher, had 21. The only other Yankee besides Ruth and Gehrig to hit more than 10 homers on the '27 team was Lazzeri (18).

The pitching between the two teams was probably a draw. Whitey Ford had his best season, 25–4; there were adequate backup starters and outstanding relief support from Luis Arroyo. But the '61 Yankees were superior defensively. Clete Boyer at third was outstanding, and Kubek and Richardson were the strongest double-play combination in the league. The team simply had no weaknesses; they were unmatchable then, and, take your pick, in '27, or anytime else.

But for as long as anyone will talk about that season, it will be about Mantle and Maris and their tag-team race to break Babe Ruth's home run record. In June, the Yankees trailed the Tigers by three and a half games, but then Maris went on a home run binge. He had twenty-seven by month's end, enough so that reporters began asking him about breaking Ruth's record. But on July 1, Mantle, who had been hitting them out with regularity from opening day, hit his twenty-sixth and twenty-seventh. It was clear to everyone that both players conceivably had a shot at the record. By the end of July, it became even more apparent: Maris had forty homers, Mantle thirty-nine. Going into September, it was Maris fifty-one, Mantle forty-eight.

The race thrilled fans across the country, and it released Mickey Mantle from the dungeon he had been living in since he joined the team. The pressure to prove that he was better than a legend was now, as though by the flip of a switch, transferred to Maris.

Maris, in his way, was even more unprepared to deal with it than Mantle. There was no talk about his being a player who had the potential of a Ruth, a Gehrig, a DiMaggio; he was presented in the media as a first-rate player but not a great one, and that is the way he was viewed by fans. He had just joined the team a year ago, so he was not a part of Yankee tradition—unlike Mantle. Yes, he could hit home runs, he had a good arm, and he played hard—but he was no Mantle. He would never hit .300—not that year, when he hit .261, and not any other year—unlike Mantle.

And if Mantle was surly and uncooperative with the press, Maris had his own problems with the unprecedented media onslaught that accompanied his record chase. He, like Mantle, came from a small town, but unlike Mantle, he never took to the excitement of the big city. The trade to the Yankees, far from making him feel like he had been blessed, was unwelcome and unwanted; New York was never a place where he wanted to play. As the season wore on, New York became to him a kind of United Nations of abuse—literally. "There were reporters not only from every city in the country crowding around him," said Tom Tresh, a rookie then who had been called up to spend the last month of the season with the team, "but there were guys from every country around the world. It was amazing. They would ask him every day about every at-bat, even every pitch he saw in the game. It was just incredible." Unlike Mantle, who had his light moods and an ability to sometimes deflect reporters' questions with down-home humor, Maris was nearly always unsmilingly to the point, finally becoming sullen and angry as the crowds of reporters grew around him.

Mantle, who dressed directly across from him, often found himself alone in these last weeks, particularly after he dropped out of the home run derby with an injury. He had become a witness to the spectacle, and he understood exactly what Maris was going through.

"There was one ball game, I forget who we were playing, but we were tied in a low-scoring game in the eighth inning and we had a man on third with one out and Maris came up," Bill Kane recalled. "At this point, he had fifty-something home runs, so every at bat was important. So what does Roger do in that situation? He squeezes home the runner with a perfect bunt. One of the things people forget about him was that he really knew how to bunt. Okay, so we win the game, 2–1 or whatever it was, and when the reporters crowded around his locker afterwards, wouldn't you know it, one of them says, 'Roger, why did you bunt when you had a chance to go for a home run?' Well, Roger exploded. 'To win a ballgame, you stupid cocksucker, why do you think?' I'm standing over by Mickey and Mickey just cracks up at this, he waves a towel around and says, 'Go get 'em, Rog!' There were many times when I'd see Mickey sitting off by himself—and he'd be happy they weren't bothering him. He expressed it later on, that he was glad that he wasn't the center of all that attention. See, the thing was, I don't think he ever could have been comfortable in that role—not because he was from Oklahoma, but because I don't think he ever realized how big he was."

Mantle from his freer vantage point often turned to ribbing the reporters. When an overeager writer asked him one day where he lived, he gave the address of another player who was standing alongside him. Another time he told reporters, hanging on an answer he was about to give on his race with Maris and Ruth, "On the last day of the season I can see it. Roger and I are tied for the home run lead. Roger's on first, and I hit a home run, and Roger gets halfway to second and runs back to first. I can just see the headlines: 'Maris Fucks Mantle.' "

In reality, the home run chase brought out the best in Mantle. The countless stories about the two stars' feuding were untrue; when Mantle saw how intense the pressure was on Maris, he decided to room with him. He, better than anyone else, knew what Maris was up against.

Maris had been sharing an apartment that year with Bob Cerv. The apartment was in Queens, not far from LaGuardia and Idlewild (now Kennedy) airports; it was exactly the kind of nondescript place in a nondescript neighborhood that a player wanting to stay out of sight would find for himself. A friend of Maris's, Big Julie Isaacson, said it was Maris's idea to invite Mantle to join them, while Bob Cerv thought that it was Mantle's idea.

"The first year Roger was here, 1960, Maris was starting to get recognized and it was getting to be too much downtown," Cerv said, "so we got that apartment together. Then Mantle came on board. 'Hey,' Mickey said, 'Can I move out with ya?' Just like that. Nothing more. 'Sure,' I said, 'we don't care.' "

Tony Kubek believed Mantle wanted to make the move for a couple of reasons: one, because he was going broke living at the St. Moritz Hotel; and two, "because Mickey also knew that this would be a difficult season for Roger in that the press and fans were putting a lot of pressure on him. Mickey had been through it so many times that I really believe he thought he could help Roger by moving in and giving support."

Cerv said they lived quietly; they had a phone—which no one knew about—and the only problems they had were when they had to go to the ballpark. "That was the only time we ever got bothered," Cerv said. "Yeah, one year, Maris got into it with Jimmy Cannon the writer, got into it with him real good because of something he wrote. What any of them said about him just didn't match the guy we knew. He was just a great guy. I don't think anybody realized what he was going through."

Mantle apparently did. He and Maris spent hours together doing the sorts of things that college roommates might have done to keep an apartment. One time, in a local supermarket, a clerk standing on a ladder by some high shelves saw Maris and Mantle wheeling a shopping cart down the aisle. He thought he was hallucinating. He went and got another clerk, told him he thought he saw Maris and Mantle. The second clerk said that was impossible, but then when they saw the two famous players coming down another aisle, they became so excited they spilled the contents of the shelves they were working on onto the floor.

Maris and Mantle had very different lifestyles. Though Maris, according to Bill Kane, "would have his beers," he was never into the New York nightlife as Mantle was. In their entire time together, he ran with Mickey only once, staying out all night, getting back in time the next day on unsteady legs. Mantle's legs were even unsteadier; in the game that day, Mantle homered, but going down to first in his home run trot he kept going until the first-base umpire, Ed Runge, nudged him toward second.

David Halberstam insisted the friendship between Maris and Mantle was "real but cool." But even if that was true, that is entirely consistent with Mantle's being the sort of team leader Ralph Houk hoped for. Luis Arroyo, the relief pitcher, had come to the Yankees in 1960, the same year as Maris. He was little used by Stengel, but he became a key to the team's success under Houk, who used him almost exclusively as a closer. In 1960, under Stengel, he pitched 40 innings and saved 7 games. In '61, he threw 119 innings and saved a league-leading 29 games. Arroyo credits Mantle with providing the kind of help he needed most. "I'll never forget this," Arroyo said. "We're in this real close ball game, a tie game, I'm supposed to go out and pitch the next inning. We the need the game real bad, I know. Mickey comes over to me and says, 'How you feeling?' I say to him, 'I'm a little tired.' He says, 'Don't worry about it, I'm the next batter, this game's over.' And just like that he goes up to the plate and hits one out. Won the game. We beat Detroit, the team that was right on us. So we go home. And he did that."

Arroyo also had a view from the inside of the home run race. "We on the team felt, like everybody else in the city of New York, that Mickey would do it. I don't think as players it made any difference, because we were for Roger, too. But I would say eighty percent of the ball club, the organization, were hoping that Mickey would make it."

John Blanchard backed him up. "That's about right. It wasn't like we weren't pulling for Roger, too. We were. But Mickey was special to us, to the fans, to everyone. We were professionals first, but I think secretly we were all pulling for him."

Whitey Ford, though closer to Mantle than anyone else, agreed that Mickey was loved by his teammates. "But so was Roger, though you'd never know it from what the sportswriters wrote about him. I don't agree that eighty percent of us were pulling for Mick over Roger. But I'll tell you one thing, Roger was lucky to have Mickey hitting behind him that season because they couldn't walk him. They had to pitch to him."

Indeed, in all the flap that followed Maris's record, there was no more salient point about how Mantle helped Maris than where they were located in the batting order. Several years ago, the Elias Sports Bureau, the game's official number crunchers, came up with a picture of Maris as a hitter with Mantle hitting behind him as opposed to when he was followed by others. The numbers are startling. With Mantle on deck, Maris, in 478 at bats, had 54 home runs, 130 RBIs, and a batting average of .293. With others on deck, Maris, in 115 at bats (a fairly significant quantity), had 7 homers, 12 RBIs, and a .174 batting average. It is simply fact, not speculation, that Maris got a huge boost in his race with Ruth by having Mantle waiting there bulging in the on-deck circle.

On the other hand, Maris's gift to Mantle, though not statistically measurable, was also inestimable. All the grumbling about how unworthy Maris was as a successor to Ruth made it clear at last how worthy Mantle was and had been for most of the last ten years. He had the same frame, the same lope, the same speed, power, arm, and temperament, and the same Oklahoma accent, but now instead of being the target of abuse for what he was not, he was receiving cheers for precisely who he was.

Mantle was a player who gave his heart and soul to his work, no matter what he did off the field. Everyone had known about the injuries, of course, but now that he went out and played injured seemed to make him larger, more heroic than he had ever been before.

Bill Kane, in his first year with the Yankees, was initially anything but a fan. He had grown up in Brooklyn rooting for the Dodgers, and was simply grateful that the Yankees had given him a job. But he was a perfect representative of all those who now began unabashedly cheering Mantle every time he took the field.

Kane, who had been severely handicapped by childhood polio, recalled the first time he became aware not only of the extent to which Mantle played through injury, but also of how much he wanted to keep that from view, even from his own teammates.

"I remember the time perfectly," Kane said. "I used to have to get the lineups in the dugout, and I hadn't realized it but as I was walking through the clubhouse Mickey was sitting there alone. I'd heard about his injuries like everyone else, but now I caught him there. He was all by himself, wrapping up both legs from his ankles to his hips, and I was kind of amazed that he had to take care of his legs that much. He caught me staring at him, gaping at him, and he kinda looked up and kinda smiled at me. 'Yeah,' he said, 'pretty soon, Bill, I'll be as bad as you.' He said it sweet not mean, so it wasn't a put-down. But I could tell that he didn't want anybody seeing him doing that."

What Kane saw in private suddenly everyone else saw, dramatically, in public. Going into September neck and neck with Maris in the home run race, Mantle missed nineteen games when a flu shot he received became infected, and a deep abscess formed. The missed games cost him a chance at the record, but then his return in time for the World Series was more than Bernard Malamud could have invented and more than any fan could have hoped for.

Mantle had the abscess cut from his body. The surgical wound was almost four inches by two, and it was so wide and deep it could not properly be closed. "It was from the bone up, not from the skin down," Johnny Blanchard said. "The way the wound was dressed was first with a coating of sulfur right down on the bone, by the hip where it was, then it was covered with gauze and then bandaged over. It was unbelievable this guy could walk, much less play."

Mantle was told that playing was impossible, but he insisted and finally was allowed to start in the third game of the World Series in Cincinnati. "When he came to bat, you could see a spot of blood on his uniform by his hip; we all could see it," said Blanchard.

Mantle played through the third game, which the Yankees won 3–2, going hitless in four appearances. In the fourth game, he started again. In the bottom of the first inning, he extended himself in catching a fly ball in deep right center field, and when he came back to the bench and sat down, blood from his wound had soaked through his jersey. Every teammate saw it, and fans in the stands could see it when he came to bat. He stayed in the game through the fourth inning—when his pal Whitey Ford broke a Series consecutive scoreless inning streak that had been set by Babe Ruth—then came out of the game for a pinch runner after he singled and set up the Yankees' first run of the game.

Jim Murray, a couple of years later, celebrated the courage Mantle had shown. "I remember Mantle clearest in the World Series of 1961," he wrote. "He could barely stand. A strange infection in his hip had not responded to penicillin and had abscessed and been cut out. He had a silver-dollar hole in his hip. In batting practice, he hit five balls out of the lot, two off the scoreboard and one off the left fielder's belt buckle and a man, presumably a National League rooter, climbed up the Crosley Field tower and got ready to jump.

"The next day in a game, he hit one off the center field fence but barely made first base like a guy crawling with an arrow in his back. 'Look at his pants!' someone cried. They were covered with blood. He was hemorrhaging."

But for Mantle, the 1961 season was not about courage or the determination to play as long as he could stand; these were the characteristics that had made him the ballplayer he was all along. More than anything, the season was about the lifting of burdens, the exorcising of old ghosts. This great winning season had in it, first and foremost, the ease and the joy he found in playing. Before one game in Washington in August, he took part in a home-run hitting contest. As he stood at the plate, a long, raucous boo greeted each swing he took. When he looked around, it was Whitey Ford, standing on the front steps of the dugout, his hands cupped over his mouth, playfully deriding him. Mantle roared with laughter.

That winter, Mantle and Maris made a movie together, *Safe at Home*. And that winter, too, he made an appearance at the New York Baseball Writers dinner. Mantle, normally uncomfortable in the role of after-dinner speaker, was additionally distressed that night by having to follow Casey Stengel. One of the press wags cracked that Mantle following Stengel as a speaker was "like a dog act following Bob Hope."

Stengel regaled the writers as though they were all once again in his office during his best days. When it was Mantle's turn to speak, he looked numb, as though he was genuinely bewildered by the task before him. He stared at the audience, seemingly as withdrawn and uncommunicative as he was at his locker after a bad game.

"I came out of the hotel last night," he began, "and who do I meet but Casey. He's looking kind of low, so I ask what's the matter. 'I gotta make a speech at the dinner,' Casey told me, 'and I don't know what to say.'

"It just happened, I had my speech in my pocket, so I gave Casey mine," Mantle said. It took a few seconds before the writers caught on and erupted with laughter. But by then it was too late. Mantle, with a sly grin and a wave, had slipped away and gone off to enjoy the night and the new life that it had taken so long to find.

Chapter 10

With the 1962 season, Mantle began to understand, as the Willie Nelson song goes, that his todays were going to make wonderful yesterdays. He was thirty years old, at the top of his game, and appreciated as never before. When he took the field at Yankee Stadium, the cheers rang out for every home run, every hit, every running catch in the outfield, every time his name was announced in the lineup.

Roger Maris, on the other hand, inherited the inexplicable derision that had once gone Mantle's way. He was frequently booed at home and on the road, no matter the situation. He told Mantle and others that if he knew that breaking Ruth's record would have caused him such grief he would gladly have skipped it. In a game at Detroit, a bottle was hurled at him from the grandstand, just missing his head. At Yankee Stadium he was pelted with eggs. In April and May, Mantle ripped through American League pitching, leading his team in all offensive categories, while Maris, hitting behind Mantle, was at a solid .300 pace. But the season seemed to nose-dive on a single play.

In the last of the ninth inning of a game against the Twins at Yankee Stadium, Mantle chopped a ground ball to shortstop

Zoilo Versailles. He broke all out from the batter's box, but a quarter of the way down the line, he suddenly collapsed. Because his forward momentum was so great, it seemed impossible that he could hit the ground the way he did.

"God, he hit the ground like a ton of bricks," said Johnny Blanchard. "I never saw anything like that in my life. It was as though he had been shot. And in fact a lot of us thought he had been. A number of players came to the top step of the dugout and looked back into the stands to see where he had been shot from."

Mantle had completely torn a hamstring muscle in his upper right thigh—and then, twisting on his other leg as he fell, he tore ligaments and some cartilage in his left knee. A stretcher was brought out, which he declined to use; instead, he was helped from the field, hanging onto the shoulders of his teammates.

Several days later, Whitey Ford was injured, hurting his arm in the midst of a shutout against the Los Angeles Angels. With both stars gone at the same time, the team slipped from first place all the way to the middle of the pack. In Mantle's absence, it became apparent to everyone just how important he was to the entire team's fortunes—and especially to Maris's. Everyone—fans, writers, asterisk-givers—all could plainly see that with Mantle out, Maris was simply not the same hitter.

Mantle somehow managed to return to action in a month, an almost unbelievably short time considering the injuries he had sustained. He went on an immediate hitting binge, getting six homers in four games in early July, maintaining a near .500 batting average. Then, too, Maris resumed hitting. By month's end, with Ford back as well, the team was once more in first. The Yankees took the pennant that year by five games over the Twins, and then beat the San Francisco Giants in a dramatic seven-game World Series that went down to the last pitch.

Mantle was named MVP that season, the third time he had won the award. A case might have been made for the Twins' Harmon Killebrew, who had better power numbers. Though he hit eighty points lower than Mantle, he led the league in homers, with 48, and in RBIs, with 126; Mantle's numbers were 30 and 89, though in nearly two hundred fewer at bats. But the vote, more than anything, was about Mantle's value to his team—exactly what an MVP designation should mean.

Apart from producing on the field, Mantle was the undisputed leader of his team that Houk had hoped he would be. There is no standard of measurement for the sort of leadership he provided. "Just from his playing every day and never complaining, he was the leader," Johnny Blanchard said. "You never had to tell him to hustle or go all out, and everybody knew that and tried to emulate him, tried to give that little extra simply because they knew what he was doing. We all knew he was hurting and tired, and he would never ask out of the lineup. If you saw that over and over again, day after day, season after season, you'd know what an inspiration that really was." The players who were there with him, particularly the younger ones, loved him even as they idolized him. All through these years that proved to be the twilight ones in his career, Mantle was the heartbeat, the soul of his team, though he kept insisting that he be taken as just another player.

Phil Linz was one of a brace of rookies that joined the Yankees in '62. Along with Tom Tresh, Joe Pepitone, and Jim Bouton, the new players represented a well-established Yankee tradition: that change was an inevitable part of the business of continuing to win pennants and championships.

The new players were all minor-league stars who came in with advance billing. Tresh was considered the hottest of the prospects; he was the "next Mickey Mantle," the media said, a switch-hitter with power and an erratic shortstop who might better be used in the outfield. Pepitone was probably the most talented of the group; flashy, brash, fearless, he was an authentic hitter, a potentially intimidating player on the field, a lover of good times away from it. Brooklyn born, he came from a broken family and a rough neighborhood. He had once been shot in the stomach as a teenager and was lucky to be alive much less a Yankee. Linz had just won a batting championship playing in the Texas League; he had speed and range in the field as a shortstop but could, like Tresh, play any number of positions.

Linz has never forgotten the ways in which Mantle made it easy for him and the other young Yankees.

"I knew I was coming up into a tough situation. I could hit, yeah, but I could really steal bases—shoulda been a National Leaguer, probably, but if you make it here it's better than making it anywhere.

"The Yankees then were a team that didn't steal bases. You know, you got on and you waited for a guy to hit the long one," Linz said, "so it was tough. I didn't know Mickey at all, I had just seen him on TV and all I knew about him was what a great competitor he was. So I was feeling a lot of pressure. I can remember as clearly as yesterday one of the first spring training games I was in. I hit a double, drove in a run, stole third, and then at the end of the inning when I went to take my position at shortstop, Mickey came running past me. He said, 'Nice going, Phil,' just like that, and he kept on running. That was a big thrill for me. He knew I existed, that I was on that team. I can't tell you what a difference that made."

The initially awestruck youngsters saw that Mantle really was a teammate, not a demigod. "The whole thing about him was that he was a regular guy. He was like an average person," Linz said. "All Mickey ever wanted to do was play baseball, be one of the guys. I don't think he could ever put up with being treated special."

Linz lockered right next to Mantle for four years. He was close enough to feel the wash of the spotlights spilling over. "Mickey resented people who were into the magnitude of his personality and physical abilities. He didn't want that, didn't need it, sometimes didn't know how to handle it."

The biggest surprise, said Linz, was that Mantle became a friend, a real friend as well as a teammate. "I never knew I would hang out with him; I figured he was a veteran, we were rookies. But he was just a regular guy. If he liked you—and he didn't like everybody—you were flattered, sure. But when he picked up the phone and said come on over and hang out, you just knew that was really sincere."

The young players were initiated into the Yankee fraternity by Mantle, Ford, and some of the other veterans in the same way they themselves had been initiated when they were rookies. It was understood that they would be gofers at the same time that they were shown the ropes and the lights.

"Once when Joe and I were hanging out with Mickey and Whitey in Chicago, we were in a nightclub," Linz said, "and they entered us into a twist contest. Mickey said, 'Why don't you two enter the contest?' So of course we did. And you know what, Joe won first prize and I won second! Mickey and Whitey couldn't get over that."

Mantle and Ford were also instigators of a more well-known and somewhat nervier prank. "They asked Joe and me if we wanted to go out to dinner with them one night in Detroit. We said sure. It was a great honor to be asked out by Mickey and Whitey, you know. They gave us the address of a supper club called The Flame, told us what time to be there, the whole bit. So we got a cab," Linz said, "told the driver where we wanted to go, and pretty soon we're noticing that this ride is gonna cost us a fortune. This place was like thirty miles out of Detroit. I remember saying, 'Joe, I don't think they're going to be here, this place is too far away.' 'Oh yeah, oh yeah,' he says, 'they're going to be here.' Now we're going through a really bad section of town and that's where the guy lets us off—that's the address, that's the club. We pay off the cabby and we walk up to the front door.

"Well, if it was a movie, what you'd see is these two dumb white guys in the dark, the glare of neon on their faces, opening the door and suddenly the music stops and everyone turns around and stares at you. We were the only white guys in a place that was packed with black people. I said, 'I don't know, Joe.'

And Joe says, 'I think we got taken.' So we did a U-turn and hightailed it outta there.

"We didn't know where we were or what to do. The cab that brought us was gone, so we walked up and down looking for another. We finally found one and we went back to the hotel. On the way, Joe says that when we see the guys tomorrow, we should apologize to them, tell them we were sorry that we hung them up but that we had to do something else. So, sure enough, we get on the team bus and we say, 'Gee, we're sorry about last night, we got tied up, hope you had a good time anyway.' Mickey and Whitey looked at each other then at us and then we all started laughing—we all really enjoyed it."

Mantle presided over the clubhouse with bawdy good humor, more like Falstaff than Henry V.

"One of my favorite Mickey stories was a night in Baltimore when eight or ten of us went out to dinner after a flash flood had washed away the game," Tony Kubek recalled.

> We left the restaurant, and on the way back to the Lord Baltimore Hotel, Mickey said we should play follow the leader. It was still pouring, and the water was rushing down cobblestone streets and flooding out the gutters and onto the sidewalk. Mickey and Whitey flipped a coin to see who would be leader. Whitey won and off we went. It was about 1 A.M., and we were chasing Whitey through alleys and leaping over garbage cans and fire hydrants. Whitey vaulted over the railing of a row house and lost his balance, landing on some cement steps directly on his left shoulder. Mickey was laughing and he sent Whitey to the end of the line.
>
> Mickey led us to the Lord Baltimore, which had a marble floor in the lobby. We were all soaked, and water was dripping off us onto the floor. Suddenly, Mickey decided it was time for the grand finale. He took off and slid headfirst across the lobby in his Nieman-Marcus suit. Since it was so late, there was no one operating the elevator. The door was open, and Mickey's slide didn't stop until he went through the lobby and headlong into the back of the elevator. He got up holding his head and rubbing his right shoulder.

One of the most valuable pieces of cardboard ever: the 1952 Topps Mickey Mantle card.

15

Mickey, with druggist Ott Chandler and writer Ben Epstein in Commerce. Some of Commerce resented its successful native son, a factor in the Mantle family's move to Dallas.

16

17

Hunting with Billy Martin in the early 1950s.

18

Mantle's lunging catch of Gil Hodges's fifth-inning liner proved to be the crucial defensive play in preserving Don Larsen's perfect game in the 1956 World Series.

Mantle holds the ball he hit 565 feet in Griffith Stadium; he is pointing to the dent where the ball hit a house after clearing center field.

20

Mantle tries on the crown he was awarded as the outstanding hitter in baseball in 1956—his Triple Crown season.

Mantle signs his 1957 contract. Looking on are Stengel, Lee MacPhail, and George Weiss (who had balked at Mantle's demand for $65,000, and tried to blackmail him into signing a lesser deal).

21

The dotted line traces the path of Mantle's 1963 blast against the facade in Yankee Stadium, off Bill Fischer of the Kansas City Athletics. 22

23

Relaxing with Roger Maris during spring training of 1961—when it was still possible for both of them to relax.

24

Mantle lies crumpled in the first base line after injuring both legs on the same play. First baseman Vic Power has come over to express concern.

As Mantle's career progressed, the pain he had to overcome just to play became more and more obvious.

26 The Mantle family in Joplin, Missouri, in June 1961, by the pool at the Mantle Motel; from left: Mickey, Danny, Mickey Jr., Billy, David, and Merlyn.

In spring training, 1967, Mantle was shifted to first base to ease the strain on his ailing legs, which were no longer up to playing the outfield.

27

On Mickey Mantle Day, June 8, 1969, Mantle's number 7 was retired. He was only the fourth Yankee—after Babe Ruth, Lou Gehrig, and Joe DiMaggio—to receive that honor.

29 Once legend and heir apparent, by now the co-idols of all Yankees fans, Mantle and DiMaggio salute the crowd on Old Timers Day in 1972.

Mantle and his buddy Whitey Ford, on the day when they were both elected to the Baseball Hall of Fame in 1974.

30

Two unlikely personnel entrepreneurs open another office of the employment agency Mantle Men and Namath Girls in December 1969. The business lasted just a few years before going under, like so many of Mantle's postbaseball ventures. 31

Mantle with Greer Johnson, in the early 1990s, pursuing the vocation that made him a living in the memorabilia boom of the 1980s and '90s: being Mickey Mantle.

32

33

Greer, Mickey, and Billy and Jill Martin celebrating Billy's birthday at the Regency Hotel in New York.

34

George Steinbrenner, Mickey, and Richard Nixon bow their heads at Billy Martin's funeral at St. Patrick's Cathedral, December 29, 1989.

35

The three men who stirred a million street-corner arguments in New York in the '50s—Duke Snider, Willie Mays, and the Mick—gather at the Baseball Writers Dinner in New York in January 1995.

36

Mickey, Greer, and Moose Skowron celebrate Mickey's sixty-second birthday at the Harbor Club in Greensboro, Georgia.

David Mantle, left, and his brother Danny listen to a news conference updating their father's condition after his liver transplant on June 8, 1995.

37

Merlyn wipes away a tear as she speaks to the media the day after Mickey's liver transplant.

38

Yankee Stadium fans show their support for their stricken hero. 39

40

Mickey listens as doctors discuss his condition a month after his transplant.

"I really liked his sense of humor and his boyishness," Jim Bouton wrote in *Ball Four,* "the way he'd spend all that time in the clubhouse making up involved games of chance and the pools he got up on golf matches and the Derby and things like that.

"I once invested a dollar when Mantle raffled off a ham. I won, only there was no ham. That was one of the hazards of entering a game of chance, Mickey explained.

"I got back by entering a fishing tournament he organized and winning the weight division with a ten-pounder I'd purchased in a store the day before. Two years later Mantle was still wondering why I'd only caught that one big fish and why all the other fish that were caught were green and lively while mine was gray and just lay there staring."

Bouton, Linz, Tresh, and Pepitone all remember other, very different sides to Mantle. He could be genuinely supportive in ways that were astonishing coming from a player with his celebrity. "I remember the time I won my first major league game," Bouton wrote. "It was a shutout against the Washington Senators in which I walked seven guys and gave up seven hits and had to pitch from a stretch position all game. . . . When the game was over I walked back to the clubhouse and there was a path of white towels from the door to my locker, and all the guys were standing there, and just as I opened the door Mickey was putting the last towel down in place."

He extended himself in ways that went far beyond the playing field or the locker room. Pepitone, advertised by many, including himself, as the next Great Yankee, recalled that in his first year, when he was in the middle of a divorce, Mantle heard about his problems and invited him to move in with him at the St. Moritz.

"I stayed with him for a month. We'd go out to dinner, just have a great time together," Pepitone said. "He came to me and said, 'I heard about what's going on with you, come and live with me, don't worry about it.' He taught me a lot about a lot of things—feelings, the way I handled myself. See, he had been taught by guys like Hank Bauer when he came up, so he told me about all the things I'd have to deal with, the fans, the media, the other players, how to stay straight, make sure I didn't go out and get a beer gut right in the beginning. He told me that it took a special person to be a superstar ballplayer. He has to be able to do everything."

But since Mantle was constitutionally incapable of disguising himself, these young players got to see him close-up in his darker moods, too. All of them knew he drank heavily and that he was a prodigious womanizer. None of that was especially remarkable on the team or in its time. Steve Boros, who played for the Tigers through the '62 season, noted that the Yankees had a leaguewide reputation for playing hard and partying hard. "It was the culture of the game then; they were able to do it a little more because they kept winning."

But the young players saw something else. "I guess the kind of life he had took its toll," Pepitone said. "It's a funny game. You go on the road, it's really a lonely life, nowhere near as glamorous as people make it out to be. If you've been around enough, you see the damage it can do. One year, two years, three, you think you've seen it all, you go the ballpark, play a game, then you either go home or go out, have a drink, have a cocktail. Guys learn that from the minor leagues all the way up. But Mickey was such a superstar and there were always so many people after him. You get tired after awhile, you get angry, you want to get away from it, get a little happy. You get phone calls all hours of the night, so you just stay out. You can't carry all of that twenty-four hours a day."

Phil Linz believed the toughest thing for Mantle was that it was almost impossible for him to enjoy any kind of privacy. As much as he wanted to be, Mantle simply could not be "just a regular guy." Linz said that while he regarded him as a friend, he was in awe of him—not only because of his unsurpassable talent, but because of how he had to deal with being Mickey Mantle out in public.

"I saw a guy who had a lot of resentment about how he was

treated. They didn't give any consideration for his privacy," Linz said. "I got to see that maybe it wasn't so good being a superstar. You know, we used to go out to a club together, a restaurant—P. J. Clarke's, say, where you'd sit in the corner and they'd have to rope off that section so we could eat in peace. Anywhere we went, people would slap him on the shoulder, just like he was their best friend or something. People say he was mean, that he had a temper, but if you would step in his shoes for a day or a night you might feel the same way."

Linz and the other players used to try to protect Mantle from the crowds that inevitably boiled up around him. They tried to be the ones to say no before Mantle had to. But that only made more apparent just how different he really was.

"I think there's a deep loneliness when you're special," said Linz. "You can be out there with many people, but you're still very lonely. No matter how much he was a regular guy, he was still looked upon as separate, he was always a special person in the group, he never experienced like I did or other players did being the least in the group. No matter what he did he was always separate."

What the players saw but could not fully acknowledge was how much the drinking had come to dominate Mantle's life. In '63, Mantle suffered another major injury. In a game in Baltimore in the beginning of June, he caught his spikes in a chain-link fence leaping after an outfield fly. He fractured his left foot (when the results of X rays were announced to the crowd, they cheered). There was a strong likelihood he would be finished for the season. After missing almost a hundred games, however, he made it back. His return was triumphant, almost otherworldly—but for reasons that had nothing to do with any damage he had suffered on the field.

Late in the summer, while he was healing but still on the disabled list, the team made another stop in Baltimore. Since he was still on the disabled list, he and Whitey Ford, who was not scheduled to pitch the following day, and several others spent all night obliterating themselves at a rural farmhouse. When Mantle arrived at the ballpark the next day, Hank Bauer, by then an Oriole coach, handed him a bottle of mouthwash so he could hide the smell of liquor on his breath. Mantle and Ford took shelter on the far end of the bench and tried to nap. Around the seventh inning, Houk came to Mantle and told him to hit. He looked at Houk like he was crazy.

"I'm on the D.L.," he said.

"Not anymore," Houk said. "You were activated this morning. Get a bat and hit."

Somehow, Mantle wobbled to the plate and not only managed to make contact, he hit a home run. "Mickey told me he saw three balls at the same time and managed to hit the right one," said Johnny Blanchard. Mantle said, "I came around second, aiming for third, and saw Brooks Robinson standing on the bag, his hands on his hips, shaking his head in utter disbelief."

It was in this same period, Mantle recalled, there was another, far more serious incident. "Merlyn and I were having dinner with Yogi Berra and his wife, Carmen. Now, Yogi always drank straight vodka on the rocks. He'd have a limit, maybe three or four, and that was it. Me, I'd be just starting. On this particular night I was drinking fast and furious. At the end of the dinner, when it was time to leave, Merlyn got in the passenger side of the car and I got in the driver's side. Yogi hollered, 'Merlyn, I wouldn't ride with him!' Good old sensible Yogi.

"On the way home I'm going about sixty or seventy miles an hour and Merlyn is trying to get me to let her drive. She's going, 'Oh oh, you're driving too fast. Slow down, will you?' Then she hits me with her purse.

"I reach over to take her purse away. Then I see a telephone pole coming straight at us. We hit it head on; Merlyn went through the windshield; the rearview mirror just creased the top of her skull."

When the police finally found them and took them to a hospital where Merlyn received multiple stitches to close her head wounds, no DWI charges were filed. Mantle was let off with a comparatively small fine, and news of the accident was kept from the media. What also remained unreported was that alcohol not only was a controlling part of Mantle's life, but had also been part of Merlyn's for almost as long.

"Everyday was a cocktail party, that was our lifestyle," she recalled. "We were just country people when we first came to New York. We didn't have anything, and suddenly Mick was the toast of New York. It scared us both to death. We were both very shy people, and I guess this was our way to cope with it."

It seems unarguable that the most serious injury Mantle played through during his career was the one he inflicted on himself and others by consuming prodigious amounts of alcohol. No single injury by itself did more to compromise the people he loved, his overall health, his physical condition, and his ability to play the game he cared so much about at the level he expected of himself than his chronic drinking. But if there is one enduring portrait of Mantle, it is as a Wounded Hero, and if those wounds came not solely from the impersonal fates but by his own hand, then they only make him seem more like a classical tragic hero undone by a fatal flaw. His greatness made him awe-inspiring, his flaw and his struggle against it made him all too human.

Though Mantle was just thirty-one as he entered the 1963 season, the great years were over. The team was still, in most fans' eyes, the best around; the Yankees were the class of the American League, and they handled their opponents that year no differently than they had over the last decade and a half. They expected to win every time they took the field. That was their invisible advantage, just as their opponents' invisible disadvantage was the expectation that, somehow, the Yankees would find a way to beat them.

The team took a small lead into July that year, but by August they had blown the race apart. They won 104 games and took the pennant by $10\frac{1}{2}$ games over the second-place White Sox. In the World Series that followed, however, it was the Dodgers, not the

Yankees, who took the field with the expectation of victory. Their pitching staff, led by Sandy Koufax and Don Drysdale, was the best in the game. Maury Wills keyed a Dodger offense that featured team speed unseen since the days before Babe Ruth, but that would soon become the standard. The result was a shock: They won the series in four straight. The games were all close, but it was as if the Dodgers, as the Yankees had in the past, were toying with their rivals, gracing them by being on the same field with them, but never once giving them a real chance.

In '64, the Yanks won the pennant again, for the twelfth time in Mantle's fourteen years. The race this time was closer, so close that anyone bothering to watch could see this was not the same Yankee team that had so dominated the game for so long. From the start, there were injuries. That was not new. But there was a new manager, and that did seem to have an effect—for the worse. Yogi Berra was handed the job following the '63 season, when Ralph Houk moved upstairs to take over as general manager. Almost from day one there was grumbling. Johnny Blanchard, who had played as Berra's understudy for so many years, expressed what many felt when he said that Yogi had been handed a job he wasn't up to. That was soon the feeling in the front office as well. By midsummer, with the team floundering, it was decided that Berra would go at season's end, no matter how the race came out.

Berra's hold on the team was shaky. He was incapable of disciplining star players and old friends like Mickey and Whitey, so he all too often took out his frustrations by dressing down second-line players in front of the whole team. One notorious incident occurred in late August, after the team had lost ten of fifteen games and four straight to the White Sox in Chicago. On the team bus going to the airport, Phil Linz, responding to the gloomy silence on the bus, whipped out a harmonica that he had gotten that day along with a toot-along book of tunes and began to play.

Linz, who was always considered something of a flake, insists that there was something more than mere horseplay in what he did. "This thing got reported a certain way, as a funny story, you know, because there were all kinds of UPI guys on the bus, and so what they said came out like a fluke incident. It really wasn't. What happened was this," Linz said.

"Yeah, I had a harmonica, I got it that day, it was one of those small marine band harmonicas. Came with a learner's book with arrows that pointed up and down and had numbers so you could play a tune by blowing in and drawing out. So I take the thing out and I start to play 'Mary Had a Little Lamb.' I'm following it by the numbers on the sheet and it sounded terrible. So then Yogi says something from the front of the bus, and I say, 'What did he say?' And Mickey says, 'He said play it louder.' Well, I keep playing, then Yogi gets up, turns around and starts coming back. 'Shove that harmonica up your butt,' he says—only he didn't say butt. Well, I got pretty upset, and so did Yogi. I jumped up on my seat, threw the harmonica at him, and he threw it back to me. He said something else I didn't make out and he went back to his seat.

"So now I'm thinking, what the hell's wrong with him? I'm still standing on my seat, and I yell at him, 'What are you getting on me for? I'm on the bench. I didn't play the whole series, why don't you get on some of the guys who did play?' All my resentment came out, and that's what it was really all about.

"What was really incredible, was that the next day, they started selling out harmonicas all over New York City. Anyway, I go into Yogi's office that night and I apologize. I said I'm sorry, I shoulda listened to you, I was upset because I wasn't playing, that's all. He said, 'No problem.' We shook hands and he said, 'Lookit, I gotta fine you for what happened. Two-hundred and fifty bucks. I don't want to, but the writers all know, I gotta do it.' I said, okay, I deserve it. I shouldn't have done it in the first place. He fines me and the day after that, though, the Hoehner Harmonica company calls me and they offer me $5,000 to endorse their harmonica. So, I took it. Got fined $250, made $5,000, and I'll always be part of Yankee history. Every time they come up with some kind of argument or controversy over the manager they always go back to the harmonica incident in 1964."

But the real problem with Berra's leadership was that he, unlike past Yankee managers, didn't really have the troops. It was mostly the frontline pitching that got them through to one more pennant, their last until 1976. Position by position the team was older and slower. Key players had either retired or been traded or had broken down. Berra, Bauer, McDougald, Skowron, Turley, and Duren were all gone. Kubek was chronically hurt, as was Maris, who was no longer the player who won back-to-back MVPs.

And then, of course, there was Mantle. He rebounded from his injury-plagued '63 season for his last big year in '64. He hit .303, knocked in 111 runs, hit 35 home runs, and led his team into the World Series against the Cardinals. The Series went seven tense games, full of heroics on both sides, and was one more occasion for Mantle to take center stage. In the third game, with the teams having split the first two, Mantle came up in the last of the ninth inning with the score tied 1–1. He was the leadoff batter against the Cards' Barney Schultz. Schultz was a knuckleballer who had saved the first game and had been bombed in a brief ninth-inning appearance in game two. As Mantle was standing on deck watching Schultz warm up, he turned to Elston Howard who was waiting next to him and said, "You might as well go on in. I'm going to hit the first pitch I see out of the park."

Schultz threw just one pitch and, good as his word, Mantle deposited it deep in the right-field stands. The win put the Yankees up two games to one, and the homer was Mantle's sixteenth in World Series play, breaking Babe Ruth's career Series record.

Mantle hit two more in the games that followed to set a mark of eighteen that will be hard for anyone to break so long as teams and rosters are impossible to hold together for more than a few seasons. But in a real sense, the home run off Schultz represented a valedictory even more than it did a victory.

People who understood the game, who watched it with coldly clinical eyes, understood all too well what was going on. Mantle was not the same player even then that he had been. Injuries had permanently slowed him; his once blazing speed was no longer a threat. He was an adequate but no longer an exceptional outfielder.

Hoot Evers, an old Tiger outfielder, was then scouting for the Cleveland Indians. Just prior to the Series, he filed a standard player report on Mantle. His findings were startling. In a rating system in which one was excellent, three average, four below average, and five poor, he gave Mantle threes and fours in every category: hitting ability, base running, arm strength and accuracy, and fielding. Only in the category of power did Evers rate Mantle highly, giving him a two. In his written comments, he emphasized, "Increased leg problems may end this man's career sooner than expected. . . . He has meant something to this club through the years, and he might have been the best ball player of his time if it were not for his legs."

There were other scouts, of course, who did not see Mantle as Evers did. But then they, too, were looking at a future full of wonderful yesterdays. The cruel truth was that Mantle's era ended in 1964, four years before his career did.

Chapter 11

In the middle of the Yankee pennant drive in 1964, the team was sold. On August 13, news got out that the team's owners, Dan Topping and Del Webb, had sold the ball club to CBS. The deal was complex, though by today's standards it seems as simple as making an over-the-counter purchase at Sears—and at unheard-of summer bargain rates, too. CBS bought 80 percent of the most prestigious franchise in sports for $11.2 million, with an option to buy the rest. As incredibly small as those figures seem today, they represented an off-the-chart earthquake in the financing of American professional games.

The true significance of the sale was summed up later by David Halberstam: "Nothing better demonstrated the changing nature of sports in general and baseball in particular than the sale of the Yankees, for it reflected both the rising value of a team and the increasing importance of television in sports. It was an important benchmark in the rising commercialism of sports. In the nineteen years since Topping, Webb, and Larry MacPhail had bought the team from the Ruppert estate for $2.8 million, the value of the major league team, the ball park, and its principal farm operations had gone up seventeen fold. Nor was this an isolated phenomenon. Throughout sports the impact of television was becoming clearer and clearer. The huge salary soon to be paid to Joe Namath reflected the fact that an experienced network, NBC, which scheduled the fledgling American Football League, needed important stars in order to be competitive."

CBS had its most important star in Mantle, but one whose value—like that of the franchise itself—was based on past accomplishment. When it came to the present, there was trouble from the first flip of the channel switch. The Yankees' loss of a second straight World Series became the pretext for the front-office decision that had been made the previous summer to look for a new manager, one who would have better control of the team, be better able to instill a necessary sense of discipline. Immediately following the series, literally before the bodies had cooled, the Yankees announced Berra's firing. And then, when they hired Johnny Keane, the manager of the winning St. Louis Cardinals, the new regime looked even more coldheartedly efficient than the old. But the move was a fiasco, from the bad press it received to the upheaval it caused in the clubhouse.

The team, though it had been divided and uncertain under Yogi's "soft" leadership, had at least won a pennant. Keane was hired not only because he was a respected baseball man from a top organization, but also because he had a reputation for being a drill sergeant. He was the worst possible choice for the hard-playing, hard-partying Yankees.

Keane let his players know right away that curfews would be obeyed, rules followed. Boozing, partying, living it up were out; the only reason anyone was there was to play and win baseball games. He might as well have been speaking in Sanskrit. Players not only resented him, they ignored him. After a couple of weeks in spring training, after Keane had taken to sitting in the lobby of the team hotel to check when players got back to their rooms, he called a team meeting and warned them against the kind of carelessness they were exhibiting. This struck the team as hilarious.

"I remember sitting in a bar with the guys, and I would say, 'Should we have another round?' " Jim Bouton told Peter Golenbock. "And they would say, 'I don't know. It's awfully careless of us. Should we be doing something so careless? Yeah, let's.' "

Among the players on the team, Mantle took to Keane less than almost anyone. "We were used to Casey and Ralph, who didn't even have a curfew, and Yogi who didn't really enforce one," Mantle said, "Now all of a sudden, here's this guy coming in like a drill sergeant."

Mantle kept his distance from Keane; the closest he got to communicating with him was through staring and glaring. The managers he had played for knew all about his drinking because at least two of them had shared late nights with him. Bill Kane, who believed that Mantle's drinking was a way of relieving pressure, said, "Yogi and Ralph actually preferred that he tie one on the night before so he'd be more relaxed." Quite possibly, the benefits of keeping a tightly muscled and nervous young superstar well oiled had not been lost on Casey Stengel, either.

In any case, Mantle learned early that Keane was serious about closing the spigot. "Right off at spring training, Keane went after me," Mantle said. "After a night when he knew I'd been out late —I had a hangover—he sent me out to center field. He grabbed the fungo stick and a bag of balls, about fifty of them, and started hitting them out—to my left, to my right, behind me, until the bag was empty.

"Now I had been in center field in the major leagues for about fifteen years. I knew how to catch fly balls. I knew he wasn't providing any instruction. He was trying to make me sick, trying to set an example."

Mantle says that he ultimately responded to this regimen by one day coming in short on a fly ball, taking it and flinging as hard as he could directly at Keane. Keane ducked as the ball sailed over his head. Mantle later said that he was mortified by what he had done and that Keane was the one manager he played for to whom he owed an apology. But there was no apology then, only a season where foul lines suddenly seemed to become lines drawn in the sand.

The Yankees nose-dived under Johnny Keane. The team finished sixth, with a losing record for the first time in forty years. It was not Johnny Keane but the team itself that was the problem. No matter what any player said, the Yankees had been a decaying institution for years. Where once teams like the Yankees and Dodgers had simply been able to buy young talent, forcing up the price other teams would have to pay to remain competitive, the major leagues initiated an amateur draft system—still in effect—in 1964. It was no longer possible for a Paul Kritchell or a Tom Greenwade to simply walk up to a Lou Gehrig or Mickey Mantle and lure him to the Yankees; there was now a pecking order with the worst teams getting first choice. The Yankees' once-vaunted farm system was also in disarray. The minors had been shriveling for years, largely as a result of teams' spending more money to secure talent; the Yankees had severely cut back, too. The players who were coming up or were available via the Kansas City Express were not named Mantle, McDougald, Skowron, or Roger Maris but Roger Repoz, Horace Clarke, and Fred Talbot. The well was dry, and the Yankees' day—as Dan Topping and Del Webb knew very well when they sold the team —was done.

The highlight of the season for the Yankees, CBS, and Mantle, was Mickey Mantle Day at the Stadium on September 18. Scores of gifts, ranging from a six-foot-long, 100-pound salami to a brand new Chrysler, were paraded before him to the roars of a nearly filled park. The affection and generosity were real, but day-to-day reality was something else. Mantle played in only 122 games that season, hounded by a series of strains and muscle pulls. His .255 average was the lowest in his fourteen-year Yankee career. His power numbers had fallen just as precipitously.

That fall, during a game of touch football with his twin brothers, Ray and Roy, he seriously injured his right shoulder. He thought then that the injury might be career threatening, but even before then he had been aware that his skills were eroding. Over the winter, bone chips and calcium deposits were removed from his shoulder. By spring he was healed, though he would never be able to throw with force and accuracy from the outfield again. He began the '66 season more convinced than ever that he was not the player he used to be.

Getting off the team bus in Chicago one day, he told Bill Kane to keep an eye on his career batting average. "He told me right then that when his average got down near the .300 mark to let him know, because that was when he would quit," Kane said. "I think his biggest disappointment in his whole career—and he told me this again and again later on—was that when he finally did retire, his lifetime average had dropped just below .300. He always believed he was a .300 hitter and he wanted to go out that way."

But Mantle, for a variety of reasons—beginning with the fact that he needed his now-annual one hundred thousand dollar salary—did not go out that way. He stayed on through several years of organizational ruin that no doubt contributed to his own decline.

Mantle's friends understood his special dilemma and the nature of his commitment. Whitey noted that if Mickey had a fault, it was that he trusted people too easily and was too careless about money. He had made bad investments in the past because he had been unable to say no to people who were only looking to make a buck off him. But he had been doing better in these later years, Ford said, adding that Mickey happened to be one of those spenders "who was always ready to pick up a check or give someone a big tip." He had a lifestyle that always placed his earnings in jeopardy.

But it was more than money that made Mantle stay on. "While you're playing ball," Mickey said, "you're insulated. All the ballparks and the big crowds have a certain mystique. You feel attached, permanently wedded to the sounds that ring out, to the fans chanting your name, even when there are only four or five thousand in the stands on a Wednesday afternoon."

He kept drawing strength from the team even as the team drew continuing inspiration from him. "I don't think anyone ever had any idea how much this guy lifted us every day, just by being there," John Blanchard said. "When you knew the sort of pain he played with every day, never complaining, never asking out, he made everyone around him want to do better. He was the standard and all of us wanted to play up to it."

By then, Mantle's injuries were more talked about than what he could do on the field. The spectacle was no longer his ability but his ability to continue. "Watching Mantle hobble off the team bus reminds a viewer of an arthritic senior citizen," wrote a reporter for *The Sporting News*. "He enters the park, hits a homer, steals a base or somehow helps win a game. Then he climbs laboriously back on the bus for the return to the hotel. . . . That has happened so often it is almost normal now."

Mantle made it a point to buttonhole reporters in an effort to get them *not* to mention anything about his injuries. It hardly mattered; everyone knew how battered he was. Joe Soares, the Yankee team trainer then, said, "Mickey has a greater capacity to withstand pain than any man I've ever seen. Some of the things he has done while in great pain are absolutely unbelievable. . . . I think I can say beyond any doubt that no athlete has ever continued to play so effectively after so many crippling injuries as Mantle. He is as amazing a medical case history as he is an athlete."

Going into the '66 season, Jimmy Cannon articulated what it meant to have Mantle simply being there and playing the game:

> The big words turn meaningless. Their majesty has been defaced. There should be a special vocabulary to describe Mickey Mantle on the sports page. It demeans Mantle to tell what he is in the banal language of flattery that has been squandered on the description of three-foot putts.
>
> It might be enough to say that Mantle is a ballplayer as they should be. He comes to us out of all the old myths, and makes them true. I don't claim perfection for him. But in his heart he is the pure ballplayer. His spirit is intact. He is immune to adversity. . . .

The wrong people hear the applause as the freak is taken seriously in a time of trouble. We celebrate jerks because they temporarily distract us. On the sports pages the clowns are celebrated. The great words are their reward. You get around to Mantle and it would insult him to commemorate him with the splendid phrases that have been frayed by repetition.

He has to be the greatest athlete of these times. He performs on a plateau above ability, on the peaks of mountains no other athlete can scale. In him are the virtues on which competition in sports are founded.

The code goes back to antiquity, and the good men have cherished it eternally. It may be insignificant because Mantle lavishes it on a game. But it is rare no matter where it happens, and it exalts the human race.

The adulation, as pleasing and revealing as it surely was, was still not the motivating force that kept him in the game. The most elemental need of all was satisfied in feeling that he belonged to his team. It was his family in ways that no personal family could be for him. Like a caring father, he continued to be needed by younger players.

"I idolized Mickey from the time I was seven," Steve Whitaker, who joined the club in '66, said. "When I came up at the end of the season, to become his teammate, I was in a terrible state. How would I talk to him? Should I call him Mr. Mantle? How could I play ball in the same outfield and keep my mind on the game?

"The day I reported, however, Mickey came over to me and said, 'What took you so long? I thought you'd be here a year or so ago. Anything you need, let me know.' Man, I didn't recover from that greeting for a long time.

"There were many times when I was down on myself, but Mickey would invite me to have dinner with him. I often visited his apartment and he would sit and talk to me for hours. He told me how he had gone through the same things, tried to help me raise my spirits."

In the midst of his teammates, away from reporters and fans, from all those who wanted from him something he could never give, Mantle was more genuinely at ease than he had ever been in his life. He was an oracle from Oklahoma aboard team flights, full of sly humor and honky-tonk wisdom. He and Whitey, the Chairman of the Board, always had adjoining seats in the left front of the rear compartment of the planes they flew. And around the two players, others would congregate for games, jokes, and drinks. Mantle was fond of a word game called "jumbles," which involved scrambling and unscrambling big words. He delighted in stumping teammates with prairie nonsense words.

Over the years, he had become close to some players whose tastes and temperaments were very different from his own. One player he became especially friendly with was Bobby Richardson, the straight-living member of the Fellowship of Christian Athletes who later became a minister and spoke at Mantle's funeral. Richardson, in those days, was an organizer of Baseball Chapel, and Mantle tried as best he could to assist him. He actually attended one early morning meeting, was asked to recite the Lord's Prayer, could not, and never went back. Still, over the years he always made appearances when Richardson asked him to help out at fund-raisers for charities or church-sponsored events. And always, Richardson said, he was good-hearted and fun to be around. One time the team was late in arriving in Minnesota on a Saturday night. On the way to the hotel, an announcement was made aboard the team bus about the next morning's Baseball Chapel meeting. Mantle wisecracked, "It's gonna be a short night if we all get up that early. I suggest we all have our meeting right now, so let's all sing." Mantle, Richardson remembered, launched into a rousing Christian hymn and had the whole bus rollicking along with him.

But the team was going nowhere. Twenty games into the '66 season, Johnny Keane was fired, and Ralph Houk returned to the bench—and nothing changed. The team never came close to the

.500 mark and, in September, plunged into last place, where they finished for the first time since 1912. The seemingly endless stream of top players that had so regularly moved in and out during the championship years continued to dry up. The younger players, like Kubek, Richardson, Turley, or Tresh, were suddenly older, damaged by time and injury. Veterans like Moose Skowron, Yogi, and Hank Bauer had long since moved on; others, like Maris and Elston Howard were soon to go—as was Whitey Ford, who increasingly found it hard to raise his left arm, much less to pitch effectively. In '66, Ford won only two games, appearing in twenty-two. In '67, he made seven appearances before finally calling it quits after sixteen seasons.

Mantle increasingly was playing in a vacuum; his opposition, like a solitary runner's, was what was in himself. There were occasional bursts of effectiveness. In '66, Mantle hit eleven of his twenty-three homers for the season in eleven days. Four times in that splurge he had two-home-run games. Some of his home runs were milestones; these were increasingly impressive accomplishments, but they were the coda to a great individual career and not the prelude to better days for his team. In '66, he surpassed Lou Gehrig's career mark of 493 homers. On May 13, 1967, he hit his 500th homer off the Oriole's Stu Miller at Yankee Stadium. On September 19, 1968, he hit his 535th, putting him ahead of Jimmie Foxx on the all-time list. The one before that, which tied him with Foxx, was a ninth-inning pinch-hit homer.

In 1967, the Yankees finished next to last, and the season saw a big change for Mantle when Ralph Houk asked him to shift to first base. At the end of the previous year, it had become as clear to management as to opposing teams that he could no longer handle center field. During the season he missed more than fifty games with a broken toe and a severe injury to a finger; he was then switched to left field because it was felt he would handle fewer chances and that the demands on both his throwing arm and his legs would be reduced. The decision to move him to first base was made to prolong his career. He was the only draw the team had left. Joe Pepitone was switched to center field—an indication of how thin the Yankees had become in filling everyday positions—and Mantle groped and fumbled his way at a position totally unfamiliar to him.

As it became clear that he was nearing the end, team owner Mike Burke asserted that Mickey could surely play for a few more seasons and that he would be a Yankee forever—but by now those were words no one wanted to hear. Nearly all the cartilage in both of Mantle's knees was gone. When he hobbled to and from the batter's box, just getting there involved a scraping of bone on bone. He could not hit at all from the left side; when he swung and missed a pitch batting left-handed, he corkscrewed around, grimacing in such obvious pain that the shockwaves of effort and pain were as palpable in the grandstands as in the dugouts of opposing teams.

Yet for all the pain he endured, those final years represented a kind of payback for the years when he played brilliantly to hoots of derision. Wherever the once-hated but now toothless Yankees went, the crowds turned out to see and cheer him, as though his mere presence carried with it an indefinable but necessary reaffirmation of what was best in baseball. Mantle, whether he wanted to be or not, was an ambassador from baseball's past. From 1965 on, it was generally acknowledged that the deterioration of his talents was almost complete. Toward the end of the '66 season, when Mantle was only thirty-four, Cleveland scout George Strickland filed a report where he refrained altogether from grading Mantle. Instead, he wrote: "This guy is aging and he's showing it and I really don't feel he should be playing right now. The injuries are just too much for this guy to overcome. If he comes back it won't be for any length of time, because there is just too much chance for him to re-hurt himself and he's just got too much going against him with the bad arm and the bad legs. He can't throw at all right now and it is just tough to see a great player get old and lose it so quick."

But that somehow was beside the point. First, to anyone who

cared to notice, Mantle played his new position well. He had no range, and he was not quick, but his hands were good and he worked at his game. He said that the short, choppy movements of infield play better suited him than the extended movements required to cover ground in the outfield. Some of his old teammates from Independence and Joplin probably smiled when he acknowledged to the media that the most difficult play for him at first was an infield pop-up. As Mantle explained it, it was because it was somehow harder to follow a ball coming down at him from straight overhead than coming toward him over a distance. But the point of it all was that he covered his position. He had little trouble scooping balls from the dirt. Over time he became familiar enough with the footwork around the bag so that he didn't feel—as he did initially in the spring—that he was groping blindly for the bag. He committed eight errors in '67, fifteen in '68, and went from city to city around the league as one of the game's great stars, universally respected and applauded.

While the crowds that stood and cheered him were by now part of the daily copy attaching to Yankee games—almost the only positive part of the story for the team—the respect and affection accorded by other players and teams was just as impressive, if not more so.

Dave Nelson was a rookie second baseman for Cleveland in 1968, Mantle's last year. He was not much of a hitter, but he was quick, could steal a base, get his bat on the ball, and make the plays in the field. His first trip to Yankee Stadium, he said, was memorable in ways he never anticipated.

"I was just a young kid then, had just turned twenty-three, I think, and there I was in the big leagues, in Yankee Stadium, and I'm just in awe of the place. I don't remember for sure who was on the mound—maybe it was Al Downing," he said, "but Mickey was on first—and I knew his knees were gone. I had no clue at that time that other clubs had decided some things among themselves out of reverence for him. So, in this one at bat, I pushed the ball, push-bunted right between the pitcher and first base and they had to go for it. I had great speed so it was a base hit. I turn around halfway down the right field line, and there's our first base coach walking towards me, and he stops me and tells me, 'Hey, Dave, we don't bunt on Mick out of respect for him.' I go to myself, 'Oh-kayyy.' So then I walked back to first base and I'm standing next to Mickey Mantle. I'm looking at this guy's arms and they look like tree trunks, and I'm saying, 'Man, he's gonna pinch my head off,' and then he pats me on the butt and he says, 'Nice bunt, rook.' And I look at him and say, 'Thanks, Mr. Mantle.' "

There was a far more controversial tip of the hat in what proved to be Mantle's farewell season. When he hit the home run that put him ahead of Jimmie Foxx into third place in the career home run standings (behind Ruth and Willie Mays), it was off Tiger pitcher Denny McLain in Detroit. McLain that year won thirty-one games, a total unmatched since, leading the Tigers to a pennant and an eventual championship. With the Tigers ahead 6–1 in the top of the eighth and the pennant already clinched, McLain watched Mantle settle into the batter's box. There were two men out and no one on. Aside from occasionally drinking with him, McLain had grown up idolizing Mantle. "I think everyone then wanted to be Mickey Mantle for at least one day in their lives," he said. He looked in at his catcher, Jimmie Price, and summoned him to the mound. "We had already won the pennant, in fact, we won it two nights earlier against the Yankees, 2–1, and this Thursday afternoon was the last game Mantle was going to play in Tiger Stadium," said McLain. "So when Price came out . . . well, first of all he says to me, 'What the hell is going on, there's two out, let's go home.' I said no, I got an idea. I said, 'This is Mantle's last at-bat in Tiger Stadium. Let's see if he can whack one,' and Price says, 'You've got to be kidding.' I said, 'No, let's let him hit one, let's at least let him try.' I said, 'You go back there and you tell Mr. Mantle to be ready.' Well, the last thing in the world that a hitter wants to hear is somebody saying to him, 'Be ready.' I mean, that's like telling a hitter what's coming, and they don't want to know that unless they can be sure you're telling them the truth. Well, Mantle always knew I was a little wacko to begin with, so when Price goes behind home plate and says, McLain says to be ready, Mantle says, 'What the hell does that mean?' And Price says, 'Just be ready.' Mantle took the first two pitches down the middle for strikes. I mean, they were fastballs about 45 miles an hour with an arc, and he took both of 'em. Then he looks out at me and he says, 'Are you gonna do that again?' And I said, 'Yeah, just be ready, my God, HIT ONE OF THOSE!' So I came in with the next pitch and he fouled it off, then I finally looked at him and I said, 'Where the hell do you want the pitch?' And he put his left hand out over the plate and said 'I want it here, belt high inside part of the plate, put it there.' And I put it there and he hit a line drive into the upper deck in Tiger Stadium."

William Eckert, commissioner at the time, heard about what had happened along with the rest of the baseball world and sent McLain a letter accusing him of attacking the integrity of the game. No action was taken, however. "Somehow he got over it and I got over it," McLain said.

The reaction of the crowd at Tiger Stadium and of McLain's teammates was unforgettable. The Detroit crowd, always partisan and anti-Yankee, rose to its feet cheering Mantle as he made his way around the bases. "We all had goose bumps," McLain said. "I think most of us on our club thought of him perhaps if not the greatest player in the history of the game, certainly as one of the top two or three, what with his magnetism and all of his ability. As he went around first base, our guys were applauding him. I mean our infielders were applauding him as he went around first, went around second base."

Mantle knew that that trip around the bases at Tiger Stadium was in all likelihood going to be his last. The decision to retire, which he had postponed for three seasons, seemed more inescapable than ever. He had managed to play 144 games, but his .237 average in 435 plate appearances was the lowest of his career, and his 54 RBIs matched the level of his run production for the last few seasons but was woefully below his norm. He could still hit with power—when he got his pitches. Denny McLain believed that even at the end, as a right-handed hitter, he was as formidable as anyone in the league. Dave Nelson, who never bunted on Mantle again, remembered making an infield play against him on a ball that was the hardest hit he had ever seen. Bobby Murcer recalled that Mantle's strength then was still astonishing. "I remember standing at third base one time—it was spring training—and he was batting right handed, and he hit a ball just to my left, and it was hit so hard I couldn't react to it. I mean, you're gonna react in one way or another on almost anything hit your way, but that ball was by me before I could move a muscle. I can only imagine what he must have been like at the peak of his career."

But much of the fun was gone in the last seasons. Whitey Ford's retirement had left a void in his baseball life that he simply could not fill just by being a teammate. The new players were just that—new and unfamiliar to him.

Mantle did not announce his retirement immediately. Instead, he spent the winter playing cat and mouse with the media and the front office, though he almost certainly knew that he was not going to continue. He was not trying to deceive anyone, there was just no reason to rush into a future that loomed before him like a blank plain. All he had ever known was how to be a ballplayer, and there was no way for him to simply and neatly become someone or something else. Ralph Houk believed there was a chance he would be back; so did Yankee president Mike Burke. Ford, who had rejoined the team as a pitching coach, may have been prompting his friend to reconsider when he pointed out in the season's last weeks how well loved Mickey had become throughout the baseball world and how important he still was to the game.

But Mantle, when he spoke at all on the subject, was suggestive enough. He told columnist Dick Young about how much he was needed at home, how much his children wanted to have him around. The words were not those of someone thinking about one more season.

"The main thing is how I do," he said. "Whenever I'm going good I enjoy playing as much as ever. The only thing is, those good days don't come around as often anymore.

"People tell me I have to change my values because the values of baseball have changed. I'm supposed to think that .250 is a good batting average. It is now, I guess, but it's tough for me to think that way."

Ultimately, Mantle held off his announcement because he was asked to. Teammate Steve Hamilton urged him to delay making an announcement until the beginning of the next season. Hamilton was the Yankees player rep, and at the time he was deeply involved in helping get the Players Association off the ground. Simply having Mantle as part of the cast lent credibility to their organizing efforts and to their threatened player boycott over pension rights. When the '68 season ended, noted David Halberstam, the issue of free agency was just beginning to surface, and Mantle, though he was not a "union man" or particularly political, was sympathetic enough, unlike some other star players of the day who had actively spoken out against the union's activities. Mantle remembered all too well his salary fights with George Weiss.

Mantle waited until spring training to announce his retirement. He told the front office, told his manager, then appeared at a press conference at the team's Yankee Clipper Hotel. Reporters at the time noted that he seemed unusually calm and composed. He spoke only briefly, from a prepared statement, but he could not have been more direct. "I just can't play anymore," he said. "I don't hit the ball when I need to. I can't score from second when I need to. I can't steal when I need to."

In June, the team gave him another day at Yankee Stadium. His number was retired, his uniform folded and handed to him on the field. Sixty thousand fans got to see him ride slowly around the warning track of the ballpark, waving up to the crowd. When he finished his sentimental journey, he went to the press room below the stands. He posed for pictures, stood patiently under the glare of television lights, and answered questions for a while. A reporter asked who he thought was a better ballplayer, he or Willie Mays? "Willie Mays is better," Mantle said, without hesitation. "I don't mind being second to Willie. If I'm second, I'm pretty good."

And then he was gone to the rest of his life.

Chapter 12

Anyone taking a look at Mantle's career record will likely be surprised by what is not there. Alongside other great players, his numbers seem to belie the stature he attained. His career batting average is nowhere near the game's best. Even among sluggers, his lifetime .298 average is low; Babe Ruth's lifetime average, never mind the 714 homers to Mantle's 536, was .342. Lou Gehrig hit .340 for his career, and his 1,990 RBIs, third all-time, dwarfs Mantle's 1,509. The player Mantle is most often compared with, Willie Mays, outdistances him in almost every category. Mays's lifetime average was .302, he hit 660 homers, drove in 1,903 runs, stole 338 bases to Mantle's 153, and scored 2,062 runs in his twenty-two years (fifth all-time), while Mantle scored 1,509 in eighteen seasons. Mantle knocked in 100 or more runs only four times in his career; Mays did it ten times, Ruth thirteen, and Hank Aaron eleven. The only major category in which he topped the all-time charts is an ignominious one: strikeouts, a mark he set some four years before his retirement. Statistically, Mantle just does not seem to belong in the very first rank of the game's players—that is, until one takes a second and closer look.

When Mantle retired, he was one of eight players with five

hundred or more home runs. Only Mathews had a lower career batting average, .271, than Mantle's .298 mark. But of the six players who've joined the list since, not one had a higher career average than Mantle, and only Frank Robinson, at .294, was within twenty points of him. Mantle played at a time of relatively low batting averages; his two nearest contemporaries on the five hundred run list in 1968, Mays and Hank Aaron, finished their careers with averages only slightly better than Mantle's, .302 and .305 respectively. It is worth noting, too, that Mantle and Mays are the only postwar players to have two fifty-home-run seasons; only twelve players in baseball history have managed even one. And for those who wish to argue that Mantle benefited from the short right-field porch in Yankee Stadium, forget it. In his career, Mantle actually hit four more home runs on the road than at home, 270 to 266, despite playing twenty-three fewer games on the road. He was probably hurt as much by the Death Valley in left center as he was helped by the porch in right.

In recent years, many fans and observers of the game have devised intricate formulas to measure a player's total performance. One of the most publicized of these is given the name Total Average by Thomas Boswell of the *Washington Post.* Total Average combines the total number of bases produced by a player, figuring in the full value of his extra-base hits, walks, stolen bases, and divides it by the number of outs he was responsible for at bat (taking double plays into account) and through times caught stealing. By this measure, which considers all aspects of a player's offensive contribution, Mantle ranks in the top ten of all time, tied for eighth with Rogers Hornsby. Of the players whose careers overlapped his, only Ted Williams is ahead of him.

Mantle's strengths as a hitter went beyond just hitting home runs. It is true that he struck out more times than anyone before him (seven players have since passed his total). But it is also true that only four players ever walked more times than he did, and he led the league in walks more often than he did in strikeouts.

Mantle's walks indicate considerably more patience at the plate than he was generally given credit for, and how much opposing pitchers feared him. His presence in the lineup not only benefited anyone who hit in front of him—remember the Maris numbers—but also gave good hitters behind him a chance to drive in runs—which they did, often. Mantle was one of the great run scorers in baseball history. He led the league in runs scored six different times; only Ruth, who led the league eight times, did so more often. Mantle accounted for runs one way or another on a team where run production was spread up and down the lineup, a team that played station-to-station baseball, never allowing him to utilize his great speed to steal bases.

There is no current measure for a player's ability to take an extra base, getting himself in position to score. Yet that was as much a part of his game as walking or hitting home runs. Frank Crosetti, the longtime Yankee coach, said Mantle could see better than his coaches exactly when to move from first to third or to score from second on a single, or to stretch doubles into triples. He had a kind of perfect baseball sense, Crosetti said, which people rarely gave him credit for.

Mantle's 1956 season, when he was completely healthy, was one of the best single seasons that any player has ever had. In that one year he not only hit .353 and hit 52 homers, but also led the *major leagues* in six different offensive categories: batting average, on-base percentage, homers, RBIs, slugging percentage, and runs scored.

No matter how the numbers are juggled, Mantle was one of the most feared hitters who ever lived, and almost certainly was the most feared hitter of his day. And when he left the game, there was an aura about him that exceeded anything he had done on the field.

"He's the last of the Yankees," wrote Jim Murray in 1969. "He might have been the best of them, considering night games, the slider, the big parks, the trappers' mitts, and the fact that he would have been a certified cripple in any other industry. He was rejected four times by the military, afraid he couldn't keep up with a Fourth of July parade.

"I know one thing: those monuments in center field are going to be awfully lonely this summer. Their last link to the present is gone."

Of course, Mantle did become a monument himself after he left the game. Following the obligatory wait, he was elected to the Hall to Fame in 1974. He was named on 322 out of 365 ballots, which meant that forty-three writers who had the opportunity to make him one of their ten selections that year somehow did not. Still, the election on his first attempt traced the straightest of lines between his retirement and election to the Hall.

The occasion was doubly pleasing because he was inducted in the same year that Whitey Ford was. Ford had missed the year before, and the oversight allowed the team within a team to step up together.

In New York, before the trip to Cooperstown, the days and nights were filled with cocktails, press conferences, and get-togethers with old friends. At the Royal Box Club in the Americana Hotel, Mickey and Whitey held forth. At forty-three, Mantle seemed a little corpulent, decidedly past his playing days. But his after-dinner manner had mellowed considerably.

"I'm surprised I got as many votes as I did," he said without the least trace of affectation. "The first five years I was in the majors, people thought I was aloof. But, really, I wasn't aloof. I was scared." The implication was that if some writers had been turned off by his manner, enough to vote against him, it was *his* fault, not theirs. He reminisced about his career, but he talked not about his achievements but rather his youth, his early days on the Yankees. He remembered rooming with Hank Bauer and Johnny Hopp, and the apartment they shared over the Stage Delicatessen.

A voice from middle of the room yelled out, "Put a glass in their hand, it'll make 'em feel more natural." It was Toots Shor. The crowd of writers and friends, Mickey, and Whitey all laughed. Mickey went on, telling everyone how particularly thankful he was to Billy and Whitey for showing him the ropes.

"We used to pal together and they were pretty brash," Mickey said. "I was quiet, I just listened. They did all the talking."

Someone asked what possible chemistry there could be between people as different as the Oklahoma Kid, Billy the Kid, and the Kid from Queens?

"We all liked scotch," Mantle said with perfect timing.

"Be sure to tell 'em everything!" Whitey piped up, sitting next to him. Mickey gave Ford a look of mock innocence and went on. A newspaper account the next day mentioned that each of the men held forth with a Bloody Mary in hand as they answered questions. When they moved on to Cooperstown for their great day, the *Daily News* headlined the event, "Drinks Are on Mickey and Whitey."

For induction day, Mantle rented a charter bus from the city for the long trip to Cooperstown. Merlyn, his four sons, the Rizzutos, and friends from Texas and Oklahoma went with him. At the ceremonies, he was introduced by Commissioner Bowie Kuhn, who catalogued his career achievements.

When Mantle stood up to make his speech, it was clear he was moved by the occasion, but his words and thoughts were all jumbled together, disconnected and emotional. He began by talking not about his successes but about his failures, thanking the commissioner for not mentioning the number of times he struck out in his career. "I was the world champion in striking out and everything I'm sure," he said. That made him think of the World Series. "I don't know for sure, but I must have had that record in the World Series, too." That made him think of Babe Ruth. "I broke Babe Ruth's record for all-time strikeouts. He had only like 1,500. I think I ended up with 1,710."

In his entire speech, which went on for ten or fifteen minutes, there is little mention of his Yankee days or of any of his achievements. He talked about his childhood, about his father and mother and their love of the game and how much they had devoted themselves to him so that he could play ball. But his love of the game ruined his brothers' chances to play ball, he said. On the farm in Whitebird, he remembered, "We dozed a little ball park in the pasture out there and I think that probably I burnt my [twin brothers] out on baseball. They were supposedly one day gonna be an all-Mantle Yankee outfield, and I think by the time the twins got old enough to play ball they were tired of it, because I used to make 'em shag flies for me, and play ball all day, and I think I probably burnt 'em out on baseball."

The twins and playing all day made him think of Baxter Springs and the Whiz Kids, and the Whiz Kids made him think of life back home and the fact that he had moved away, to Dallas. Mantle remembered an Oklahoma friend of his, Harold Youngman, whom he credited with helping him out with investments in the early days when everyone had a scheme for him.

"Probably the worst thing I ever did was movin' away from Mr. Youngman," Mantle said. "We went and moved to Dallas, Texas, in 1957, but Mr. Youngman built a Holiday Inn in Joplin, Missouri, called it Mickey Mantle's Holiday Inn. And we were doin' pretty good there and Mr. Youngman said, 'You know, you're half of this thing so why don't you do something for it?' So we had real good chicken there and I made . . . and I made up the slogan for our chicken, and I said to get a better piece of chicken you'd have to be a rooster! I don't know if that's what closed up our Holiday Inn but we didn't do too good after that."

When Mantle got to the end of his speech, he introduced his family. He gestured to Merlyn, saying, "We've been married twenty-two years. That's a record where I come from." He introduced his four sons. And then, in closing, he mentioned that he had been to a dinner the night before for Hall of Famers only. Mantle looked over his shoulder at the other great players on the platform and said, as though his own membership among them somehow was still in question, "I just hope that Whitey and I can live up to the expectations and what these here guys stand for. I'm sure we're going to try to."

Mantle's speech gave a strong hint about the road he had traveled since he left baseball. If there was a map that marked the way from the day of his retirement to the library steps at Cooperstown, it would have looked more like a maze than an expressway.

In all those years, Mantle had been thinking, speaking, even dreaming like a ballplayer. At thirty-eight, when he retired, that was all he knew. In the days before he was inducted into the Hall of Fame, he revealed that he had been having recurrent nightmares, all of them about baseball. In one of them, he said, "I pull up in front of Yankee Stadium in a cab and over the loudspeaker I can hear them announce that I'm gonna hit. But the guy at the door won't let me in. I try to crawl through a hole, but I get stuck and I can't get in. Then I hear Casey Stengel asking the players, 'Where's Mickey?' and they tell him, 'He's coming.'

"In the second dream I'm coming up to the plate left handed and I'm always hitting at fastballs. But I can't hit them. I keep fouling them off and I say to myself, 'That's it, I can't hit anymore.' "

On the surface, the dreams were about making a comeback. For a while, he said, he gave some thought to coming back as a player, but every time he thought about it his body told him what was and was not possible. He could not play; there was no choice to make. On a deeper level, though, the dreams reflected his inability to find himself a place in the game to which he had given so much.

The idea of coaching or managing came up several times. Mantle said in his later years that the idea had only limited appeal to him because he hated the travel, and even more hated the idea of feeling useless on the field. He briefly returned as first-base coach for the Yankees in August 1970 because, he said, he was "getting the itch to see my old friends. I just couldn't break away from baseball completely." But he felt lost and out of place standing on the sidelines.

The team had brought him to New York and had gotten a

suite for him at the St. Moritz, where he had had an apartment for so many years when he was a player. But the royal treatment never got him to a point where he felt at home. He returned to his suite one night, couldn't find his keys, and then smashed his fist through a glass door, slicing his hand so deeply that he needed emergency treatment and stitches to close the wound. When he showed up at the ballpark to take his place on the first-base coaching lines, his hand was heavily bandaged. If anyone in the crowd noticed, they didn't react; they went on cheering the image of Mickey Mantle, not the flesh-and-blood person standing in front of them. "I wasn't naive," he said. "I put extra people into the stands, that's all. There I was, pacing back and forth in the box, and saying, 'Let's get it going now!' and feeling like a fool when Bobby Murcer drew a leadoff walk in the fourth inning, called time, and asked me what the signs were. I said, 'Mine look good. I'm a Libra.' I was nothing more than a public relations gimmick."

Mantle's coaching career was over almost as soon as it began, but he still wanted to be in baseball. In 1969, the year Mantle retired, Billy Martin began his career as a manager. Mantle had never believed that he had the baseball mind or emotional makeup for managing that his friend did, but the idea of working as a manager attracted him far more than he ever let on. Tex Gernand, who was Martin's chauffeur and bodyguard for years and who got to know Mantle well, is sure that there was a touch of envy in the way he looked at his friend's second career. "I saw them enough to know that," Gernand said. "I know for sure that Mickey wanted to manage—but he couldn't land a job because no one was willing to risk it with him. And that got to him, believe me."

In fact, Mantle did want to manage—and he had begun actively campaigning for a job as early as 1970, before he began coaching for the Yankees. In a July 1970 interview he gave to the Associated Press, he said that even though he had disclaimed ambitions in the past to be a manager, he had changed his mind because "I'm getting to where I could manage as good as anybody." Mantle said that he doubted that he could go back and manage the Yankees, because Ralph Houk was set there. "But there are several jobs that I think are going to open," he said, "and I might consider one of them. I think probably before I become involved in managing that I would have to spend a year as a coach for somebody, to see what it's really all about."

Martin urged Mickey to come work under him as a coach in Detroit after he left his coaching job with the Yankees. Mantle turned down the offer but only because by then, he thought he might have a direct path to a managerial job.

In 1971, after the Yankee job fizzled, Mantle again publicly expressed his interest in managing. At the time, the expansion Washington Senators, owned by Bob Short and managed by Ted Williams, were planning to move to Dallas, to become the Texas Rangers. There were rumors that Williams was going to leave, either to become the team's general manager or to retire altogether. Mantle was enthusiastic about the idea of managing a team based in Dallas. In an interview with Blackie Sherrod of the Dallas *Times Herald,* he was asked point blank if he would be interested in managing the new Dallas team. "Heck, yes, I'd be interested in talking about managing," he said, imagining what it might be like to go into Yankee Stadium with his team. "They might make my whole salary back in one series if I brought a team into Yankee Stadium to play the Yankees. And how about if I was managing a team and took it to Detroit to play Billy Martin's team? That might draw quite a few at the gate. It ought to be good for something. Of course," Mantle added, "nobody's gotten in touch with me."

Short then did get in touch with Mantle. A meeting was arranged. But it didn't turn out the way he hoped. "I got worked up," he acknowledged, "and I told Merlyn, and she said, 'Mickey, that sounds great. I know you'll make a good manager.'

"Short told me to meet him for an early breakfast, and I had to get up at six in the morning to meet him. We settled down, and Short says, 'Mickey, I need a new manager, and I wondered if you had anyone in mind?' "

Mantle shrugged and said that he thought Billy would be ideal. Ted Williams stayed on for a year, and the season following, Short took Mantle's advice and offered the job to Martin.

Mantle's ineffectual campaign to become a manager showed how adrift he was in the baseball world—and everywhere else. For a brief time in 1970, Mantle became a part-time, pregame commentator on NBC's weekly baseball broadcasts, working with former teammate Tony Kubek. The move was a disaster. Mantle was uncomfortable on camera, and off camera his drinking all but guaranteed that no one in the industry would take a chance on hiring him long term.

For an NBC game in Minnesota, where Billy was managing at the time, the network decided to do a short feature with Mickey and Billy together. Tony Kubek remembers what happened when Mantle was flown in from Dallas and was taken over to Billy's house in suburban Minneapolis for the interview. "We're doing the taping on a Friday, it was going to be shown on Saturday," said Kubek. "They had a Friday night game, so Mickey's supposed to get there Friday morning at Billy's house. Well, Mickey's had a couple of beers, maybe more, and we waited and waited, finally we're waiting at Billy's house. And they had something like a semi parked in the driveway at the house next to Billy's, and there was probably a crew of fifteen people there—television was a little different then than today where you only need a couple of people—anyway, they were paying lots of guys lots of money, and hours and hours pass. Finally, it's one o'clock and Mickey shows, so we go down to Billy's rec room—he was married to Gretchen then—and Billy says, 'Come on Mickey, let's have a couple of drinks.' Billy didn't drink because he had a game that night. Mickey tells him we're trying to fill this show. Now we get in there, and there are a lot of pictures on the rec room walls, a lot of them with Billy and Mickey. I said, 'How do you want to start?' Billy says, 'Start with this picture right here, I wanna tell this story.' The picture shows them in some log cabin where they went hunting together in Texas, they were deer hunting together, and Billy is holding a .45 revolver, a pistol, to Mickey's head in this picture. So I introduced the thing, and Billy comes in and says, 'Here's what kind of buddies we are, we were just kidding around.' And Mickey comes in—it's all on tape—and says, 'The only thing is, we found out later the gun was really loaded. He's pulling the trigger, it was like Russian Roulette.' The two of them are laughing and joking and stuff. I sat up there for four hours with those two guys, just trying to get a seven- or eight-minute piece for the show. The language got so . . . Gretchen, ironically, was sitting in the mobile unit listening; and she didn't care for Mickey because she thought he was leading Billy astray. Merlyn didn't like Billy for the same reason. So there it was, in the rec room, with all of that going up to the mobile unit where Billy's wife was sitting in the truck listening."

Outside of baseball, Mantle had no idea what he might be suited for. At an age where most men are entering their most productive years, Mantle was more like a retiree casting around for something, anything new. Only he was broke—and young—and still the main support of his family. He had no skills other than those he had left behind on the ballfield. He had his name and little else. "My job is to be Mickey Mantle," he told a reporter one day. He was a corporate greeter, a golf buddy for money, a face at ribbon cuttings, department stores, country clubs, and business functions.

He tried his hand—or at least his face—at business. The results were predictable. In 1969, he became associated with Joe Namath as heads of a New York personnel agency called "Mantle Men and Namath Girls."

Namath and Mantle had been drinking buddies for years. Namath, who acknowledged a decades-old problem with alcohol in 1987, said his carousing with Mantle began at a New York nightspot, The Pussycat, in 1965. "Mick was with Whitey and Billy," Namath said. It was easy, too easy, to fall in with them.

"With the various pressures on star athletes," he said, it was just natural "to get hung up on alcohol. . . . Mick's the only male in his family to make it past age forty-one. We'd talk about that now and then—jokingly, but with some seriousness—that if he had known he was going to live that long, he'd have taken better care of himself." When Namath blew out his knee playing for the Jets that season, he said that a beer company sent a case of beer to his hospital room to help him recuperate. He and Mantle "had great times together," he said. But it took years before he, like Mantle, was able to acknowledge the effect alcohol had on their lives. "We had a lot of fun and I never saw a big problem then," Namath said.

The input of the two stars in their joint business venture was mainly ceremonial. The idea for the business came from a big New York ad agency, Lois Holland Callaway. For advertisers to go into the personnel field, and especially to link up with two top athletes, made perfect sense; a sponsor survey during this period revealed that athletes not only had better name recognition than other public figures, but also inspired more trust. Among the most recognized and trusted athletes in the survey were Mantle and Namath. Only Stan Musial was ranked higher in the "most trusted" category, and only Willie Mays had a higher recognition factor than Namath.

The advertisers who formed the agency promoted the seriousness of their front men's involvement. "Mickey and Joe will be writing letters, cracking hard accounts, having lunch or playing golf with presidents and chairmen of the board," said one of the company's executives. Instead of just taking a large fee for the use of his name, Mantle invested some of his own money in the venture. By 1972, Mantle Men and Namath Girls had filed for bankruptcy.

There were other deals, other failures. Mickey Mantle's Country Cookin' was supposed to expand from a single fast-food restaurant into a chain; the wings never spread, the chicken never flew. A chain of apparel shops opened and closed, real estate investments fizzled. In '73, Mantle became an executive—that is, a golf-playing front—for a life insurance company that went nowhere. As he was casting around for a job in baseball, Mantle told Tony Kubek that he was essentially broke, that he had been "used to making a hundred thousand dollars a year . . . but all of a sudden the money stopped coming in."

It wasn't just the money that dried up, either. His image began to change, too. In 1970, Jim Bouton published his book, *Ball Four*. At the time, the book was revolutionary in its inside look at the game. Until then, sports journalism, like much political journalism, operated with an unspoken gentlemen's agreement that allowed its subjects wide latitude in their personal and private lives. That went out the window with *Ball Four*—literally, in Mantle's case as it described some late-night Peeping Tom parties on hotel rooftops. Though tame by today's standards, the book went inside the Yankee locker room to reveal how players really behaved—mostly like adolescent boys in athletes' bodies. Bouton described midnight drinking parties, childish escapades, backroom conversations and indiscretions. Fans learned for the first time that Whitey Ford doctored baseballs when he pitched and that Elston Howard helped him by using the side of his shinguard or convenient clumps of dirt. But it was Mantle who seemed to get hit hardest. Though his drinking and difficulties with the press were well known, no one before had quite given fans the unflattering view of him that Bouton did. Bouton let people see Mantle at ease with his teammates, running betting pools on golf matches and the Kentucky Derby; but he also wondered aloud about the relationship between Mantle's injuries and his drinking, asking if he might not have healed more quickly if "he'd been sleeping more and loosening up at the bar with the boys less." Bouton praised Mantle for his generosity and humor but showed a side of him that few wanted to dwell on:

> There were all those times when he'd push little kids aside when they wanted his autograph, and the times when he was snotty to

> reporters, just about making them crawl and beg for a minute of his time. I've seen him close a bus window on kids trying to get his autograph. And I hated that *look* of his when he'd get angry at somebody and cut him down with a glare. Bill Gilbert of *Sports Illustrated* once described that look as flickering across his face 'like the nictitating membrane in the eye of a bird'. And I don't like the Mantle that refused to sign baseballs in the clubhouse before games. Everybody else had to sign, but [clubhouse man] Little Pete [Previte] forged Mantle's signature. So there are thousands of baseballs around the country that have been signed not by Mickey Mantle, but by Pete Previte.

The intent of the book, Bouton insisted, was not to tear down anyone, Mantle included, but to show the game in its everyday setting, to show players as real people speaking in real voices, people who were sometimes moving, funny, irreverent, sad, courageous but who, first and last, were ballplayers. But Bouton had trashed the most sacred rule of baseball clubhouses: "What is said and done here stays here."

The reaction to the book among Bouton's teammates was sharp and predictable. "None of that stuff is new," Whitey said. "I've read all of that before, about the ring and the mud ball. Even if you throw one once in awhile—and most pitchers do—you still have to throw 100 other pitches."

Howard denied that he used a buckle on a shinguard to help Ford. "That's a lie," he said. "As for dirtying the ball up for Whitey, all catchers do it. Any time I can scuff up a ball for a pitcher I will."

Ralph Houk said he started to read Bouton's book but put it aside in disgust. Lee MacPhail, the general manger, characterized Bouton as a "very difficult man." But the harshest judgments from nearly everyone were reserved for what Bouton had said about Mantle. "I don't think [Bouton's comments] were fair to say about a guy like Mickey after all he did for the club," Whitey said to a reporter. "I talked to . . . Merlyn and she's very upset over the story. In my 18 years with the Yankees, there has never been a player who was as generally disliked as much as Bouton was. Because of that Mickey and I went out of our way to be nice to him. We used to drive him to the park in Florida so that his wife could use the car."

Elston Howard was just as incensed over what had been said about Mantle. "I love that man," he said. A player who wanted to remain anonymous said that the only reason he thought Bouton wrote the book was for money, but that "he'd better make a bundle because he won't be around much longer. No matter how much money he makes he's going to find out it wasn't worth it."

The reaction out in the public was another matter entirely. It was the age of the antihero, and Bouton's irreverence fit the times perfectly. The book went to the top of the best-seller lists, stayed there, and went into several best-selling paperback editions. And largely because of it, sports journalism changed; more important, as far as Mantle was concerned, the uncritically adoring view the public had of him began to fade. In the years following, the public's image of Mantle was as someone who surfaced for a few weeks each spring to stand around for several hours in his old uniform and then to carouse at night.

Back in Dallas, his marriage became increasingly rocky. Mantle began an affair with a woman who was working for him as a personal assistant. The affair, like many of his others, was poorly disguised but with one difference: The woman involved happened to know and talk to a local reporter who was a neighbor of hers. She talked vaguely about the time she spent with Mantle, but more explicitly about his episodes of excessive drinking and abusive behavior. "The abuse was never physical," the reporter said, "except for one occasion when she talked about being on a yacht with Mantle when he threw her overboard. The abuse she talked about most was verbal, which apparently, according to her, could get pretty heavy."

Though the story was never made public, it was part of an undertow pulling Mantle into a kind of anonymity that was more painful than his celebrity had been. He made brief appearances at all-star games—like the '73 game at Yankee Stadium, where

Mickey's team took on a fan team headed by George Plimpton —and at other events where the sight of him stirred old memories, yet clashed with his present image for those clear-eyed enough to see through their own nostalgic mists.

For a brief period in 1973, when he needed the money, he and Whitey Ford made a series of appearances at local trotting tracks in the northeast. For a fee, the men signed autographs, mixed with the public, and also got into a pair of sulkies and raced one another. Fans saw Mantle and Ford, dressed in jockey's silks, go at it over five-eighths of a mile. After one heat at an obscure track in Pennsylvania, in which Mickey beat Whitey in what was described as "a thrilling come-from-behind victory," an official of the Grand Circuit told wire service reporters that Mantle showed "real natural ability." Never mind that it was Mickey Mantle dressed for a sideshow or that the venue was in the middle of nowhere, Mickey was just being Mickey—yesterday's hero willing to make a spectacle of himself for some needed extra cash.

By decade's end, Mantle had virtually disappeared from public view. He made what money he could by meeting and greeting, by playing rounds of golf with corporate clients. He spent much of his time at the exclusive, men's-only Preston Trail Golf Club in the suburbs of Dallas. When he wasn't drinking, he was out on the course, though his old knee injuries made it difficult for him to walk. "Everyone had their Preston Trail stories about Mickey," said Skip Bayless, a longtime Dallas sportswriter and radio personality. "The stories," he said, "are invariably sad and funny; you'd hear about him playing golf naked and drunk. There was a coed club—Bent Tree—which adjoined Preston Trail. Well, you could see one course from the other through some trees across a creek, and Mickey thought it was just great to shock both men and women by letting them stumble on Mickey Mantle playing golf naked."

In a recent article, Bayless recalled the first time he ever met Mantle, at a cocktail party in North Carolina in 1979. Until then, he had had only his childhood memories of a great player.

"I worshipped the game more than I did any one player," he said. "But I'd never seen anyone look so fearsome at the plate. The bull neck. The number 7 stretched so tightly across the muscled back. . . . But I suppose I was just as influenced by the way the media portrayed Mantle. Every mention in the newspapers or on TV hit my subconscious with religious impact. I was taught Matthew, Mark, Luke, John, and Mickey."

At that party, Bayless saw a very different person. "I was introduced to him in a cocktail crowd of 10 or 12 men and women at about 5 P.M. Mantle lived in Dallas, so he knew my work. He said loudly, 'Man, you write some weird shit.'

"The group chuckled nervously. Mickey Mantle was so drunk he was having a hard time keeping his balance. Three hours later he 'spoke' to a group of two or three hundred. His remarks lasted maybe five minutes. He told an off-color joke that embarrassed the audience. He rambled. He finally said, 'Shit, that's enough from me.' "

Bayless says that in the next few years he got to know Mantle and that he saw another side to him, a side that might have been visible all the while during his glory years but that was plainly apparent in those years when he slipped from view. Mantle was a person with a "good, big, tortured heart," he said. "All he ever was was an uneducated, raw-boned, small-town boy trapped inside maybe the most physically talented body the world has known. Mantle didn't even strike me as having any street smarts. . . . He never could quite understand the idolatry that constantly reverberated around him like a home-run roar. . . . He couldn't quite come to grips with why so many millions of people hero-worshipped what came so easily to him."

But at this point in his life, the hero worship was as far behind him as his skills. His body had become the measure of who he thought he was, and he punished it regularly. As he neared fifty, he had an old man's body, arthritic and vulnerable, which he constantly numbed and abused with alcohol.

In 1977, the damages of drinking began to catch up with him

in ways he could no longer ignore. For years, Mantle had virtually been a missing parent to his four sons. "He was gone so much, I didn't even begin to know him until I was sixteen," said thirty-four-year-old Danny Mantle in the months following his father's death. David Mantle, who grew up indifferent to baseball—"A fraternity buddy told me it was because baseball had taken my father away from me," he said—remembers that it was around 1972, when he, too, was a teenager, that he had any inkling who his father was. "I went to a Rangers old-timer's game that year and I think it really hit me when they introduced dad, you know, everybody stood up and gave him this great big ol' standing ovation. I got the goosebumps. . . . It kinda brought tears to your eyes, you know, to see old people really love him."

In '77, Mantle's oldest son, twenty-three-year-old Mickey Junior, who had been stumbling through various jobs since attending junior college, told his father he wanted to try his hand at professional baseball. It was a surprise. Mickey Junior, though the best athlete among the sons, had shied away from baseball because people's attitudes toward him as Mantle's son "took the fun out of it for me," he said. "The game had never really been worth it." But now he wanted help because there were no other avenues open. His father arranged a Yankee tryout for him, but scouts were not impressed. He was cut in spring training. Then a tryout with the Class A Alexandria Dukes was arranged; that was a flop, too. Mickey Junior, at twenty-three, the first of the Mantle boys out on his own, was totally at sea, unable to plan his next move.

Even more disturbingly, 1977 was the year when Mantle's nineteen-year-old son, Billy, was diagnosed with Hodgkin's disease, the old family specter. Billy had been troubled through much of his life, eventually becoming involved with drugs, alcohol, and weapons. When Mantle and his wife took him to the hospital to have a small lump behind his ear evaluated, they were not prepared for the grim news they received. Months of chemotherapy and radiation treatments followed. Mantle said that he and his wife used to sit around the house staring into space, unable to comfort one another.

Billy Mantle's cancer eventually went into remission. But it reminded Mantle of how he had all along been waiting for the disease to strike him. "I often wondered why the disease had skipped me after it had felled so many in my family. I had been expecting it all my life," he said.

He had been living and waiting since his earliest days in baseball for the tragedy to catch up with him, and now, in his late forties, he could no longer conquer his fears by hitting a ball five hundred feet or drinking himself into oblivion. He was ill, too; he had been having stomach pains, deep, sharp, unexplained seizures of pain that he assumed came from drinking—until he was hospitalized in June 1978. He was told he had a bleeding ulcer. "I've had a bellyache before but nothing like this," admitted Mantle. "I don't guess I've ever had anything this serious. I've been doing a lot of traveling. It seems like wherever I go, there's always a cocktail party. Maybe I was drinking too much."

The following spring, he turned up for his annual two-week stint at the Yankee training camp in Florida. There was nothing remarkable in that, except that Mantle talked about the problem of glory withdrawal he was having. "Once you've had it, it's hard to forget," he said. "It's tough to realize you're through. I don't think anybody ever gets over it, and I can see how it can kill somebody." He tried to explain what he meant. He mentioned the bleeding ulcer that he had had the previous summer, but that he was now feeling better. "But it's harder than hell," he said, candidly. "I'm fairly recognizable, and it's not been totally taken away from me. But I can see how a guy can commit suicide."

Chapter 13

In 1980, Willie Mays was offered and accepted a job as a greeter at Bally's Park Place Casino in Atlantic City. Baseball Commissioner Bowie Kuhn told Mays he had a choice: turn down the job, or accept it and be banned from all future major league employment. Mays chose to work for the casino.

In 1983, the Claridge Casino, right across the way from Bally's, offered Mickey Mantle the same kind of job, and Bowie Kuhn gave him the same choice—with the same result. The contract the Claridge offered was for one hundred thousand dollars a year, essentially for shaking hands, hanging around, and playing golf for five days out of each month. The work had nothing to do with gambling per se, and the money was more than Mantle had seen since his last year in baseball; he was not about to turn it down.

The decision to ban him, ironically, brought his name back into the headlines for a brief time. Sportswriters wrangled about Kuhn's decision; most backed Kuhn, though some, like Murray Chass of *The New York Times,* wondered whether a double standard was in use. Warner Communications had recently purchased a minority share of the Pittsburgh Pirates; three Warner executives at the time had either pleaded guilty or were convicted in fraudulent stock-purchasing schemes. One of the convictions involved charges of racketeering. Kuhn had taken no action to block Warner's involvement with the Pirates, Chass said, even though a legitimate question about "the integrity of the game" might have been raised.

The issue for Mantle had nothing to do with legal or moral hairsplitting. The Claridge had offered him a job; baseball had not. He was a baseball man who had no place in baseball. It made little difference to him to be told that he was now officially unemployable in the game because that had been the reality for him for some time. "The real pity is that there are no jobs in baseball for a Mickey Mantle or a Willie Mays that can pay them the amount of money they are getting from the casinos," said Phil Pepe, a writer close to Mantle.

Kuhn's act of banning Mantle had the unanticipated effect of reinforcing his position as a symbol of baseball's better days. Labor-management disputes over the years had transformed the game. Since 1976, free agency had become a fact of life, and between '76 and '80 the average major-league salary jumped from about $53,000 to almost $150,000—more money than Mantle had ever earned in a single season. Players began to move freely among teams, often reducing the fans' attachment to their favorite stars. A long and costly strike in 1981 wiped out the heart of that season. One result of all this was to create a sense of longing for the game as it used to be and for baseball's old heroes—like Willie Mays and, especially, Mickey Mantle. The irony, of course, was that these two heroes were banned from the game in the long shadows of the one issue—gambling—that had nearly sunk baseball earlier in the century.

There were strong voices who believed Kuhn and baseball were right to keep Mays and Mantle out. Dick Young wrote a long 1983 piece in the *New York Post* from the Yankees' spring training camp in Fort Lauderdale about the meaning of Mantle's absence from the game. As far as Young was concerned, there was little more involved than keeping Mantle off the payroll as a part-time honorary coach for a couple of weeks in the spring—which meant only that he could not be there in an official capacity but he could still party with Whitey, the pitching coach, and Billy, by then the Yankees' manager. Young's conclusion, an echo of the commissioner's, was that "there are broad misunderstandings. Mantle is not a baseball leper. He can visit his buddies here or anywhere in baseball. He can play in old timers games, same as Willie Mays. . . . Nobody is about to turn their plaques to the wall in the Hall of Fame. They are not banned from baseball. They are simply banned from holding a job in baseball while they are on the payroll of a casino-hotel."

But a year later, when Peter Ueberroth became commissioner and there was a possibility of reinstatement, the drumbeat for Mantle and Mays picked up. Jerome Holtzman reminded readers of what Mantle had accomplished, who he was and why he was so important to the game. "Mantle, at 52, is perhaps America's No. 1 sports hero," he wrote. "Like Joe DiMaggio, there is a macho quality about him that appeals to men, especially athletes, amateur or professional. Mantle played hurt. He never fully recovered from a knee injury he suffered in 1951, his rookie year, but nonetheless appeared in 2,401 games, all with the Yankees, a club record."

Holtzman wrote his piece after attending a Yankee-Dodger fantasy camp, awakening old memories. "When Mantle arrived," he wrote, "the Yankee 'students,' nine of whom were wearing No. 7 in tribute to him, were on one diamond, the Dodger students on the other. Within minutes, they had blended into one group and were worshipping at the shrine. 'I can now die and go to heaven,' said a 41-year-old pediatrician from New Jersey. 'I just shook Mickey Mantle's hand.' "

Holtzman observed other players, former stars like the Dodgers' Tommy Davis, also "worshipping at the shrine." Davis handed Mantle a box of baseballs to autograph, announcing "these will keep me in hamburgers the rest of my life."

To Holtzman, Mantle had a "magic touch" that could not be denied. The work he did for the casino included representing the hotel at charitable functions, including the annual Jimmy Fund dinner in Boston, Save-A-Heart in Baltimore, and the Special Olympics in Philadelphia. All that he was doing, wherever he turned up, was built on the glories of a career that was the common property of the game of baseball. Holtzman asked Mantle how he felt about being banned. Mickey insisted that he was not about to press for his own reinstatement, "but it would be nice," he admitted. "I don't want the day to come when one of my grandchildren says to my wife, 'Hey Grandma, how come Grandpa got banned?' "

Simple common sense finally persuaded Ueberroth to reinstate Mays and Mantle. Sentiment aside, it had become important to officially rehabilitate these old stars in the eyes of the game's paying customers, both fans and advertisers alike. Baseball's past was beginning to become a lucrative part of the game's business. The baby boomers who had idolized these players as kids were now in the prime of their earning lives, and they brought money, lots of it, to the shrine when they worshipped. They were investing in baseball cards, memorabilia, autographs, and other mementos that guaranteed an honored place for the game in the public eye.

Between Mantle's prime and the 1980s, great changes had shaken society. The country had fought and, for the first time, lost a major war. The civil rights movement had revolutionized relations between the races; federal and state laws had been overturned; political parties totally realigned. The hippie and drug cultures of the '60s and '70s transformed social and personal values, at the same time triggering new divisions based on age and gender. America's unquestioned position of economic strength had been undermined by upheavals in the world's oil markets, by serious recessions at home, and by revolutions in the third world, including peaceful ones that saw the rise of new economic superpowers like Japan and Germany.

It was no wonder that those who had been children in more secure times became nostalgic enough as adults to make the past a booming business. Whether the product was old movies, old clothes, or sports memorabilia, the new marketplace was driven by a longing for the better times of youth. The past could be recreated, reshaped in the present, and old heroes could be dusted off, refurbished, and restored to their past luster. In the baseball memorabilia business, the biggest hero of them all was Mickey Mantle.

Mantle seemed to reemerge in mint condition from inside pristine wrapping paper to satisfy this need to recreate a past that never existed. All the special qualities that made Mantle a natural for fans and writers when he played made him a gold-plated natural for collectors in the '80s. The fact that he was older, slower, heavier, and had problems with alcohol made all the more poignant who he was long ago. He was a symbol of youth, confidence, achievement, and vulnerability. He was a small-town boy, from the heartland rather than from one of the jaded coasts; and his voice, his manner, his look, even his name made his glamorous success with the nation's most glamorous team all the more significant. True, he was white—unlike Willie Mays, Jackie Robinson, or any of the great black stars who were changing the look and texture of professional sports with each passing year—but his appeal went beyond boundaries of race and class as easily as his longest home runs had cleared the fences.

Alan Rosen is one of the biggest baseball card dealers in the business. He grew up in the fifties, the son of a *Daily News* photographer, and his hero of heroes then and for many years was Mickey Mantle. Rosen has a picture of himself as a child standing alongside Mantle at Yankee Stadium in 1961. As an adult, his memories of Mantle and his childhood remained strong.

"I got out of the Army in 1971," Rosen said. "My first job was selling copy machines in New Jersey. That first job interview was quite unusual: The boss took off his watch and said, 'Alan,

I want you to sell me this watch.' . . . A couple of years later I was at the top of the division in sales. . . . I was doing pretty well. By 1974, I decided to try it on my own. . . . [Then] I got interested in antiques. . . . It was 1978, and I walked into a card show and everything started to change.

"I couldn't believe it. They were buying and selling my memories! I looked at a 1957 Topps Mantle and the resplendent 1959 Mantle card with its red background, and I was hooked. These were the cards that I remembered as a kid. People get hooked on baseball card collecting because it recaptures your past on cardboard. Here was an opportunity to go to a card show and relive your childhood through baseball cards. My favorite card in the whole world is the 1953 Topps Mantle card, and I bought one at that first show along with a 1978 Topps set."

Rosen started out in the card and memorabilia business on the hunch that his feeling for the past would be shared by others. He began working out of the basement of his house and within years was buying and selling at a pace he never believed was possible. In one year, he did $6 million worth of business. It became normal for him to spend $75,000 a week buying baseball cards from others and then, just as quickly, selling them for a profit.

The anchor in all of this remained Mantle. Mantle's rookie card, he soon found out, was worth $30,000 (compared with Mays's rookie card, which was worth about $5,000). "In a way, he's responsible for the whole memorabilia business. I can even date it exactly. It was '79," Rosen said, "because some jerk burnt a 1952 Mantle on a garbage can. He got a lot of publicity out of it—because he hated the Yankees. A lot of guys hated the Yankees and they all burned their cards. So, guess what? Mickey Mantle cards suddenly shot up three or four grand overnight."

For Rosen and other collectors, the rest was money, tons of it. Mantle was the hottest piece of cardboard going, with the exception of one old Honus Wagner card. "Mantle could have his picture on a piece of toilet paper, people want it," Rosen said. "You can have a thousand cards in your showcase—and I sold a hundred million dollars worth of cards in my life—but if you have Mickey's rookie card in there people hit their faces down into the glass squashing their noses to get a look at it. It's Mickey."

Rosen says he met his hero in 1981 at a card show. It was the first time he had seen him since that moment on the field at Yankee Stadium twenty years before. He knew Mantle was going to be at the show, so he had the picture with him and he asked him to sign it. Mantle obliged, telling Rosen with a laugh, "Looks like we've both put on a few pounds since then."

Over the years following, through the years that Mantle worked at the Claridge and then afterward when he began appearing more frequently at shows, earning more and more revenue for his appearances, Rosen got to know Mantle professionally. He began working with him, hiring him to appear at special events. The hero he cherished as a child and the one he sold for a handsome profit in his new, proliferating business were very different people. If the memorabilia business had embraced Mantle as a kind of Last Hero, Rosen discovered him to be wholly unprepared to step forward with his jaw set and cape flying.

Rosen says there was no one incident or series of incidents that disenchanted him. At dinners and social gatherings, in the company of men and women, business associates and their wives, Mantle invariably made crude and usually insulting remarks about women, Rosen said. "I was at a dinner party with him once, and all his comments were about how every piece of food was like a woman's anatomy. It was disgusting, vile."

Rosen sponsored a reunion of the 1961 Yankees at Trump Castle in Atlantic City. Thirty-four Yankee old-timers were there, including Mantle, whom, Rosen says, he paid $150,000 for three days' work. The players and other guests had waited around through the late afternoon till dinnertime for Mantle, the principal guest, to appear. Rosen finally called him on a house phone. "You know what he told me? 'Fuck your mother, fuck your show, and fuck Donald Trump!' Now, he wasn't being hired to have sex with me in Macy's window for $150,000; all he had to do was show his face. Trump's out there waiting around, so are all his old buddies—and it's in the contract that he has to be there, to take a team picture, all the rest. Was he drunk? Who cares? If he was Steve Howe he'd be in prison, but because he was The Mick it didn't matter what he said or did. When he finally did show, we had a crippled kid in a wheelchair who wanted him to sign a bat. He wouldn't do it, because one of his rules is he doesn't sign bats—he wouldn't even sign one for one of his old buddies. Moose Skowron came up to him and asked him to sign one, he had thirty-three guys who had already signed and he was missing only Mickey's signature, and he wouldn't do it."

At about the same time that Rosen began working with him, Mantle met a woman named Greer Johnson, a divorced, thirty-four-year-old elementary school teacher from Georgia. She was visiting the Claridge in 1983 with friends, including a date whom she described as "a high roller." "It was Mickey's job to entertain us, to take us out to dinner," she said. What was not part of the job description was that the two became close business associates and also fell in love.

Johnson said that when she met Mantle she had already grown tired of teaching and was looking for a career change. She never anticipated, though, that her career change would involve Mickey Mantle.

"We had known each for awhile, he had known that I wanted to do something in the business world, so one day he asked me if I had ever thought about being an agent for celebrities," said Johnson. "I just laughed. I told him, you're right, that was a course that was offered one day when I was absent, a 101 course that I happened to miss. But he kept at it. And I listened. I was single, I didn't have any children, I had no responsibilities, so I thought about it for a long time."

When Johnson finally decided to go ahead, the line of division between romance and business was missing. "It was a Cinderella story in the beginning. I traveled, met people, did things I never imagined would be possible in my life." But Johnson also took her crash 101 course seriously, and she learned the memorabilia business inside out. As a "celebrity agent," she represented Mantle and a number of his old teammates like Hank Bauer, Moose Skowron, Whitey, and Yogi, but her main client was always Mantle. She saw him from the start through very different eyes.

"I traveled with him all the time," she said. "I saw what the marketing people, the advertising people did, and I saw real early a real big need to protect Mickey Mantle—a huge need to protect him. He was like a little boy to me, he was very naive and totally inexperienced when it came to business. That was a real surprise. He thought the best of everybody, and there were all kinds of people who were willing to take advantage of him. That's what I wanted to protect him from."

When Alan Rosen's name came up, Johnson was quick to defend Mantle. "He's a guy who's very self-important, calls himself 'Mr. Mint,' or something like that, and Mickey really doesn't take to people like that. He was very outspoken and opinionated; Mickey prefers people who are more modest, so when we did a show with Alan and he wanted Mickey to do more than was in his contract, or what I had negotiated, Mickey would get his back up, yes."

But then Johnson acknowledged that Mantle indeed could be rude and crude, but to her, even that kind of behavior pointed up the need to protect him. "Mickey had a bubble around him. He had this protective wall around himself and he wouldn't let anybody in. It was amazing," she said, "he'd tell me some things, say, like what he thought about somebody, and we'd be talking and he would tell me something entirely different than what he had said before around that person. He'd know what he was feeling but he'd just hide it."

Johnson believed that Mantle trusted her completely—because he did open up to her, especially about the new and overwhelming business pressures he was experiencing.

"He was like a child in so many ways," she said. "He would

do an appearance or a luncheon, a dinner, a card show or whatever and we'd get finished and he'd wait for me to critique him. He'd ask me, straight out, 'How did I do?' "

"And I was honest with him. When he'd screw up—and he did—I'd tell him. You know, if he'd been drinking and he used foul language, I'd tell him. I wouldn't pull any punches, and I think that's what he respected and trusted. If he did good, I was the first one to praise him. I'll tell you this, whenever he got out of line, whenever he did something, the person who felt worst afterwards was him, I guarantee you."

Whether he knew it or not, Mantle was taking his own Celebrity 101 course in this period. His experiences as a star player in the '50s did not quite prepare him for making a living as a personality rather than an athlete. Johnson said that Mantle would get disconcerted at shows when people in line used the wrong pens for autograph signing, or he'd get flustered and angry at airports when people tried to catch him as he was heading toward a flight gate. "We started taking cards with us that were pre-signed whenever we went to airports," Johnson explained. Mantle seemed not to realize that most people came up to him not with the intention of exploiting or bothering him, but with gratitude and affection. "For people to come up to you that way, I explained to him once," Johnson said, "it sometimes takes a lot of courage and they must love you absolutely to death to do it. And for you then to turn around and be ugly to them, that's the only the time they're probably ever going to meet you in person—and you're their hero—and that's what they are going to take away with them and remember about you."

Johnson says that Mantle continued to wrestle with this side of himself. When he lashed out at someone, he would send Johnson out with a signed card to find the person, bring them back, do something to make amends. "He always knew," she said. "When something like that happened, if he ever knowingly hurt someone's feelings, he'd think about it for days afterwards. He could crush people and he just didn't realize it."

Mantle, with a major assist from Johnson, slowly learned to rein himself in. The business of being Mickey Mantle was many-sided, with any number of pitfalls and traps. From the start, Johnson made sure that the details of contracts and payments were always in order, open, and above board. Payments to Mantle were always made by check rather than in cash. In a business that was all too fraught with possibilities of fraud and tax evasion, this was critical, perhaps even more than his manner in meeting and greeting fans. In the tax-cheating cases involving baseball stars that have surfaced in the last years, there have sometimes been hints that Mantle too was involved in such practices. But according to Johnson, attorneys of Mantle's, and Alan Rosen, the rumors were only that.

"With Greer he did real good," Rosen said. "In the beginning guys used to slip him stuff; he'd be drinking and they'd get him to do an extra thirty to forty autographs. When Greer became his agent, she, in my opinion, really put him on the map as far as making big money and not doing anything extra is concerned. She was very professional about it, very strict with the promoters and she had everything down in writing. She had him making $50,000 a day signing autographs, and to the best of my knowledge not a penny of that was ever taken in cash."

Mantle was also becoming far more comfortable out in the business world himself. Over time, he had become far better at being Mickey Mantle than he ever had been during his career. In 1988, Mantle was approached by a group of New York businessmen who wanted him to become a partner in a restaurant they would open. The restaurant, as it was conceived, would be another *Toots Shor's*. The idea was to sell a legend, not just a menu. As Bill Liederman, one of the managing partners of *Mickey Mantle's,* put it, "We first looked downtown for a big open space for a sports bar—you know, we're gonna have batting cages, hoop shoots, but we weren't at all interested; we just looked as a courtesy to the broker. Then we went up to Central Park South and looked at this place, which had legend written all over it.

The space dictated that. You know, we stopped to think who might fit that category: Joe Namath maybe; I grew up in Princeton, New Jersey, maybe Bill Bradley; Muhammad Ali. But there was really only one guy—Mickey Mantle."

Liederman, like Alan Rosen, said Mantle was his childhood idol. But unlike Rosen, Liederman's view of the later Mantle fit the old image—sort of. "When we first sat down with him, we were really nervous. I mean, I was going to meet my boyhood idol and pitch a deal to him? My God. Well, the first thing that happened was that I noticed his size. I had been expecting to meet someone who was going to be huge, six-five, six-six, someone bigger than life. He was like five-ten, and here I am six-one, I'm looking down at him! And then you notice the arms and the neck. Well, a funny thing happened at this dinner," Liederman continued. His mother came over and was introduced to Mantle and fell all over him. She told Mantle she had been a Dodger fan all her life and that he was her favorite Dodger, that she used to go to Ebbets Field all the time to see him play. "He was so kind and sweet to her," said Liederman, "he played right into it. It was almost elegant. Then afterwards, we got around to talking about the kind of restaurant we were thinking of. We were still thinking of an interactive sports bar, and just like that, he says, 'I don't want none of that shit.' My partner and I looked at him, we both thought we had had it. What had we said wrong? Then he says, 'No, I want a place the way *Toots Shor's* used to be, where a guy my age can be comfortable coming in and eating and having a couple of drinks with friends, a place where people from my era can be comfortable."

Mantle was really saying that he knew what it was he had to sell. And he did. In 1987, on the twentieth anniversary of his five hundredth home run, Mantle sat down with an interviewer from *USA Today.* Mantle trotted out one of his favorite jokes for the occasion. "You know, I dreamed I died, and when I got up to heaven, St. Peter met me at the pearly gates and said I couldn't get in," he said, "because I hadn't always been good. 'But before you go,' St. Peter said, 'God has six dozen baseballs He'd like you to sign.' "

"Once [Mantle] had the fastest bat in baseball," the interviewer concluded. "Now Mantle, 55, has baseball's quickest, sunniest smile."

A couple of years later, Mantle agreed to a long one-on-one interview with Bob Costas that was broadcast nationwide. In the interview, Mantle was obviously at ease and in good spirits. If there was a surprise for the general public, it was in hearing how skilled Mantle was in spinning yarns. He just did it; he had no affectations, and he was always willing to tell a story on himself. He told one about getting hit in the forehead the first time he tried to catch a fly ball in the outfield, and how when he was playing first base for the first time and was instructed from the bench to go to the mound to talk to Whitey, Ford wheeled around and (expletive, expletive, expletive deleted) told him to please go back to his position. He had that rare storyteller's ability to endear himself to an audience. Among others, he told Costas the story of how he had been recruited to play football at the University of Oklahoma. It had the cadences, timing, and irony that, if not quite Will Rogers-ish, was definitely down-home Mantle:

> There was this time in 1949 when I was a senior in Commerce High School and they brought me down to OU to work out. I never did meet Bud Wilkinson, but Darrell Royal drove me all around the campus and everything and I knew who he was, but you know, he could never remember my name. Probably didn't even think about it, but about 1958 I was living in Dallas, Texas, and the Texas Longhorns was playing over at Fort Worth, playing TCU, and I went to the game and they gave me a pass to go down on the field. It was right after the World Series and I met Darrell Royal [who was coaching Texas] and he goes, "Hey, nice meeting you. I always wanted to meet you." I said, "Darrell, I met you a long time ago, don't you remember that?" I said, "You carried me around Oklahoma University in your car one day and showed me all the dormitories and tried to talk me into coming to OU to

play football." And he says, "In 1949?" I said, "Yeah." He says, "Hell, you weren't even Mickey Mantle then."

Over the years, Costas, who delivered the principal eulogy at Mantle's funeral, became a friend. The relationship, Costas said, began with his being a fan and always had some of that in it right to the end. But Costas was a reporter first and last, and he had always puzzled about who Mickey Mantle the person was when he became Mickey Mantle the icon.

"I had dinner with Mickey one night, it was in January in New York, and it was really cold. We were walking back to the Regency, where we both were staying," Costas said, "and I had noticed that Mickey had asked for a doggie bag for his dinner in the restaurant—which was sort of strange. Anyway, he asks me to take a walk with him. Now this wasn't the kind of night where you wanted to take a stroll, but I went along, over to Madison Avenue, where he knew this homeless guy who was in a cardboard box. He knocks on the cardboard and suddenly this guy pops up his head. He looks frightened—and frightening—not knowing who's there, and suddenly when he sees us, the guy's face softens. He says, 'Oh hi, Mick.' And Mantle hands him his dinner. It was clear to me he had done this many times before. Did it mean that Mickey was the greatest humanitarian in the world? No—just that that was part of him, just as an hour later he could have been drunk in a bar and told some very nice autograph seeker to go fuck himself."

Which was all too true. Because even as he had learned to better handle being a legend, he still found it impossibly hard to handle himself.

Chapter 14

In 1985, Mantle published his third autobiography, *The Mick*. Aside from being a best-seller, the book for the first time included Mantle's own descriptions of his drinking problems. The accounts of his escapades with Billy and Whitey were placed in darker shadows than they had been before. He talked openly and apologetically about the troubles he had caused others, especially Merlyn and his children. He had been on the road too much, had ignored all of them too much. And he had damaged himself. The years of boozing had all along been robbing him of his own God-given gifts, and he now understood that he could have achieved so much more if only he had taken better care of himself.

The book was written with a coauthor, but there was no mistaking Mantle's voice in it. All of the old stories were there along with some new ones. The backlighting was different, but so was the script. Mantle was using his celebrity to tell others to lay off drugs and alcohol, to take another look behind the laughs and shenanigans.

Of course, if the '50s were the years of the all-American boy and the '60s the age of the antihero, the '80s were the time of the celebrity confessional, in which dirty laundry was cleaned in public in the name of honesty and forthrightness. Stories of drug and alcohol abuse, especially among the famous, were becoming familiar; one celebrated athlete told his collaborator of how he overcame his cocaine addiction by playing golf. A good, handwringing confession, said one skeptical critic of the day, could always be an adequate substitute for the truth.

And, in truth, Mantle's book was only a half step. He was still as much denying his alcoholism as acknowledging it. "I'll say this," he wrote. "In the last few years my drinking has been confined to social occasions. Merlyn has been highly successful in reminding me if I forget. As a matter of fact, if it wasn't for her I probably would have wound up an alcoholic like so many other ballplayers who did come to a tragic end that way." On several occasions, in talking about his book, he seemed to disown it, as though he was only half committed to what he said about the damage he'd done and the hurt he'd caused.

But his drinking, and his remorse and fear over its many consequences, hounded him wherever he went and in whatever he did. All through the period when he reemerged as a hero, he had wild anxiety attacks where he would without warning begin to hyperventilate and shake. In 1985, while making a personal appearance in Portland, Maine, Mantle began suffering blinding headaches. At the same time, he noticed that lumps had formed in his neck. When he returned to Dallas, he was admitted to the Baylor University Medical Center and underwent an MRI. The suspicion was Hodgkin's disease, of course, but none was found. It was around this time that Roger Maris, who actually was suffering from cancer, took a turn for the worse. (When Maris died a few months later, Mantle was so disturbed by the news that was conveyed by telephone that he screamed and hung up, profusely apologizing afterward when the connection was reestablished.)

In 1987, following another personal appearance, Mantle was on a flight from Albany to Dallas when he suddenly felt pain in his chest and was unable to breathe. He got up from his seat, found a stewardess in the aisle, and asked her if she had ever handled a passenger aboard a flight who had had a heart attack. The stewardess, seeing that he was pale and sweating, had him take a seat where she administered oxygen. "I wasn't drunk," he said, "I knew everybody would think I had a real bad hangover. I just ran out of gas."

An ambulance was waiting for him at Love Field (where an autograph seeker approached him while he was being wheeled away on a stretcher). For a day or two, it was not clear what had happened; the scare was real, but there was no heart attack. Mantle said he felt very lucky, but that if that was a heart attack, "I've been having them all my life." A week later, he was in New York, in Yankee Stadium, at Easter time. By then the world knew he was all right. Longtime Yankee PA announcer Bob Sheppard asked the crowd to wish Mantle "a healthy and happy Easter." Mantle rose to his feet and waved from a TV booth as the crowd voiced its holiday best wishes.

Mantle tried, but he could not truly acknowledge how deeply and fully alcohol controlled his life. "I think Mick was always plagued by a sense that he did not have enough strength of character," Bob Costas said. "But even so, for ten years or more, without the press ever paying attention—you know, it wasn't like he saw the light only in the year before he died—he was out there preaching to kids to stay away from alcohol and not use him as a role model. He did a video in the late '80s where he made that a special point. He and I also did a video together called the *500 Home Run Club,* and he went out of his way to say it again." But the more Mantle preached—and could not live up to what he preached—the more guilty he became. "I think the low moments became lower and lower and worse and worse, and I think what was torturing him all along was that he understood what he should be and what he was," Costas said.

Mantle was asked in this period by an interviewer what he felt when he saw pictures and film footage of himself as a young player. He answered, "When I see, even as late as 1968, but all the way back to 1951 when I was really young, I can be watching these things and I keep thinking, you know, that I can't really hardly remember playing. It's like it's somebody else. At home in my trophy room, we have a den that we call a trophy room that's got all the Most Valuable Players and the silver bats and pictures all over the walls and everything. It's like it's somebody else. I mean, it's not like it's me, you know. I can hardly remember it."

The somebody else who was doing the watching increasingly seemed to be a bystander in his own life. It was as though there were two competing souls vying for the exclusive attention of this person, and, caught in the middle, there was no way he could manage. His marriage fell apart, and his oldest friendships, including those with Billy and Whitey, became strained or distant.

There was a rupture with Billy that was especially sodden and messy. Mantle and Greer Johnson had been spending time with Billy and his fourth wife, Jill, in upstate New York near Martin's home. The foursome had become friends with a local businessman named Mike Klepher, who Jill Martin had said was making unwanted sexual advances to her and to Johnson. Klepher vigorously denied any such behavior, and Mantle and Johnson were more suspicious of Jill than they were of Klepher. Mantle and Johnson both believed that Martin's new wife had a game plan for Billy that involved cutting him off from his friends. Mickey and Billy quarreled, and for almost an entire year, until shortly before Martin's death in an automobile accident on Christmas Day, 1989, the two friends, who had always been "as close as brothers," did not speak.

Jill Martin says that she was the one who finally reunited the old friends by persuading Mantle to make a reduced-fee appearance at a 1989 roast for Billy. That was not the way Greer Johnson remembers it. "Billy came into town one day and they began talking again, that was all. There was no deal, nothing behind it. Mickey had always loved Billy, because Billy had never wanted anything out of him."

Ford and Mantle had run a fantasy camp together for awhile but their business association fell apart. Mantle's relationship with Ford after baseball was never as close as the relationship he had with Billy. "He wasn't a hanging-out buddy the way Billy was," said John Lowy, one of the partners in Mantle's restaurant, "not in the years that I knew Mickey at any rate."

When Mantle spent time in Dallas, he drew a tight, small circle around his life. Most days he could be found at the Preston Trail Golf Club. When he went out, which was not often, there were only two places in town where he would let himself be seen: Jaxx Cafe, where there was a whole section in back of the bar roped off and reserved just for him, and an Italian restaurant, Capriotti's, where his privacy was just as zealously protected. Most of the time, he was at home—and home was falling apart. His sons, all of them, now had serious alcohol problems. His son Billy had been in and out of rehabilitation four different times for alcohol and drug abuse. Mickey Junior, who had failed to follow in his father's footsteps as a ballplayer, instead followed him in his drinking habits. Danny, Mantle's youngest son, regarded his own alcoholism seriously enough that he had begun searching around for help—for himself and for his wife. David, the next oldest son, had serious problems with addiction as well.

The sons and father had formed a partnership to run the fantasy camp, but their real partnership, Mickey said in *Sports Illustrated* in early 1994, was in passing the bottle. "I feel like I'm the reason that Danny went to Betty Ford last fall," Mickey told Jill Lieber. "For all those years I'd make him go to lunch and dinner with me. I'd get Mickey Jr. and my next oldest son, David, to go, too. I'd say, 'Hey, what are you guys doing tonight? Let's go eat.' Which would mean, 'Let's go drink.' They all drank too much because of me. We don't have normal father-son relationships. When they were growing up, I was playing baseball, and after I retired I was too busy traveling around being Mickey Mantle. We never played catch in the backyard. But when they were old enough to drink, we became drinking buddies. When we were together, it kind of felt like the old days with Billy and Whitey."

But the circle had closed. His sons were not his teammates, and he was older. His body no longer could simply accept what he was doing to it. The panic attacks he had first had years before were increasing. He began experiencing disturbing lapses of memory. When he talked about the difficulty he had remembering his time as a player, it was nothing compared with his problems in the present.

Mantle said that when he talked with his longtime lawyer, Roy True, about business matters, he could no longer follow the details of what he was being told. "I'd forget what day it was. What month it was. What city I was in. . . . The loss of memory really scared me. I told a couple of the doctors I play golf with at Preston Trail Golf Club . . . that I thought I had Alzheimer's disease, and they said, 'Well, you're probably not there yet.' . . . I was scared that the alcohol had changed my brain."

When Mantle was not in Dallas, he spent much of his time with Greer Johnson who had her business in Atlanta but had a home at the Harbor Club on Lake Ocomee in Greensboro. Though there had been no formal divorce from Merlyn, Johnson was, in every respect but the one of public acknowledgment, Mantle's second wife. The two traveled together, socialized together, shared a life together.

More than anyone else, Johnson saw what drinking was doing to Mantle. "To be perfectly honest, I'd never been around an alcoholic before," she said. Though she was hardly an abstainer, she was not prepared for what she then experienced. "When I met Mick I knew he drank, and it seemed like it got progressively worse. At first I didn't realize there was a problem. Finally, I did realize it, so I'd talk to him. I tried to have an intervention with him—and he would balk at that. We would go out and, first of all, if we were at places where I knew the bartenders, I'd talk to them and tell them, to make his drinks real light. Then he got wise to that. So I came up with a way of mixing a drink that he thought was a great drink. I'd fill the glass with ice, then three-fourths was the chaser, then just a splash of alcohol, whatever it was, right on top, and when he took a drink that's what he tasted—the alcohol—so he thought it was a great drink. I played all kinds of mind games with him. I'd fake headaches, tell him I needed to go home. Sometimes it worked, and sometimes I'd get so upset and angry with him, I'd just walk out and leave him. Usually that would make him go home, too."

Johnson believed Mantle drank because it was expected of him. Wherever he went, a glass would be put in his hand, and people would wait for him to get drunk. "I think he felt he was Mr. Personality when he drank—which he wasn't," she said. But he shared with her his growing sense that he could no longer control what was happening. "And he wanted so much to do something about it."

Pat Summerall, the broadcaster and ex-football player, was a close friend of both Mantle and Johnson, had known them for years. His friendship with Mantle went back to the days when they both played minor-league baseball. Summerall was a first baseman, with some power, for another team in the K-O-M League (or Sooner State League, as Summerall remembered it). Summerall's brief baseball career ended when he discovered that he couldn't hit a curveball. "The guy who did me in was Lindy McDaniel," Summerall said. "They signed him out of high school and he was on our team. When he got there, I volunteered to warm him up one night in the bullpen. He was already warm—and the lights were bad. The first pitch he threw whistled past my head, I was lucky it didn't kill me. The next one I managed to knock down. I knew then that I couldn't follow a good curveball. I went to the manager and asked him to let somebody else warm him up. And then, later on, he asked me if I wasn't interested in a career in pro football—which was a nice way of saying I'd never make it as a ballplayer.

"Anyway, I got to know Mick then," Summerall said. "He went on to Joplin and then to the Yankees pretty quickly, so for awhile I just followed what was happening with him, what they were asking him to do—to replace DiMaggio and all of the rest of that with all that publicity.

"I probably didn't see him then for six or seven years, but then when I was with the Giants, the football Giants, we both were playing in Yankee Stadium in those days and our seasons overlapped, so we sort of renewed our friendship then."

It was 1961 when the two fell in together, right in the middle of the home run chase with Maris. Mantle had filled out, Summerall said; he had gone from being a 160-pounder to weighing more than 200. "But personally he hadn't changed so much at all. He was still the kid from Commerce who had the twin brothers that I knew. His personal demeanor was the same. He had been with the Yankees for nine or ten years by that time, and he still wasn't aware that he was the superstar he was. That lasted to the day he died."

The two men used to frequent a bar called the Yankee Tavern, which was across the way from the Stadium. Summerall was living in the Concourse Plaza. "I used to share dishes with Bob Turley," he laughed. But that year was also Summerall's last as a football player.

When he retired, he went to work for CBS. And because CBS did Yankee games, Summerall was soon assigned to cover the team. "My first interview, my very first," he said, "was with Mickey—so that kept our friendship going for awhile. And then I lost touch with him for a long time. When he got out of baseball, I didn't really know what he was doing, other than that he lived in Dallas. He sort of dropped from view. But then beginning in the late '70s or early '80s, I ran into him again. He had an apartment in New York at the Regency. And I was spending more and more time in New York doing Giants games or on business trips, so I had an apartment at the Regency, too. At first I'd just run into him in the lobby, and then we started hanging together. We'd go out and drink and raise hell. We became pretty fast drinking buddies. Billy Martin was around all the time, and we'd go up to his apartment and we'd sit around and tell stories and, you know, talk like guys do."

Several years ago, Summerall himself moved to Dallas. He was in the midst of his own domestic problems, and he had a girlfriend in Dallas. Though he had kept in touch with Mantle in New York, he saw him more frequently in Dallas. The two often played golf and lunched together. Mantle eventually sponsored his friend for membership at Preston Trail. "So then we were golfing buddies *and* drinking buddies," said Summerall.

It was during this period that Summerall dealt with his own long-standing problems with alcohol. "I was part of an intervention," he said. "A group of my friends got together and told me they thought I was drinking too much. I was in Philadelphia and they literally had an airplane waiting for me. They said, we want you to go to the Betty Ford Center, it was all arranged.

"I was enraged. It was none of these people's business. They had ambushed me in Philadelphia, they had a plane, the whole bit. But I was also impressed that if so many people were that concerned and had put themselves out in that way, that, yeah, maybe there was a problem I needed to deal with. So I decided to go ahead. I went to Betty Ford."

Summerall described the routine at Betty Ford. "The major thing at Betty Ford is that you're nobody special," he said. "You're there for twenty-eight days—that's a magical number of some kind, but it also has to do with insurance—but my first five days weren't counted because I was so angry. Well, the first thing that happens is that they give you a roommate. There are twenty people in a dormitory, two to a room except for one room which has four people. They call that one 'The Swamp.' When Mrs. Ford went in to rehab she was one of four people in a room; they told her there were no private rooms, and when they built the Betty Ford Center they built it with one room like the one she had been in.

"In any case, you were no one special, that was the whole point. There were no other celebrities in the group I was in—if I'm a celebrity. You get up at 5:30, you make your bed, do your laundry, you must show up for breakfast—which is really difficult for those on drugs. Then you go back and you read a group devotion. You sit around, and everybody is obliged to say what they got out of the particular passage that was read. Then you go to what they call group therapy, where there are eight people involved. You sit in a circle and you start to say what it is that happened to you, what happened to you that made you need help. Then they make you write a series of letters—to your mother, your father, your alcoholism, the person who was most important to you in your youth. You keep a diary, and at the end of each day you turn it in and a counselor grades your thoughts. If he disagrees with something you said, you're told why. Then, in the afternoon, there's a one-on-one therapy session. You have a recreation period for an hour. You can do pretty much what you want there, aerobics, weight training, swimming, whatever. Then there's an evening meal, and after that you go to an AA meeting. Curfew is at ten o'clock. You're allowed to read only two books, either the Blue Book of AA—they call it the Big Book—or the Bible."

The Blue Book was put together by AA's founder, Bill Wilson, and it details the Twelve-Step program that has since become the standard. At Betty Ford and other rehabilitation centers, only the first few steps are completed before recovering clients go out on their own. The steps require an admission of powerlessness over alcohol, an acceptance of God, and a willingness to take a "moral inventory" of one's life. The last step before a client is released at Ford is to acknowledge to oneself and to another, a total stranger, the exact nature of one's wrongs. "You sit down in a room with a person you've never met before," Summerall said, "and you tell him. And one of the things you will be asked then is, what does God mean to you? Whatever God means to you, even if you have no belief, you are required to say."

When he got back to Dallas, Summerall told Mantle about what he had been through and found that his friend was a little more than curious about his experience. "He asked me when I got back, 'How was it?' I told him they had to keep me an extra five days because I was so pissed off and didn't get with the program. I told him as best I could what happened and that I sure didn't want to go back, but I thought I had actually accomplished something there. He didn't ask very much then, and I didn't say very much. I knew he had some friends in Dallas who didn't have his best interests at heart, but you can't come out and say that. There were some doctors, for example, who knew how bad Mickey's knees were, how his shoulder hurt, how much trouble he had walking or just keeping food down, and they'd just give him a handful of pills. But gradually, he started asking me more and more questions about the Betty Ford Center and what I'd learned there. I remember him saying to me at one time, 'They don't get into that religious shit, do they?' I said, 'Well, yeah, they do.' Anyway, we'd inevitably get into a conversation about his early childhood and his dad. Pretty soon, we'd both be crying at lunch, and then we'd go and play golf."

Summerall believed, as did Greer Johnson, that Mantle's interest in rehabilitation stemmed both from concern for his sons and from his own deteriorating physical condition. "Danny was in a couple of our conversations at Jaxx," Summerall said, "and then Danny used to play golf with us. But I think honestly what got to him was his sense that he was more and more dependent, and he was really badly physically deteriorating. You could see that. He had gotten to the point where he could hardly get up and down the stairs at the club, and then he started to get a pretty good gut on him. He finally went to a legitimate doctor who didn't give a damn that he was Mickey Mantle."

After a physical exam, Mantle's doctor recommended an MRI. The experience of lying in a tube for an hour and fifteen minutes was terrifying; Mantle said that it was hard for him to keep from crying. He was thinking, he said, of all that he had done to himself over the years, how he had abused his body with alcohol for forty-two years. When the results of the MRI came back, Mantle's doctor told him how bad the condition of his liver was and that the next drink he took might be his last.

Mantle began talking to Danny, who had done a stint at Betty Ford the previous fall, and to Summerall about the clinic's routines. What he feared was that he would have to stand up in front of people and talk about his feelings. He did not want to do that because he was sure he would cry—and "Mickey Mantle," he said, "is not supposed to cry."

Summerall arranged for Mantle to be accepted at the center. When he was told that a bed was ready, he called Mantle and told him. "He called me back on a Thursday night," he said, "and told me he was ready to go, but then I told him that if he went on a Friday the first days wouldn't be counted against his stay—weekends don't count. He said to me then that he wasn't going to go, that I had to call them back and tell them that those two days had to count. I did, and they said not to worry, that all of that would be taken care of when he got there. So he went on a Friday."

Summerall said that about two weeks later, though telephone calls out of the center were not permitted, he got a call from Mantle. "He asked me if I had liked that place except that his language was a helluva lot stronger. I told him, no, I didn't like it, I didn't go there for a good time. He said, 'I want you to make me a promise.' I said, 'You're not thinking about leaving?' He said, 'Hell, yes, I'm thinking about leaving.' I said 'No, you can't do that.' He calmed down after awhile, and then he said to me, 'I want you to make me a promise.' I told him I'd do whatever I could. He said, 'If we're ever together, and you see me have a drink, I want you to kill me right there.' I told him there's only one person who can do that, and it ain't me," said Summerall.

Mantle's distress at the center did not end with the call to Summerall. His desire to leave grew stronger. Toward the end, the center offered "Family Week," when a relative, spouse, or "significant other" was encouraged to visit and take part in classes, group therapy sessions, and conferences with counselors. Greer Johnson arrived for Family Week and found Mantle angry and anxious to escape. He was angry, she said, because he was not used to being told what to do by people he didn't know. "For the first time in his life, these people didn't care who he was, and they weren't gonna let him get away with anything," she said. "They'd call him down—and he wasn't used to other people calling him down. He told me that when I left, he was going to leave." Johnson says that she then told his therapists what he was thinking and of his intention to leave. She decided to stay on. "Mickey said, 'Well, I'm leaving,' and I said, 'Fine, that's your choice. I'm staying.' He said, 'You mean, you'll stay?' I said, 'Yeah, I'm staying.' So he said, 'Well, then, I'll stay.' And he stayed for the rest of his final week."

Mantle's closest friends, people who knew him and did business with him, were at least skeptical about his chances of staying sober. Because the recovery program only involved the first five of the Twelve Steps, Mantle still had much more to do. All studies of alcoholism are clear that the physiological and psychological effects of addiction are profound and cannot be "cured." Because alcoholism is a disease, not a state of mind, someone who gives up drinking is only a "recovering alcoholic," not someone whose problem is in the past. It becomes critical for a recovering alcoholic, therefore, to openly acknowledge the continuing nature of the disease, to say to others, "I am an alcoholic," even when one is dry.

But Mantle, as far as anyone could tell, stayed sober. When he was out in public, he drank soda water and Diet Coke. Al Biernat, the manager of Jaxx Cafe, noted, "There was something different about Mickey after he came out of rehab. There was a lot more laughter at that table that I noticed."

John Lowy and Bill Liederman, the restaurant partners in *Mickey Mantle's,* who had too many times over the years seen Mickey begin his days with a witch's brew of dregs from the night before called "A Breakfast of Champions," were both certain that in the last year of his life he did not drink. He had a regular booth at the restaurant, and whenever he came in, they said, he always sat there sipping water or Diet Coke.

Summerall remembered that Mantle turned in characteristic fashion to pranks about his sobriety. "His favorite day of the year was not Christmas or his birthday or anybody else's birthday, it was April Fool's Day. He calls me at home one time and he says, 'Pat, you've got to come and get me.' I thought, 'Oh shit, he's had a relapse.' I said, 'Where are you, Mick, just stay right there.' He says, 'I guarantee you I'm not going anywhere. I'm in jail.' I asked him to let me talk to the police, but he said he couldn't because the guy was black or something and I wouldn't be able to understand him, and I said, 'Oh my God, what did you do?' And he says it was a dragnet, that they got him along with a whole bunch of winos and hookers. I was out of my mind by then. I said, 'Just hold on, I'll be there in ten minutes.' Then he says, 'Pat, what day is it?' He had me cold. I tell you, it was sort of like the crust melted when he came back."

But the way back was anything but easy or certain. Within weeks of his getting out of Betty Ford, his son Billy died of a heart attack in a local drug rehab program. Around the same time, Mantle's mother died from complications of Alzheimer's disease. The strongest pressure on him to stay sober, Greer Johnson said, came from this sense of his life being overturned, and from an awareness that it was now expected of him to stay sober, just as it had once been expected of him to drink—or to excel on the ball field.

"Every time now that he'd go out, every time he was on an airplane, no matter where he was, when he would order something to drink it was like E. F. Hutton—everybody was waiting to hear what he was going to order. I think the expectations helped him," she said.

As a recovering alcoholic, there were particular requirements for Mantle in how he acknowledged his alcoholism. According to the Blue Book, without this critical step of public acknowledgment all others are said to be impossible. For Mantle, this went far beyond standing up in an AA meeting and telling people his name and that he was an alcoholic. Everyone knew; his AA group was the nation. His time in Betty Ford was a news story.

Mantle discussed his options with Greer Johnson and then

with Bob Costas. Costas had called Mantle after he had gotten out of Betty Ford just to see how he was doing. It was about two weeks after Billy Mantle's death. Costas knew as well as anyone what kind of public pressure Mantle would have to deal with, and he wanted to talk to him about it.

"At some point you're going to have to make a decision," he told Mantle. "The press is going to be all over you for this, the tabloids and the afternoon shows, you've got to decide what you want to do." Mantle asked him what he meant, and Costas explained that there were really three options: He could remain silent, he could talk to everyone, or he could decide to talk only to a select group of media. "What I think you should do is pick one broadcast outlet and one print place," Costas told him. He did not necessarily have his own program in mind. "If you want to do it with me, fine, but maybe it should be *60 Minutes*—but wherever it is, it's got to be a place that has some dignity and credibility where they're not going to chop up what you say into a thousand sound bytes and exploit it."

Mantle chose two outlets, just as Costas suggested. One was a nationally broadcast hour-long television interview with Costas; the other was an as-told-to interview he granted to *Sports Illustrated.*

In neither interview did Mantle ever acknowledge that he was, at present, an alcoholic. In the *SI* piece, he mentioned that the most difficult part of his rehabilitation at Ford was when he was asked to write a letter to his father. Mantle said he had wept through the ten minutes it took him to compose the letter. He said the most important thing he discovered was that his drinking had come from depression over never having been able to fulfill his father's dreams. Then he added "Dad would be proud of me today, knowing that I've completed treatment at Betty Ford and have been sober for three months. But he would have been mad that I had to go in there in the first place. He would have forgiven me, but it would have been hard to look him in the eye and say, 'Dad, I'm an alcoholic.' I don't think I could have done it. I would feel like I'd let him down. I don't know how you get over that. I can't hit a home run for him anymore."

What Mantle was able to do was to apologize, to convey in the most harrowing terms the sense of guilt that haunted him but never restrained him through the years. He apologized to his wife for the suffering he had caused her; to his sons for being a negligent father when they were growing up and, later, for being their Pied Piper; to fans and to the general public for the countless incidents of inconsiderate and offensive behavior. As he had in the past, he used both forums to urge kids not to drink or do drugs.

Pat Summerall was not sure the *SI* piece sounded like Mantle, but Greer Johnson was. She sat with Mantle and the reporter, Jill Lieber, at the Harbor Club in Greensboro when the interview was done. "It was his voice all right, believe me," she said. "I heard the words."

But Johnson knew the part of him that was still damaged in the present and why it was important for him to acknowledge the continuing nature of his own illness. "After he sobered up, he used to say all the time, 'I'm not much fun anymore, am I? Ever heard the song, *I'm Not Fun Since I've Stopped Drinking?*' Every time we heard that song, he'd say, 'That song was meant for me.' "

So far as anyone has been able to determine, Mantle stayed stone-cold sober to the day of his death. "I'll tell you what," Johnson said, "of all the surprises in our ten years, that was probably the biggest one of all."

For his part, Mantle had plans. He wanted to use his time differently. "I've told Joe Garagiola that I'd work with him in BAT, the Baseball Assistance Team, which helps old ballplayers who are having troubles," he said, "and I'd like to talk to kids about drugs and alcohol abuse. It used to be said I was a role model, and kids, even older guys, looked up to me. Maybe I can truly be a role model now—because I admitted I had a problem, got treatment, and am staying sober—and maybe I can help more people than I ever helped when I was a famous ballplayer."

And then he had some thoughts just for himself. Pat Summerall remembered that sometime after Betty Ford, Mantle asked him about baptism: "You know, his life until he went into Betty Ford was really an artificial one in so many ways. Somebody would tell him what time the bus leaves, when batting practice is, what time was curfew and all the rest. We used to play golf every day at eleven o'clock; even that was part of it. Until he came out. Then he just kinda sat back. He asked me once if I'd ever been baptized. I told him, yes. He said, what's it like? I said, 'I don't know, I was an infant.' He said 'You was a what?' I told him I was once an infant, and he said, 'They do something with water, don't they? Well, you know I can't swim.' It was funny. But then we had many more of these conversations."

Mantle seemed to be aware that he was facing something very different from just staying sober or having to make amends or being someone's role model. The knowledge was coming from his own body, whispering to him, as it had long ago when he first saw the face of death and was driven out into the world to find his way and defy it. Only now he was sixty-three, not seventeen.

Chapter 15

The pain was a familiar one. It was deep and unabating in the center of his body, and it robbed him of his appetite and his ability to hold down food. Because it seemed to him more like an old injury than something that would take his life, he was strangely lulled by it. As with all the physical damage he had sustained over the years, he assumed he would simply throw it off and go on. Usually the pain left in a day or so, but this time it did not, and so on June 1, 1995, he was hospitalized for what was termed "a little stomach disorder." Mantle's son David told reporters that his father would be returning home the next day; Mantle's lawyer, Roy True, assured the media that no heart problems were involved.

When it was announced to the world a week later that Mantle was suffering from liver cancer and would need a transplant to survive, the media shock waves were seismic. It was as though a president or a Pope had been stricken. Overnight there was a cottage industry that formed just to try to make sense of why the story was so important. Savants and shills, columnists and con artists were out in force. What did Mantle's illness mean? Why was its hold on the public so great? To some, it meant money:

The owner of a well-known New York memorabilia shop told a reporter for *Newsday* that Mantle's nearly priceless rookie card "would jump $10,000 overnight if his condition got worse."

But there was more than money on most people's minds.

"The first time I saw him in this town was in a World Series game against the Dodgers," wrote Jimmy Breslin, "and he hit the ball straight up. He threw the bat and ran with this furious anger towards first base. The pop fly was high over the infield and the Dodgers shortstop, Pee Wee Reese, was under it and waiting. Mantle ran. He was past first and now Reese had his hands up for the ball. Still Mickey Mantle ran. He ran with that build of a football player, his head mounted on a neck that was a size 18 at least. Now Reese caught the ball. And Mantle was past him and almost to third. If Reese doesn't catch the ball, Mantle is standing at third.

"Nobody I ever saw could run bases that fast. Nobody anybody else ever saw could do it, either.

"He kept running through all the nights. He was so sure he would never see so many of them he wanted to use them."

Robert Lipsyte believed that Mantle and America were allies in promise, vulnerability, and failure. "Like America in the '50s," he wrote, Mantle "was burdened with a distant sense of doom. For America it was the threat of atomic attack by the Soviet Union. A generation of sports fans grew up with the Mick and with 'duck and cover' air raid drills in school. For Mantle it was the Hodgkin's disease that killed most males in his family before they reached 40. . . .

"The threats to America and Mantle ultimately proved empty, but they dominated the psyche of the country and the center fielder and gave each an urgency and a poignancy that affected behavior in often destructive ways. America abused itself with the cold war. Mantle had booze."

The news of the gravity of his illness was quickly replaced by fresh headlines about the liver transplant he received at the Baylor University Medical Center on June 8. Because there was so little time—twenty-four hours—between the announcement that a transplant was needed and Mantle's actually receiving one, his identity was again magically transformed. "Mickey Miracle," screamed one tabloid headline after the operation. Another paper, and many reporters questioning doctors at the Baylor Center, suggested that the real "miracle" had to do with a famous and privileged patient receiving preferential treatment.

Mantle did not have to answer for America's failures or for the judgments made by doctors and administrators handling a famous patient, but he did have to answer the long-delayed demands of his own body.

When his cancerous liver was removed, additional cancer was found at the site of the bile ducts, strongly suggesting that his survival would not be long term. The questions raised about whether the new cancer was found early or late in the surgery mattered to the hospital and its reputation, but either way, Mantle was left to cope with the difficult aftereffects. He was on a regimen of both immunosuppressive and anticancer drugs, the one to prevent organ rejection, the other to fight tumor growth. The drugs counteracted each other and, said many specialists, may have had the effect of spreading his cancer throughout his body. The cancer became a wildfire. He lost almost forty pounds in a little less than three weeks when he was finally released from the hospital and allowed to go home.

One of the last times Pat Summerall saw him was at the men's grill at Preston Trail. His friend was sitting there, waiting for him. Though he had seen photographs of Mantle at his hospital news conference, Summerall was still not prepared for what he saw with his own eyes. Mantle rolled up his trousers and showed him his legs. "He said, 'I want to show you my damn legs. You know I used to have pretty good legs.' His legs were like—not a pencil, but the pencil lead. They were all black and blue from where he had taken the chemotherapy treatments."

Then the men went out and got a golf cart and followed some other Preston Trail members, Lanny Wadkins, Freddy Couples,

David Graham, and David Frost around the course. "We rode about nine holes, I guess," said Summerall, "and during that time he told me that they had found some cancer." Mantle was about to start a new round of chemotherapy, and he very quickly began looking and feeling worse. Mantle managed to get to the club a few more times, but by then he was too weak to do more than poke his head out the door and look at the course. "The week before he went back into the hospital for the last time, I gave him my house," Summerall said. "I was going to be out of town, and he wanted to get away from all the pressure and the phone calls and the publicity. When I told him to take my house, he said to me afterward, 'You know, you gave me your damn house—no strings, no nothing, you just gave me your damn house. That's the nicest thing anybody has ever done for me.' He really said that."

In that last week, Greer Johnson lived with Mantle and looked after him at Summerall's house. Johnson sensed the gravity of Mantle's condition merely from his appearance, but she insists that neither she nor Mantle were really aware of just how little time was left. "I will tell you," she says, "that neither one of us really knew how bad he was. No matter what was said. You know, he was making all these plans to come back to Georgia and then go to Hawaii." The couple had been celebrating honeymoons for years, she said, and "he was talking about going to Hawaii because we had never been there."

Johnson also said she was reinforced in her sense of hope by talking with the family. She had had cordial relations with Mantle's sons over the years, and they were the ones informing her of what the doctors were saying. They were always upbeat, she said, even then.

"I'd ask his attorney and his son Danny, is anybody saying anything, is anybody talking about a time frame on Mickey's life? They were all saying, no, no, no, he's gonna be fine, everything that's going on is by the book, he's reacting just the way he's supposed to be reacting. I don't know if they did that to keep me away and to keep me from panicking. But why would they have done that? For ten years I had done everything I could to respect the family and not to hurt anybody's feelings or to cause a problem."

During that week, though, Mantle again talked about baptism, and in just the way he had with Summerall. "The week I was with Mickey in Dallas before he passed away," she said, "we talked about baptism, and he asked me one night, out of the clear blue, 'Have you ever been baptized?' I said, yeah, when I was about nine years old. He said, 'Do you have to be dunked to be baptized?' I told him, no, they can just kinda sprinkle your head with water. He said, 'Does it have to be done at a church?' I said, 'No, Mick.' " All through the week, she said, they kept talking about it. "Sometimes he'd joke about it," she said, "that he was gonna let me sprinkle water on his head and baptize him."

Johnson had come from a religious family, and belongs to a church in Greensboro that she had been urging Mantle to attend for years. He had half-reluctantly, half-playfully gone along with her at first, she said. One morning, instead of remaining behind while she went to church, he got dressed and went with her.

"We sat real close to the rear door so when the service was over he could get up and run out," she said. "He just didn't want to . . . well, he knew everybody there would have loved for him to stay around and talk . . . anyway, he got to like our minister a lot, played golf with him and so forth. One Sunday, we went to church and I didn't realize there was going to be communion that day. Mickey didn't understand what communion was. I tried to explain it to him, and he says that he can't go up to the front and kneel because his knees were so bad—said he'd never be able to get up. So I went down and had communion, and as the minister came by with the bread I took an extra piece. He looked at me like, what was I doing? I winked at him and nudged my head back towards Mickey, and he grinned. Then he came around with the wine—which was grape juice, wouldn't you know it—and Mickey tells him, 'If I had known you were gonna have bread and wine, I'd have brought nachos and Kendall Jackson!' "

Mantle never was baptized. Because his condition deteriorated so rapidly, there was time for very little. He kept in touch with his sons, his attorney, and a handful of friends. Even though Summerall had turned over his house to him so he could live for a time without the phone ringing, a few people managed to find out where he was. One of them was Ted Williams. Unlike DiMaggio, who had been aloof and almost petty in his dealings with Mantle over the years, Williams had always gone out of his way to acknowledge Mantle for all he had meant to the game; when Williams opened a baseball museum dedicated to great hitters, Mantle was an honored guest. Another caller—and fellow member of the five hundred home run club—who somehow knew where Mantle was staying was Harmon Killebrew.

But nothing could slow the wildfire.

Johnson says that she did not really understand that she and Mantle were saying good-bye when he left Summerall's home to be readmitted to the hospital. They both were still talking about the future. "On that Friday when I left him—we had been talking about it all week—he said, go back to Georgia and find where I can take chemo," said Johnson. "Emory University was right there in Atlanta, and that's where he was talking about getting it done."

Summerall remembered that when he saw the two of them together for the last time, Mantle emphasized to Greer Johnson how much he loved her.

"I thought about it a lot when he left here," he said, "that he was shutting the page on that part of his life—that he knew that was the last time he was going to see her. But I'm not sure he knew that. I think he did, but I'm not sure."

At Baylor Medical Center, he was placed in a private suite with an adjoining room where guests and his family could stay. Merlyn and his sons were with him constantly. Merlyn, who had long since made a life for herself apart from him, once more stepped into the spotlight that had always been as uncomfortable for her as it had been for him. "He's a tough old bird," she said, "and he's a fighter. If anyone can make it, it's Mick." She was talking as much for Mantle, who had a television set in his room and was able to follow all of the news beamed to the outside world about his condition, as she was for public consumption. Merlyn and his sons stayed with him till the end. Mantle received blood transfusions the Friday he checked back into Baylor, and then again on Sunday. He was initially listed in stable condition. But three days later, it was announced that the cancer had spread beyond his lungs and his condition was downgraded. The following day, Thursday, Johnson spoke with Mantle by phone for the last time. He was still talking about the future.

On Saturday, the day before he died, Johnson met with Roy True and True told her then, for the first time, how grave his condition actually was. "Two to four days, he told me," said Johnson. "I asked him then if there would be any problem of my coming to the funeral. He said there would be none."

Earlier in the week, True had contacted Mantle's old teammate, Bobby Richardson, in South Carolina and asked him if he would officiate at the funeral when Mantle died. He agreed immediately. Richardson was an evangelical lay minister and had been friends with Mantle since their playing days. "Actually, even before," said Richardson. "I was just seventeen when I came up for a brief look by the Yankees, and I remember standing there just looking bewildered, not knowing anyone or what I was supposed to do. Mick came over to me, put an arm around my shoulder, and then cleared some guys out of the batting cage so I could hit. I'll never forget that. I went down to the minors for two years before I came back up."

Over the years, Richardson said, Mantle had always been generous with his time and energy, helping with different projects for charity. In 1976, when Richardson ran for Congress as a conservative Republican, Mantle also flew in to offer help. "But you know Mick, how he always kids around. He got on a local CB radio and told the listening audience that he wouldn't vote for Bobby Richardson for dog catcher! But then the next day he did a benefit and raised all kinds of money."

Richardson vividly recalled when Mantle was a pallbearer at Roger Maris's funeral. Richardson conducted the services that day, and at one point Mantle approached him, visibly shaken. He explained that he had always thought that Maris would outlive him, and the idea of his dying so young was impossible for him to accept. "Then he said to me, 'Bobby, I want you to handle my funeral.' Just like that." Richardson said he was so taken aback that all he could do was make a joke. "I told him that he was such a clean liver that he'd outlast me by twenty years. But I always remembered that and so when it came time I did what he wanted."

At the mid-July 1995 all-star game, held in Arlington, Texas, Richardson called Mantle to see how he was getting along following his transplant surgery. "He told me then that he was really hurting," Richardson said, "and then the next morning, at around six o'clock, he called my hotel room. My wife answered the phone and Mickey said 'Betsy, let me talk to Bobby, I want him to pray for me.' " Richardson said he then got on the phone and for a brief time prayed together with Mantle. They had two or three additional conversations like that before he went back to South Carolina, Richardson said. Then, weeks later, on Wednesday, August 9, True summoned him to Dallas.

Richardson said he and his wife got to Dallas that evening. The next morning, Richardson went alone to visit Mantle at the hospital. Just before he got there, Mantle had a visit from Whitey Ford, and it seemed to pick up his spirits. He stood back in the room for a while as Ford left and Mantle seemed to doze off. When he opened his eyes again, there were just the two of them in the room, and Richardson said Mantle recognized him and smiled.

It was Richardson's understanding—though he could not be specific—that Mantle's doctors had "leveled with him" about his condition and that he knew he was going to die. "What he didn't know was when—and he didn't want to know," Richardson said. Then he said Mantle told him that he had accepted Christ as his savior. Later in the day, Betsy Richardson visited. Mantle's sons David and Danny helped their father from his bed and got him to a chair where he sat for awhile. "Betsy sort of knelt down by him and held his hand and shared her testimony with him," Richardson said. "Then she asked him the question, 'Mickey, if God were to stand before you today and say, "Why should I let you into my heaven," what would you say?' He kind of picked up and said, 'We're talking about God?' She said, yes, that's right. He then quoted John 3:16." A little while after that, Richardson said, they left Mantle for the day, and by the following morning, Friday, he was incoherent, slipping in and out of consciousness.

Other friends and teammates visited Mantle that last Thursday. Hank Bauer, Moose Skowron, and Johnny Blanchard came and left together. Bauer, seventy-five, had been through cancer surgery himself; Skowron, sixty-five, only recently had had heart bypass surgery. The old teammates helped Mantle from his bed to his reclining chair so he could watch a golf match on TV for a while. Sometime later, the three men helped Mantle to the bathroom. Bauer and Blanchard held him by the arms, and Skowron walked alongside, wheeling a tree of IV medicine bags. When they got him back to bed and Mantle, exhausted, closed his eyes, Bauer motioned for them to go. Mantle then opened his eyes.

"You guys ain't leavin' already are you?" he asked. The men stayed a little longer.

Bauer says he did not know if Mantle was aware that he was going to die, but his teammates were conscious of it all the while they were there. Before they left, Mantle dropped off to sleep. Bauer noticed that his ankles were terribly swollen. He reached out and touched them before leaving the room. "His ankles were ice cold," Bauer said.

On Saturday evening, Mantle's doctors told the family they did not think he would last the night. Sometime after midnight, the family gathered at his bedside. Mantle was not conscious. Merlyn held one hand, his son David held the other. Then, for just a moment, he opened his eyes.

"Hi, Mick," Merlyn said. He said nothing. Forty minutes later he was dead.

In those last days and weeks, even as his body was breaking down, he acquired, quietly and with an almost ethereal elegance, a strength and dignity he did not know he possessed. He faced his own death with that strength—whether or not he chose to acknowledge its imminence—and became a new kind of hero. He was as heroic in the manner of his dying as he ever was in his greatest seasons on the field. There was something in the images of his shrunken frame that were as inspiring as they were haunting. Shriveled, with a white ball cap on his skull, and an old man's sweet, vacant smile on his face, his eyes blinking into bright lights, he implored others not to be like him and asked people to think of signing organ donor cards. He was a man of many summers long ago in the final minutes of his final summer, and his voice was weak and frail, but his words were strong. In his last months he stopped worrying about what others wanted him to do for them, and he urged them to take time out to do something for each other.

Mantle's funeral was held on a bright, blazing Texas day at the Lover's Lane United Methodist Church in Dallas. Originally, the family had wanted a private service, but they yielded to the intense demand for something more public. There was a private wake held before the noon service that day, but the service itself was for the nation and the world.

Though there was room for fifteen hundred people in the church and another three thousand standees outside, the mourning for Mickey Mantle was nationwide and involved millions. When Mantle's death was announced that Sunday morning, there was a ball game scheduled at Yankee Stadium. The huge videoboard in center field that day showed Mantle's number, along with the words "Mickey Mantle A Yankee Forever." Forty-five thousand fans took part in the hastily arranged tribute that followed, and in every major-league ballpark around the country, similar outpourings of affection and remembrance took place. Film clips of Mantle's youth and career played everywhere.

The evening news showed players in places like Fenway Park standing solemnly at attention, some even applauding as they watched the ballpark video of Mantle that played in the background. In the press box at Yankee Stadium there was a flurry of rumors that Mantle would actually be brought back to New York and his body briefly placed in state in the ballpark—as Babe Ruth's had been. But the funeral took place in Dallas and, though public, was relatively small. It was a baseball funeral. The greats of the game—most of them—were there. Joe DiMaggio chose not to attend, issuing a statement of tribute in which he felt obliged to mention that Mantle had to be sent back to the minors in his rookie season.

It was a family funeral, too. The Mantle family along with honored guests were seated in the front of the church, near the casket. Greer Johnson was assigned a seat near the back of the church. Pat Summerall sat with her until an usher came down the aisle and told him that a seat had been reserved for him in the first rows. Summerall frostily told the usher he was quite happy sitting where he was.

The service was simple and, by Dallas standards, modest in the extreme. Bobby Richardson, true to his word, was in the pulpit for the service. He recalled some of the good times as a teammate of Mantle's, some of Mickey's practical jokes, and then talked about his friend's underlying fear of death, which seemed to drive him first to bright lights and then to the light of God.

Bob Costas delivered the principal eulogy. He spoke not as a broadcaster, he said—Mel Allen was the eternal voice of the Yankees—and he was not even there to speak solely for himself, but for the "millions of baseball-loving kids who grew up in the '50s and '60s and for whom Mickey Mantle *was* baseball."

Costas pointed out how uncomfortable Mantle had always been with the fuss made over him. It was not really because of his basic shyness, he asserted, "but because he was always too honest to regard himself as some kind of deity."

In his eulogy, Costas said there was something poignant about Mantle "before we knew what poignant meant." Weeks later, the word was still on his mind. "A columnist mentioned—and it's true—DiMaggio had preceded Mantle and had those 361 home runs and 369 strikeouts, a stunning combination of skill and control," he said. "Well, with Mantle it was all or nothing, you know, you could practically feel his heart bursting. Everything about him was so emotional and at the same time so poignant and flawed."

The whole truth of Mantle, Costas said earlier at the funeral, could never be found on a box of Wheaties or in the back rooms of all those bars, nor in those countless locker room pranks nor even when, for a time, he was clearly one of the best baseball players ever. The whole truth of the man was all and none of the above, but there was something in his last days, his final inning, that made who he was and what he did both moving and large. "Our last memories of Mickey Mantle are as heroic as the first," Costas said. "None of us, Mickey included, would want to be held to account for every moment of our lives. But how many of us could say that our best moments were as magnificent as his?"

Mantle had wanted a song sung for him at his own funeral. As he had asked Bobby Richardson to preside at his service, he had many years before asked Roy Clark, the country-and-western star, to perform the song "Yesterday When I Was Young." He had befriended Clark when he first heard the song. Clark had consented, never imagining that he would actually have to do it. "It wasn't supposed to happen this soon," he said.

The song is a lamentation for a life wasted, life as sweet as rain, played at as foolishly as a game. Clark sang on an unamplified guitar, so the words and music seemed more elemental and simple than the service itself. Pat Summerall believed all of Mantle's life was contained in the song, and so did many of the mourners gathered there. It was almost possible to imagine Mantle's presence hearing and feeling the words:

> *I ran so fast that time and youth at last ran out. . . . There are so many songs in me that won't be sung . . . the time has come for me to pay for yesterday when I was young.*

The pallbearers who took Mantle's coffin from the church were his old teammates, including Whitey and Yogi, Bauer and Skowron, Bobby Murcer and Johnny Blanchard. Outside, the milling crowd included other old teammates and former stars, among them the hero of Mantle's own youth, Stan Musial.

The procession that wound through suburban Dallas to the Parkman Hillcrest Mausoleum, where Mantle was laid to rest next to his son Billy, passed by two ball fields, one directly across the way from the crypt.

But Mickey Mantle had left baseball fields behind long ago—when he was young.

Afterword

In the basement of *Mickey Mantle's* restaurant in New York City, there are cartons of letters and cards that were sent to him between the time he received his liver transplant in June and the time he died on August 13, 1995.

The letters and cards came from everywhere in the country and around the world. Some of them are elegantly printed as though from someone's desktop publishing mill; others are crudely hand lettered, full of misspellings and cross-outs. Some are religious, some decidedly secular, but all of them have in common a thread of intense and intimate feeling, as though each writer had been a close personal friend.

There is a letter from a person who identified himself as a certified public accountant but who had once been a batboy for the Chicago White Sox. "Over 30 years ago," said the writer, "a kid approached you declaring that his American history teacher said anyone making over $100,000 owned a yacht, so would you please sign baseball saying that you don't own a yacht. You the took the time to sign the ball with, 'I don't own a yacht.' I will never forget you for that."

Another person wrote: "Hey Mick, remember me? I was the

guy who saved your life when you got stuck in that phone booth in the airport in Philadelphia."

Mrs. Eldred Lehmke wrote to Mantle about the need to focus on God and to trust in His mercy and benevolence. The Marians of Immaculate Conception from Stockbridge, Massachusetts, sent him a Certificate of Enrollment for fourteen years of spiritual benefits. Someone from Peoria, Illinois, wrote Mantle, signing off with a happy-face drawing of two eyes and a smiling mouth. The writer said, as though he were Mantle's brother, "I hope you're doing okay and getting better. I'll be praying for you. You listen to what your doctors say, but don't eat the hospital food. Hang in there, buddy."

A recovering alcoholic wrote to Mantle, thanking him for being so brave and honest in acknowledging his drinking problems. He was an example, the writer said, "for all of us who have been caught in the same hell and tried to fight our way out."

Someone who identified himself as an old Negro League fan confided that he had been hospitalized for depression and that Mantle had always been his inspiration. Another writer said, "Thank you for being an honest man with a good heart and willing to express yourself so that we could all grow a little more in the right direction. Your influence has positively enhanced my life."

And another: "Mr. Mantle, if I could, in my entire lifetime affect only a handful of people you've been able to shine for, I don't think I could ask for a greater reward in life."

This one, from a Queens, New York, resident:

> It's been 32 years since I last saw you in person. I used to live at the Van Wyck Apartments. You and Roger and Yogi and the guys used to come in from practice. You helped us always with our batting, fielding, etc. I remember going to Hal Reniff's apartment one day and having a soda. Roger and you came in one day and saw us playing. You stopped and taught us how to catch a fly ball in the sun. Those are days that will live with me forever.

One day, the whole team comes over and signs my mitt. So thrilled being only seven.

I wish my son had someone to idolize these days, as long as I have idolized you.

The letters and cards were the private and secret springs of a broad and deep river of public affection. Mickey Mantle was worshiped as few athletes of his or any other time have been. There was something about him that went far beyond athletic accomplishment, though his accomplishments were stunning enough. He hit 536 home runs in his career and more home runs than anyone else in World Series history. Some of those homers were among the longest and most memorable ever. Bob Costas believed that that alone was enough to make Mantle stick in people's minds. "There's something about the idea of knocking the ball out of the park, there's something about the idea of no boundaries in baseball as opposed to any other team sport—and I don't mean at all to push the romance of 'The Game,' which too many people do—but in baseball the ball just disappears, it's gone, lost, where it's never been before. You can only run a hundred yards in football, Michael Jordan does things that people haven't done, same as Jim Brown and Gale Sayers—but to me the idea of hitting it out of the park where it disappears, there's something mystical about it."

There was something about him that touched people's deepest longings and dreams. He was a hero beyond stadiums, stats, facts, or plaques. He was a phenomenon in exactly the way Marilyn Monroe, James Dean, and Elvis Presley—those other damaged heroes from his generation—were.

Tom Tresh was one of scores of younger teammates of Mantle's who grew up worshipping him. "When I was a kid, I used to go to Tiger Stadium and sit in the center-field bleachers and watch him play," Tresh said. "In high school, I kind of mimicked everything he did, mimicked his run, the way he hit. I was a switch-hitter, and I watched how Mickey stood at the plate, his mannerisms, everything. If you look at some of my home runs when I was playing with the Yankees, if you look at the footage of me running around the bases, I probably went around a little faster than he did, but I also kinda tilted my head like he did. When I used to go to the outfield, I think I unconsciously limped sort of the way he did. I have a son named Mickey. When he was born he weighed seven pounds, seven ounces, and he was born on the 19th of October. Mickey Mantle's birthday is October 20th. I told my wife, if you could just bear down a little bit, if you could just hold on for another sixteen hours, we'd hit his birthday, you know?"

Bill Kane, the Yankee statistician and publicist, after he had been paralyzed by polio as a child, spent seven years in a Catholic charity hospital, where he determinedly learned to walk with the aid of crutches. More than anything else he wanted to be a competitive athlete. He played sandlot football—on crutches—and whaled at opponents with them in the midst of pileups and tackles. After he came to the Yankees, Mantle was his favorite player—because he so often played injured and had such obvious heart.

One time, Kane was mistaken for Mantle—and he played out his role with Broadway bravura. "It was in Chicago after a game when I was having a few beers," he said. "This guy thought I was Mickey, and he insisted I give him my autograph. He was winging around all over me, so I gave him my version of Mickey's signature. Now the guy really went wild. He kept hanging around and finally asked me about all the injuries I played with, you know, he particularly wanted to know about my bad leg. Well, I'd had a few by then, so I told the guy, 'I'll show you how my leg is,' and I rolled up my pants leg and showed him my leg, which of course looks like a toothpick. The guy went absolutely berserk, started saying to everyone that Mickey Mantle was the most amazing player ever. I told Mickey the story the next day and he laughed like hell, and from that day he always used to ask me, 'How's the leg, Mick?' "

Mantle never saw himself as a hero, never felt comfortable in the role, and he rebelled against it. His drinking and carousing, in part, were a way of getting away from it; so was his humor, which could be funny or, at times, obscenely earthy. After he had been out of the game for several years, he was contacted by the Yankees, who wanted information from him for a publicity package they were preparing for an upcoming old-timer's game. As with other players, Mantle was sent a questionnaire asking him to describe his most outstanding experience at Yankee Stadium and then to give details of the experience. In his own hand, Mantle wrote a wildly unprintable account of a sexual encounter he had with an unnamed partner "under the right field bleachers by the Yankee bullpen." After giving the details in the most graphic terms possible, he signed the questionnaire, placing an asterisk next to his name. The asterisk was explained at the bottom of the page: "The All-American boy."

Weeks before his death, while he was in the hospital for treatment, he was still up to his old tricks. Somehow he managed to find time to send off a package to one of the nation's most well-known memorabilia collectors. When the collector opened the package, he found a pair of stained surgical gloves with a note from Mantle saying that he thought he might be able to make use of them, explaining in precise terms what the gloves had most recently been used for.

Mantle could no more escape who he was than could any character from mythology who was burdened by fate. But his own fate took time to see, a lifetime rather than a season or a career. He came into our consciousness first as an unguarded innocent, a rookie in Babylon, with his fresh smile, scrubbed face, and bent ball cap. He was the Next Great Yankee. But then, when he was not quite Babe Ruth on the field, he became the Babe off it. He was the King of New York on one leg, and when he failed, he won and was loved. When he left the game he left it more like a prodigal son than like an old ballplayer put out to pasture. He came back to us larger than ever, a memory we needed to heal *our* wounds. Then we learned just how deep his own wounds went, and like the prodigal son who returned or the blinded king who had finally seen, he became a wholly different kind of hero at the end.

Pat Summerall said that in these last years Mantle seemed to be someone who was trying to make amends. There were no songs and no sermons in the effort he was making; if somehow he had been miraculously healed, he likely would have gone out to Preston Trail as usual with a rubber snake hidden in his golf bag, looking to surprise some unwitting friend or associate in an afternoon's game. Mantle believed he could never make amends for the life he felt he had wasted; that was his torment, his boundary. But as he had once shattered a game's boundaries by swinging from his soul, so did he break his own bonds in his final years by determining to make himself a better person. The miracle of his last days was that in them he transformed his life, and made himself into an even more enduring kind of hero.

Acknowledgments

Special thanks to my editor, Jeffrey Neuman, for help in so many matters large and small. I also want to acknowledge the assistance of all those who helped make this book possible, the people who were willing to share their memories of Mickey Mantle with me. Their names are in place in the text, but are herein gratefully thanked. Thanks also to Marty Appel, Ira Berkow, Darryl Berger, Rob Butcher, Joanne Curtis, Bob Creamer, David Feiman, Michael Gershman, Pete Golenbock, Fred Kraly, Lee Lowenfish, Bob Lipsyte, Bobby Murcer, Larry Ritter, Ray Robinson, Harold Rosenthal, Frank Scatoni, and Andrew Siff. For support and encouragement, thanks to Ellen and Matthew Alcorn, David Black, Jenny Dowling, and Joan and Dan Siff. Additional special thanks to Skip Bayless, Bob Costas, Nick Ferguson, Greer Johnson, Bill Liederman, John Lowy, and Pat Summerall.

About the Author

David Falkner is the author of seven previous books, most recently, *Great Time Coming: The Life of Jackie Robinson, from Baseball to Birmingham* and *The Last Yankee: The Turbulent Life of Billy Martin.* A frequent contributor to *The Sporting News,* Falkner lives in the Bronx, New York.